D1756332

The Radical and Socialist Tradition in British Planning

Focusing on the key period between the late 18th century and 1914, this book provides the first comprehensive narrative account of radical and socialist texts and organised movements for reform to land planning and housing policies in Britain. Beginning with the early colonial settlements in the Puritan and enlightenment eras, it also covers Benthamite utilitarian planning, Owenite and utopian communitarianism, the Chartists, late Chartists and the First International, Christian Socialists and positivists, working class and radical land reform campaigns in the late 19th century, Garden City pioneers and the institutionalisation of the planning profession.

The book, in effect, presents a prehistory of land, planning and housing reform in the UK in contrast with most historiography which focuses on the immediate pre-World War I period. Providing an analysis of different intellectual traditions and contrasting middle class-led reform initiatives with those based on working class organisations, the book seeks to relate historical debates to contemporary themes, including utopianism and pragmatism, the role of the state, the balance between local initiatives and centrally driven reforms and the interdependence of land, housing and planning.

Duncan Bowie is a senior lecturer in planning and housing at the University of Westminster, where he is course leader on the MA Urban and Regional Planning. He has worked in senior posts in housing and planning for the Mayor of London, the Housing Corporation, the London Docklands Development Corporation and London boroughs. He is a member of the policy council of the Town and Country Planning Association, as well as the executive committees of the London Labour Housing Group, the Socialist History Society and the London Society.

The Radical and Socialist Tradition in British Planning

From Puritan colonies to garden cities

Duncan Bowie

Routledge
Taylor & Francis Group

LONDON AND NEW YORK

First published 2017
by Routledge

2 Park Square, Milton Park, Abingdon, Oxfordshire OX14 4RN
711 Third Avenue, New York, NY 10017

Routledge is an imprint of the Taylor & Francis Group, an informa business

First issued in paperback 2018

Copyright © 2017 Duncan Bowie

The right of Duncan Bowie to be identified as author of this
work has been asserted by her in accordance with sections
77 and 78 of the Copyright, Designs and Patents Act 1988.

All rights reserved. No part of this book may be reprinted or reproduced or
utilised in any form or by any electronic, mechanical, or other means, now
known or hereafter invented, including photocopying and recording, or in
any information storage or retrieval system, without permission in writing
from the publishers.

Notice:
Product or corporate names may be trademarks or registered trademarks,
and are used only for identification and explanation without intent to
infringe.

British Library Cataloguing-in-Publication Data
A catalogue record for this book is available from the British Library

Library of Congress Cataloging in Publication Data
Names: Bowie, Duncan, author.
Title: The radical and socialist tradition in British planning : from Puritan
colonies to garden cities / Duncan Bowie.
Description: Abingdon, Oxon ; New York, NY : Routledge, 2016. |
Includes bibliographical references and index.
Identifiers: LCCN 2016004020| ISBN 9781472479020 (hardback) |
ISBN 9781315553672 (ebook)
Subjects: LCSH: City planning—Great Britain—History. | Regional
planning—Great Britain—History. | Land use—Great Britain—
Planning—History. | Urban policy—Great Britain—History. |
Housing policy—Great Britain—History.
Classification: LCC HT169.G7 B693 2016 | DDC 307.1/2160941—dc23
LC record available at https://lccn.loc.gov/2016004020

ISBN: 978-1-4724-7902-0 (hbk)
ISBN: 978-1-138-61656-1 (pbk)

Typeset in Sabon
by Florence Production, Stoodleigh, Devon, UK

Printed in the United Kingdom
by Henry Ling Limited

Contents

Acknowledgements

I would like to thank numerous colleagues who have commented on drafts of this book at various stages: the late Sir Peter Hall who commented on an early outline, Michael Hebbert, Martin Crookston, Michael Edwards and Tony Manzi as well as the publishers' anonymous referees. Hugh Ellis gave me access to the TCPA's attic and the short loan of some early volumes of the *Garden Cities* journal, while Gavin Parker escorted me into the RTPI's basement archive. I would like to thank Ron Heisler and Andrew Whitehead for information on the O'Brienites, as well as my colleagues from the Socialist History Society for their interest in the project and invitation to give a talk on the subject of the book. My thanks go to the librarians of Southampton University and Warwick University in making available copies of unpublished MA dissertations. My thanks also go to those librarians and archivists who have digitised rare pamphlets, especially those of the British Library and the University of Michigan, to the reprint publishers of India and to second hand booksellers everywhere. I would also wish to acknowledge the proofreading services provided by my wife, Jackie, as well as guidance from my son, Chris, on rewriting the introduction, and the suggestion from my daughter Jenny that I should shorten my paragraphs and sentences. Finally, I would like to record my appreciation for the help of the editorial and production teams at Routledge, as well as copy editor Alice Stoakley, in assisting this text through the publication process.

1 Introduction

Radicalism, socialism, planning and planning history

Many practitioners and commentators, including this author, take the view that planning has lost its way. In the British context, and more specifically within the planning regime in England, there is now little notion of a public purpose, and the role of planners is seen by government and by political and economic thinkers as primarily to enable the private market to respond to the challenges of growth. We have largely lost any concept of a social purpose for planning, and the success of planning practice is largely judged on whether planners have facilitated development in terms of contributing to economic growth, with little consideration of what could be termed as the wider 'public good'. As a historian and a professional planner engaged in the development of planning policy as well as teacher of practising planners and potential planners, I have written this book on the presumption that knowledge of the history of planning can inform both academic discourse and planning practice.

In political theory and practice, planning has traditionally been associated with the 'left', or to be more precise, with a number of left traditions – Fabian, social democratic and communist. Most of these traditions are perceived as centralist and state dominated. Other more pluralist traditions recognise that the state and planning can operate at a number of spatial levels – international, national, regional, sub regional, local and neighbourhood level, and that a centralist perspective is not necessarily the most democratic. While anarchists may seek to limit or abolish the role of the central state, libertarian socialists generally accept the principles of subsidiarity – that governance and planning should be undertaken at the most appropriate level which is closest to the individual and the community. This is the starting point for the federalist and pluralist traditions of socialism and an approach to planning which rejects centralised – and by extension – authoritarian decision making. In a context of localism, consumer choice and deregulation, the dominant paradigm across the contemporary political spectrum, planning is widely seen as out of step with current political thinking, both in practice and in dominant conceptualisations within contemporary political science. This book is therefore seeking to use the historical record as a basis for challenging the dominance of neo-liberal perspectives within contemporary discourse.

However, both planning in the broader sense and spatial planning specifically, are critical to the delivery of progressive policy outcomes – the term 'progressive' being used here in a broad sense to incorporate radical and socialist perspectives across an extensive chronological period. This study seeks to reassert the positive role of planning as understood in previous historical periods in contrast with the contemporary context, in which planning is widely regarded as a negative factor. The object of the book is to provide an understanding of the past, but also to provide inspiration for those working within such a negative and hostile contemporary environment. It is my hope that today's planners will have time within their day to day pressurised and constrained work situations to read about the struggles their predecessors fought and to understand that there is another more positive role that they as professionals can play in society.

Taking a historical perspective does demonstrate the positive role of planning in contributing to the delivery of public policy objectives and recognises that this positive function does involve constraining the operation of the market and the behaviour of individuals where this conflicts with public policy objectives. This is essentially a Benthamite perspective – that planning should be about achieving the greatest good in terms of benefit to the greatest number of people.

Planning is not about consensus as perceived by the current UK government. It is about making explicit choices between different and often conflicting options. Planning decisions should not only involve assessments of who benefits from a policy or a specific development, but also an assessment of who is disadvantaged – who loses out. This brings us to the fundamental question as to what should be the explicit socialist objective of planning – beyond the general Benthamite concept of 'the greatest good'. The concept of public gain from private development value has been a core part of the discourse about the role of planning throughout most of the period covered by this study. The role of planning as constraining the operation of the land and property market is itself part of the neo-classical paradigm. The neo-liberal perspective that planning should facilitate the operation of the market is not accepted by this author. State and market are in fact interdependent – planning impacts on the market but the delivery of planning policy objectives is impacted on by market factors. In practice, in most countries where the private sector is dominant, the role of public sector planning is to seek to regulate the operation of the market. A neo-liberal position would seek to minimise the degree of regulation and state intervention, while a Benthamite perspective would argue for the minimum level of intervention necessary to achieve the 'public good'. An explicitly socialist perspective might seek to use planning for redistributive purposes – to advance the interests of households with less wealth and income and access to the market, to mitigate the negative impacts of a free market in land, property and development and to seek to achieve a more egalitarian society.

Despite common assumptions to the contrary, planning as policy and practice has always been related to other key components of state governance such as investment and taxation. Planning cannot be considered independently of consideration of the control and use of land or of the provision of new and improved homes. Planning cannot be considered independently of consideration of provision of schools, health facilities, leisure and access to open space. This narrative seeks therefore to relate the debate over planning and the perspective of liberal, radical and socialist reformers across the period covered to debates over land, housing and public health more generally. This book discusses radical and socialist visions of new communities but it is fundamentally about the reforms of policy and more broadly the political reforms necessary for the achievement of these visions.

Many histories of UK planning, housing and land reform start in the late 19th century with Ebenezer Howard, Octavia Hill and Henry George. References back to previous periods tend to be brief and lacking in detail. This book seeks to provide the prehistory and to demonstrate that these three reformers were perhaps less original in their ideas than is perceived by many historians and in fact derived many of their ideas from earlier reform campaigns. The book seeks to focus on the activities of working class radicals and socialists to provide a counter-narrative, or at least supplementary narrative, to those narratives which focus on a small group of middle class philanthropists and writers whose prominence generally rests on their authorship of texts which are perceived as 'classic' and remain in print and on course reading lists.

It is important, however, to acknowledge that there are a few exceptions to the traditional historiography. Academic writing on utilitarian planning of the late 18th and early 19th century is limited to Hyde's essay (Hyde, 1947), though it should be acknowledged that Home's pathbreaking study of British colonial planning, *Of Planting and Planning* (Home, 1997), also makes the link with utilitarian philosophy, as does the more recent study on the planning of Adelaide by Donald Johnson *Anticipating Municipal Parks* (Johnson, 2013). In this work, I also draw on the extensive primary and secondary literature on early colonial planning in America and Australia – for non-indigenous Americans and Australians, this was, after all, the beginning of their national history. It is however important to recognise that much of the planning of the settlements in these new countries was actually undertaken in England as the colonising country and can be related back to British politics and ideology and should therefore be seen as part of British planning history.

Eldon Barry's *Nationalisation in British Politics* (Barry, 1965) includes a survey of the mid and late 19th century land reform movement, including the Chartists, the Land and Labour League and the land nationalisation movement of the 1880s and 1890s. I should also acknowledge the anonymous pamphlet on *Land Nationalisation in Britain* published by the History Group of the Communist Party (Communist Party History Group, 1957), which covers, if somewhat briefly, the activities of some of the organisations studied in Chapters 5 and 7 of this book, although I will admit to only discovering this rare mimeographed pamphlet after I had largely completed my research. David Englander's unpublished Masters dissertation on the Workman's National Housing Council (Englander, 1973) provides a detailed narrative study of working class campaigns on housing reform in the 1890s and early 1900s while A J Peacock's study of the Land Nationalisation Society and the English Land Restoration League, also an unpublished Masters dissertation (Peacock, 1961), has proved invaluable. It is highly regrettable that neither of these works has been published – Englander's published study, *Landlord and Tenant in Urban Britain* (Englander, 1983) uses very little of his earlier work. The classic study by Avner Offer on *Property and Politics 1870–1914* (Offer, 1981) should be acknowledged as setting the land reform movements of that period within their wider economic and ideological context. It is also important to pay tribute to Anthony Wohl's pioneering study of late 19th century housing reform, *The Eternal Slum* (Wohl, 1977), which is still unrivalled for its coverage of the subject, and first led me to a recognition of the relationship between political history, housing and planning.

The only work previously published which analyses the relationship of early 19th-century socialist theory and politics to the built environment, as far as I am aware, is Frederic Moret's study *Les Socialistes et La Ville* (Moret, 1998) which is a comparative study of individuals and organisations in France and Great Britain. It is perhaps significant that it was a French academic who saw the impact of political theory on built environment practice as significant. Bronstein's comparative study of land reform movements in Britain and the United States (Bronstein, 1999) also includes useful material on Owenite and Chartist initiatives.

It should be acknowledged that there is a significant literature on communitarian settlements, with copious volumes on the Owenite experiments and increasing academic study of Owenite followers and their religious tendencies, for example Latham's study of James Pierrepoint Greaves (Latham, 1999). Some studies of the post-Owenite settlements however tend to be more in the form of inventories rather than critical studies of the politics and ideology of the settlement's founding, progress and dissolution. In contrast, the home colonisation experiments of the late 19th and first decade of the 20th century, with their links to socialist agitation, have been subject to very limited study by academics though they are touched on in the works of Brown (1971) and Harris (1972). Ebenezer Howard and Patrick Geddes have both been the subject of numerous published works, and it could be asked whether there is any point in subjecting them to further study. The later chapters of this work do take a somewhat different perspective in seeking to examine the extent to which these 'founders of British planning' took ideas from previous socialist, radical and anarchist thinkers. In this context, the recent study by Scott and Bromley of Geddes' early sociological studies is enlightening (Scott and Bromley, 2013).

This work therefore attempts to provide a chronological narrative of radical and socialist planning and pioneers from the 1790s to the outbreak of the First World War, while also seeking to demonstrate that utilitarian planning at the beginning of this period itself drew on earlier examples of settlement planning, dating back to the Puritan settlements of the mid-17th century. This book is not intended as a history of urban form or as a comprehensive history of British town planning in this period. This can be found elsewhere, not least in the works of Ashworth (1954) and Benovolo (1971) and I do not attempt to cover those settlement initiatives, which were part of Britain's programme of imperial conquest and based primarily on military objectives, such as the creation of new fortified towns as part of the Ulster plantation of the late-17th century. In contrast to some of the works referred to above, this book has the explicit intention of linking the narrative of reform to political organisations and parties and to situate the debates over planning, housing and land within the wider context of political and social reform. By using primary sources, the book gets both underneath and beyond the more familiar representations in the established secondary texts. It is recognised that this work is ambitious in its time span. History is most often told in episodes. Episodic history has its limitations – to fully understand the significance of a historical event, it is necessary to know what happened before and what happened after. Few students, practitioners or politicians have much knowledge of past reform movements and policies. An understanding of the past can also inform how we respond to the current context and this book therefore seeks to fill a significant gap in the literature.

The chapters in this book are arranged chronologically with extensive quotation from primary sources. Each narrative chapter focuses on a specific chronological period and on a specific 'movement' or 'discourse'. Chronological developments and specific interventions in terms of both theoretical contributions and policy initiatives can however be related to a number of key themes, which are relevant to contemporary debates. These key themes are:

1 The contrast between middle class philanthropic reformers and 'grassroots' campaigns originating within working class based radical and socialist organisations; the extent to which these represent distinct ideological positions and whether there is a clear separation of ideological traditions across the historical timescale.

2 Comparing utopian and pragmatic approaches to constructing a 'New Jerusalem';

3 The role of the State in the initiation of new settlements.

4 The role of local initiatives relative to centralist reform.

5 The inter-relationship between policy on land and taxation, policy on housing and policy on planning, and the inter-dependency of these three reform objectives.

The chronological narrative covers the development of initiatives in colonial and domestic planning in the late-18th century as well as taking the narrative to 1914 with the introduction of the first planning-specific legislation and the emergence of a planning profession. There remains a difficulty with the selection of any chronological period, and as the initiatives of the late-18th century drew on past precedents, the first two narrative chapters briefly review the progressive initiatives of the earlier Puritan and enlightenment periods. Chapter 4 considers the role of the utilitarian followers of Jeremy Bentham in planning in Britain and the colonies. Chapter 5 reviews the communitarian initiatives of the socialist Robert Owen and his contemporaries. Chapter 6 examines the influence of the French utopians, Saint-Simon, Cabet and Fourier, on communitarianism in England in the early Victorian period. Chapter 7 focuses on debates on land reform in the mid-19th century within the Chartist movement and among English working class radicals involved in the First International and the development of a distinct working class reform agenda. Chapter 8 provides a contrast by reviewing the reform agenda of the middle class philanthropists and intellectuals of the same period in the public health reform movement, focusing on the role of Christian socialists and positivists, working through organisations such as the Social Science Association and the Industrial Remuneration Conference. Chapter 9 returns to the working class reform movement, with the revival of the socialist movement in the 1880s. It examines the policies and agitation of the Social Democratic Federation, the Socialist League, the Independent Labour Party and the National Workman's Housing Council, while also considering the influence of the Fabian Society, the role of the progressives in the first years of the London County Council and of working class Members of Parliament in both Liberal and Labour Parties. Chapter 10 examines the ideology of the garden city movement in the early years of the 20th century, with a scrutiny of the influences on the first generation of modern British planners – Ebenezer Howard, Patrick Geddes and Raymond Unwin and their successors. The final narrative chapter examines the institutionalisation of planning and housing in the English governmental system and the genesis of the 1909 Housing and Town Planning Act. The concluding chapter reviews the evidence of the historical narrative in relation to the five themes introduced in the first chapter, seeking to relate the historical experience to contemporary debates.

The book is largely dependent on the use of primary sources – the plans and polemics of the numerous radical and socialist planners, architects, social reformers and political activists across the period studied. I am grateful both to those booksellers across the world who have been prepared to sell pamphlets and other documents which have generally not been used by other historians, but also to those libraries, notably the British Library and the University of Michigan, and those reprint corporations which so often seem to be based in India, which have made available digitised copies of original pamphlets. I was repeatedly surprised that some obscure pamphlet referred to in the footnote of some secondary work was actually available. Much of the primary material was obtained from bookshops in Australia, New Zealand, South Africa and the United States, taken into exile or emigration by British radicals and socialists.

I have used secondary sources where they have supplemented the primary material, but my preference as a historian has always been to focus on the primary sources rather than engage in an academic discourse with other historians over competing interpretations of the past, or seek to reinterpret the past through the prism of contemporary concepts. This is not to be seen as a lack of knowledge of the literature, which is the output of certain tendencies in contemporary academic writing, although it can be rightly perceived as an antipathy to such approaches. A study of 19th-century political ideology and activism does not in my view require the retrospective application of such contemporary theorisation.

I should also acknowledge that this is an intentionally partisan history. It is selective in its subject matter as well as its use of sources. It has not been my intention to provide a comprehensive history of British and colonial planning. It has however been my objective to focus on radical and socialist intellectual traditions and to examine both the continuities and divergences within these traditions. This is a study which seeks to complement the existing literature rather than replace it and I hope that readers will share my view that this is an exercise which has travelled across new ground and has recovered a historical narrative that had largely been hidden.

References

Ashworth, W (1954) *The Genesis of Modern British Town Planning* (London: Routledge: Kegan Paul)

Barry, E (1965) *Nationalisation in British Politics: The Historical Background* (London: Jonathan Cape)

Benovolo, L (1971) *The Origins of Modern Town Planning* (Massachusetts: MIT Press)

Bronstein, J (1999) *Land Reform and Working Class Experience in Britain and the United States, 1800–1862* (Stanford, CA: Stanford University Press)

Brown, K D (1971) *Labour and Unemployment 1900–1914* (Newton Abbott, UK: David and Charles)

Communist Party History Group (1957) *Land Nationalisation in Britain. Our History* pamphlet No 8 (London: Communist Party)

Englander, D (1973) *The Workman's National Housing Council* (unpublished MA dissertation, University of Warwick, UK)

Englander, D (1983) *Landlord and Tenant in Urban Britain* (Oxford: Oxford University Press)

Harris, J (1972) *Unemployment and Politics. A Study in English Social Policy 1886–1914* (Oxford: Oxford University Press)

Home, R (1997) *Of Planting and Planning: The Making of British Colonial Cities* (London: Spon)

Hyde, F E (1947) 'Utilitarian Town Planning 1825–1845' in *Town Planning Review*, Vol 19, pp. 153–9

Johnson, D L (2013) *Anticipating Municipal Parks* (Kent Town, South Australia: Wakefield Press)

Latham, J (1999) *Search for a New Eden. James Pierrepoint Greaves. The Sacred Socialist and his Followers* (Cranbury, NJ: Associated University Presses)

Moret, F (1998) *Les Socialistes et La Ville: Grande Bretagne, France 1820–1850* (Lyons, France: ENS editions)

Offer, A (1981) *Property and Politics 1870–1914. Landownership, Law, Ideology and Urban Development in England* (Cambridge: Cambridge University Press)

Peacock, A J (1961) *Land Reform 1880–1919* (unpublished MA dissertation University of Southampton, UK)

Scott, J and Bromley, R (2013) *Envisioning Sociology: Victor Bramford, Patrick Geddes and the Quest for Social Reconstruction* (New York: State University of New York Press)

Wohl, A (1977) *The Eternal Slum: Housing and Social Policy in Victorian London* (London: Edward Arnold)

2 Radicals and planning in Britain and the colonies

From the Puritans to the Restoration

The egalitarian objectives of the early colonisers

Many studies of 18th and early 19th century English planning focus on the development of the aristocratic estates of the west end of London. These studies present the narrative of the emergence of the pattern of squares in Bloomsbury and Belgravia, which culminate in the work of John Nash with the creation of Regent's Street, Portland Place and Regents Park in the 1820s. Some studies also refer to the development of the new town in Edinburgh in the 1770s following the 1767 plan of James Craig (Olsen 1964; Bell and Bell, 1969; Summerson, 1991; McKellar, 1999). This is a familiar historiography.

Rather than focusing on the grand design of the architects working to the commission of the aristocratic owners of the great estates, this chapter instead considers those early planning experiments, which were drawn up as part of an explicit radical political or social agenda. The intention is to present a political and ideological context for the planning of new settlements.

The focus is on a range of early colonial initiatives by colonisers with explicit political objectives originating in a perspective of seeking to establish more egalitarian communities, free from the aristocratic domination prevalent in the home country. The general presumption of these colonisers was that the New World, whether in the Americas, Africa or Australasia, presented a *tabula rasa* – a clean slate on which their ideals of town form and governance could be established.

The first two narrative chapters seek to serve as a prelude to the main focus of the study which is in effect of the 'long 19th century' to 1914, by reviewing both colonial and domestic developments in planning concepts and practice from the perspective of radical thinkers. This chapter considers the radical influences on early colonial settlement, contrasting them with the establishment planning of the Shaftesbury model. The following chapter considers the experience of planning in the enlightenment period, including considering radical interventions in the debates on the management of the development of London, which was not just the capital of the British empire but becoming the first global city of the industrial age.

British Puritans and colonial settlement: John Winthrop and the 'city on a hill'

The first British colonial settlements in the Americas were born out of religious dissidence and political opposition. The first Puritan settlers, led by William Brewster,

John Carver and William Bradford and known as the 'pilgrim fathers', who sailed from Plymouth to Massachusetts in the *Mayflower* in 1620, were both religious dissenters but active in the political opposition to the Stuart monarchy, known as the 'country party'. As pointed out by Fries (1977, p. 43), the colonising companies that received patents in the 1620s and 1630s were dependent on the Puritan leaders of the parliamentary opposition such as Lord Say and Sele, John Pym and Nathaniel Rich. The Puritan ideology was based on self-supporting agriculture, and when the Massachusetts Bay Company was established, land allocation was to be based on each adventurer paying £50 to receive 200 acres of land. The townships were established as nucleated villages surrounded by apportionments in arable and meadow lands and common fields. Thomas Graves, appointed engineer surveyor to the Massachusetts Bay Company in 1629, put forward plans for the townships of Cambridge and New Haven based on a gridiron plan. It is likely that he was the author of a pamphlet setting out the principles for township development in an *Essay on the Laying Out of Towns*, probably written about 1635 (Fries, 1977, p. 48). This pamphlet suggested a square of six miles for the town with a centre of three square miles with a meeting house with no house more than 2500 paces from the meeting house. The farm lots should be 40 acres. The plan presumed individual ownership of plots (Fries, 1997, pp. 48–9).

There were a number of Puritan settlements in the late 1620s and early 1630s. John Endecott of the New England Company for a Plantation in Massachusetts had led the settlement of fifty planters and servants at Salem in 1629. The first settlement by the Massachusetts Bay Company at Shawmut, which was to become Boston, was self-governing. The Company charter established itself as a commercial enterprise. The stockholders were to meet four times a year as a general assembly 'to make, ordeine, and establishe all manner of wholesome and reasonable orders, lawes, statutes and ordinances and instructions ... not contrarie to the lawes of this our realme of England' (quoted in Rutman, 1965, p. 41). Once a year, the assembly was to elect from among themselves a governor, a deputy governor and a court of eighteen assistants 'to take care for the best disposing and ordering of the general business and affaires of ... the said landes and premises ... and the government of the people there' (ibid.). The original intention was that the settlement be governed from England. However, the settlement party insisted that the settlement be self-governing. The assembly of the colonists which met before sailing for New England elected John Winthrop, a Puritan landowner from Groton, Suffolk as governor, Thomas Dudley as deputy governor as well and ten assistants.

Winthrop set out his vision of a Puritan community in his sermon *A Model of Christian Charity*, which compared the Puritan settlement in the New World with the biblical exodus of the Israelites from Egypt to the promised land:

> For we must consider that we shall be as a city upon a hill. The eyes of all people are upon us ... But if our hearts shall turn away, so that we will not obey, but shall be seduced and worship other Gods, our pleasure and profits, and serve them; it is propounded unto us this day, we shall surely perish out of the good land whither we pass over this vast sea to possess it. Therefore let us choose life, that we and our seed may live, by obeying His voice and cleaving to Him, for He is our life and our prosperity.
>
> (Winthrop, 1630, p. 8)

Winthrop served twelve annual terms as governor seeking to balance the interests of the radicals and the conservatives. The radical group included Sir Henry Vane, who was briefly elected governor in 1636 at the age of twenty-three, and who was ousted a year later after a religious dispute, with Winthrop being re-elected as governor, and returned to England in 1637 where he became a leading parliamentarian and supporter of Cromwell during the English Civil War (Rowe, 1970, pp. 4–7). Another radical, Hugh Peters, was to return to England in 1641 as agent for the colony and then became chaplain to Cromwell's New Model Army. Winthrop's son, the younger John Winthrop, became governor of the colony of Connecticut. John Davenport and Theophilus Eaton left Boston in 1638 after the antinomian religious dispute to found the colony of New Haven (Archer, 1975).

Theocratic planning: New Haven

The colonisers of New Haven sought to base their planning and governance on a purer form of Puritanism – they considered that the victors in the Boston disputes, including the moderate Winthrop, had compromised the principles of Puritanism. Davenport and Cotton and their colleagues based their claim to land in the new settlement on purchase of land from the Indian population rather than on any colonial grant or charter. They therefore considered that they owed no allegiance to either the King or the Massachusetts Bay Company. Instead they first established a church government based on old testament principles and the civil government established later was to follow biblical principles in a more extreme form than that established in Boston and the other Massachusetts Bay settlements.

Archer (1975) presents a detailed argument that the plan for the layout of the town of New Haven was based on an interpretation of the layout of the temple in Jerusalem as described in the Old Testament, drawing references from a range of Christian thinkers such as the 1619 *Christianopolis* plan of the German theologian and Rosicrucian Johann Valentin Andrae and the commentaries on Ezekiel and the design of the Temple by the Spanish Jesuit Johannes Villalpandus. New Haven was laid out on the rectilinear principle, based on nine squares, with the government buildings in the central square, a design which replicates a view of Old Jerusalem published by Villapandus in 1604. The system of government established in New Haven was influenced by John Cotton's *Discourse about Civil Government in a New Plantation Whose Design is Religion*. Only free burgesses 'in fellowship of the church' had the right to participate in the government. With the absorption of New Haven into the colony of Connecticut in 1665, the theocratic governance structure established by Davenport and Cotton was superseded (Levermore, 1886; Calder, 1930).

The Restoration establishment: the re-planning of London and the Shaftesbury model for the planning of colonial settlement

British planning of the 18th and early 19th centuries can be seen as having two origins – the re-planning of London after the Great Fire of 1666, and the establishment of principles for the planning of new colonial settlements, also developed in the Restoration period. The debates over the redevelopment of London, and the plans by Christopher Wren, Robert Hooke, John Evelyn, Richard Newcourt and others have been subject to a number of scholarly studies. However, the principles and practice of early British colonial planning have received far less attention, though both their radicalism and the fact that unlike the plans for London, some were actually brought into effect, means that they are perhaps of greater significance and a sounder starting point for this study. The plans for the rebuilding of London are only referred to here so far as they were seen as having a potential influence on the planning of new settlements.

The plans of John Evelyn and Robert Hooke had similarities with the Wren Plan. All three plans had reference to the pre-fire features – London Wall, the Tower of London, St Paul's cathedral, the Thames and the Fleet ditch. It is however Richard Newcourt's grid square based plan which set out a framework for development which was to become familiar in early British colonial planning, and which is quoted as a precedent by historians of American colonial planning (Reps, 1965; Fries, 1977).

It has been argued that Newcourt's plan bears a strong resemblance to plans of Roman military encampments. The only pre-existing topographical feature it recognises is the River Thames. It is perhaps the ultimate *tabula rasa* plan for an existing capital city, comparable with Le Corbusier's 1925 *Plan Voisin* for the redevelopment of central Paris, though that city had not been subject to a devastating fire.

There has been extensive discussion as to the origins of the different plans for rebuilding London and the failure to implement any of these grand designs, beyond Christopher Wren's achievement of the building of St Paul's cathedral (Reddaway, 1940; Whinney, 1991; McKellar, 1999; Baker, 2000; Jardine, 2002; Darley, 2006; Hollis, 2008; Cooper, 2012). It is however worth noting that one study of the design of the cathedral presents a case that Wren was strongly influenced by features of the design of biblical Jerusalem, an argument which, as discussed above, was also made in relation to the development of New Haven in the Massachusetts Bay (Gilbert, 2002).

Robert Home in his fascinating history of British colonial planning sets out the principles of the model of colonial planning established in the 1670s by Lord Ashley, 1st Earl of Shaftesbury, Lord Chancellor to Charles II in the restoration period.

> 1. a policy of deliberate urbanisation, or town planting, in preference to dispersed settlement; 2. land rights allocated in a combination of town, suburban and country lots; 3.the town planned and laid out in advance of settlement; 4. wide streets laid out in geometric usually grid-iron form, usually on an area of one square mile; 5. public squares; 6. standard-sizes, rectangular plots, spacious in comparison with those in British towns of the time; 7. some plots reserved for public purposes; and 8. a physical distinction between town and country, usually by common land or an encircling green belt.
>
> (cited Home, 2013, p. 10)

It should be noted Shaftesbury was patron of the philosopher, John Locke, with whom he collaborated to write the constitution for Carolina.

William Penn, Thomas Holme and the planning of Philadelphia

In 1681 King Charles II handed over part of his land in North America to William Penn, as settlement of a debt owed to Penn's late father, Admiral Penn. The younger Penn was a Quaker leader and political radical and author of a number of tracts arguing for religious freedom and political reform. He was a supporter of the radical republican Algernon Sidney. In his 1679 polemic *England's Great Interest, in the Choice of this New Parliament Dedicated to All Her Free-Holders and Electors*, Penn argued for electors to choose as their representatives, independent individuals who were neither Roman Catholics nor government placeholders. The pamphlet set out the core principles of the radical Whig agenda: the right to property; the right to make laws; and the right to contribute to the application of justice through the jury system. Despite his religious and political dissidence, Penn was a member of the restoration court circle and a friend of the Duke of York, who was to become King James II. Penn already had a financial interest in the Quaker colonies in East and West Jersey, having had a role in assisting them in drafting the colonists; constitutions and in 1681 was appointed Governor and proprietor of the new area which became known as Pennsylvania (named after the father not the son).

Penn had the intention of using this land to undertake a 'holy experiment', which was not possible in England. Penn sent out three commissioners – William Crispin, John Bezar and Thomas Allen, to establish the colony (Bronner, 1978). He also appointed his cousin, William Markham, to travel with the commissioners and to act as governor on his behalf until he arrived. In the following year, he appointed Captain Thomas Holme as surveyor general, to survey a site suitable for the new settlement – the site on the river Delaware of the settlement which was to become Philadelphia, though it has also been suggested that the site was actually selected by the colonists before Holme arrived (Reps, 1965, p. 161). Penn had given the commissioners a set of instructions on the criteria for selecting a site.

Holme published in 1683 in London *A Portraiture of the City of Philadelphia*, which included a map accompanied by a description:

> The City (as the model shows) consists of a large Front-street to each river, and a High-street (near the idle) from Front (or river) to Front of one hundred Foot broad, and a Broad-street in the middle of the City, from side to side, of the like breadth. In the center of the City is a Square of ten acres; at each angle are to be Houses for Publick Affairs, as a Meeting-House, Assembly or State-House, Market-House, School-House, and several other Buildings for Publick Concerns. There are also in each Quarter of the City's Square of eight acres, to be for the like uses, as the Moorefields in London, and eight streets (beside the High-street), that run from Front to Front, and twenty streets (besides the Broad-street) that run across the City; all of these streets are of fifty foot breadth.
>
> (Holme 1683, cited in Reps, 1965, p. 161)

Reps considers the possible influences on Penn's plan, noting the reference to Moorfields and the fact that Penn had been at Lincoln's Inn and would have been familiar with the squares of Covent Garden, Leicester Square and Bloomsbury but then points to the similarity with Newcourt's plan for the redevelopment of London. He notes that irrespective of the origin of Penn's and Holme's ideas, and which of the two was responsible for the concept and its modifications, Philadelphia was the first American city to be laid out on a grid pattern. The plan provided for wide major streets and green spaces and the four squares anticipated later principles of neighbourhood parks. The development was compact and uncrowded and the 'liberty lands' to the north of the city functioned as a green belt (Reps, 1965, p. 172).

It is however necessary to consider the governance arrangements. Penn was a dissident as a Quaker but he was also proprietor governor on appointment from the King. It was therefore Penn who allocated lots of land to individual colonists. Penn had originally intended a city of 10,000 acres, but the initial area was reduced to 1200 acres. According to Lingelbach (1944), Penn's idea seems to have been to establish a province of landed gentry with large town houses, but due to the settlers mainly being persons of more moderate means, the blocks were subdivided and backstreets provided. The right to private property embedded in the governance of Pennsylvania was later to be embedded in the constitution of the United States with no provision for communal ownership or concept of 'the commons' as advocated by the Digger tradition.

These first settlement initiatives were to influence the next generation of colonial planners, those of the enlightenment period, though as will be discussed, these later initiatives being based on more rational 'enlightenment' thought, had less regard to the rules set out in ancient religious texts.

Primary sources

Cotton, John (1663) *Discourse about Civil Government in a New Plantation Whose Design is Religion* (Cambridge, MA)

Evelyn, John (1661) *Fumifugium* (London: Godrid, Bedel and Collins)

Evelyn, John (1666) *Londinum Redivinum* (edited by De Beer, E S, Oxford: Clarendon Press 1938)

Graves, Thomas (c 1635) *An Essay on the Laying Out of Towns* (Charles Town)

Holme, Thomas (1683) *A Portraiture of the City of Philadelphia* (London: Andrew Sowle)

Holme, Thomas (1683) *A Short Advertisement of the Situation and Extent of the City of Philadelphia* (London: Andrew Sowle)

Penn, William (1683) *A Letter from William Penn to the Committee of the Free Society of Traders* (London: Andrew Sowle)

Winthrop, John (1630) *A Model of Christian Charity* (Republished Boston, MA: Old South Association, 1916)

Secondary sources

Archer, J (1975) 'Puritan Town Planning in New Haven' in *Journal of the Society of Architectural Historians*, Vol 34, No 2 (May), pp. 140–9

Baker, T M (2000) *London. Rebuilding the City after the Great Fire* (London: Phillimore)

Bell, C and Bell, R (1969) *City Fathers The Early History of Town Planning in Britain* (London: Cresset Press)

Bennett, R ed. (1993) *Settlement in the Americas. Cross-Cultural Perspectives* (Newark, DE: University of Delaware Press)

Bronner E (1978) *William Penn's 'Holy Experiment': The Founding of Pennsylvania* (Westport, CT: Greenwood Publishing)

Calder, I M (1930) 'John Cotton and the New Haven Colony' in *New England Quarterly* III, pp. 82–94

Cooper, M (2012) *A More Beautiful City. Robert Hooke and the Rebuilding of London after the Great Fire* (London: Sutton)

Darley, G (2006) *John Evelyn: Living for Ingenuity* (New Haven, CT: Yale)

Fladeland, B (1984) *Abolitionists and Working Class Problems in the Age of Industrialization* (Baton Rouge, LA: Louisiana State University Press)

Fries, S D (1977) *The Urban Idea in Colonial America* (Philadelphia, PA: Templeton University Press)

Gilbert, A (2002) *The New Jerusalem. Rebuilding London, the Great Fire, Christopher Wren and the Royal Society* (London: Bantam)

Hamer, D (1990) *New Towns in the New World* (New York: Columbia University Press)

Hollis, L (2008) *The Phoenix: Men who made London* (London: Phoenix)

Home, R (2013) *Of Planting and Planning*, 2nd edn (London: Routledge)

Hough, O (1895 and 1896) 'Captain Thomas Holme, Surveyor General of Pennsylvania and Provincial Councillor' in *The Pennsylvania Magazine of History and Biography*, Vols XIX and XX.

Jardine, L (2002) *On a Grander Scale: The Outstanding Career and Tumultuous Times of Sir Christopher Wren* (London: HarperCollins)

Levermore, C H (1886) *The Republic of New Haven* (Baltimore, MD: John Hopkins University)

Lingelbach, W E (1944) 'William Penn and City Planning' in *Pennsylvania Magazine*, LXVIII, pp. 396–418

McKellar, E (1999) *The Birth of Modern London: The Development and Design of the City 1660–1720* (Manchester, UK: Manchester University Press)

Olsen, D (1964) *Town Planning in London in the Eighteenth and Nineteenth Centuries* (New Haven, CT: Yale University Press)

Reddaway, T F (1940) *The Rebuilding of London after the Great Fire* (London: Edward Arnold)

Reps, J (1965) *The Making of Urban America* (Princeton, NJ: Princeton University Press)

Rowe, V (1970) *Sir Henry Vane the Younger* (London: Athlone Press)

Rutman, D R (1965) *Winthrop's Boston: A Portrait of a Puritan Town 1630–1649* (New York: W W Norton)

Summerson, J (1991) *Georgian London* (London: Penguin)

Whinney, M (1991) *Christopher Wren* (London: Praeger)

3 Enlightenment planning

James Oglethorpe and Savannah

The Shaftesbury principles discussed in the last chapter were applied in the design of colonial settlement, including the settlements in Ulster, notably in Londonderry, and in the new colonial settlements in America, such as Savannah and Charles Town. It is difficult to conclude that liberal principle principles were applied in the case of the Ulster settlements. However, the settlement of Savannah does create some interesting precedents for the later work of the utilitarian planners.

James Oglethorpe, the founder of the colony of Georgia and planner of Savannah was a British army general, born in Surrey, who became the MP for Godalming in 1722. He was involved in a number of philanthropic initiatives, including campaigning against poor conditions of sailors in the Navy and in 1728 as chairman of a parliamentary committee on prison reform, he argued for the improvement of conditions in debtors' prisons. This led to many debtors being released from prison but without means of support. Oglethorpe viewed this as part of the larger problem of urbanisation, which was depleting the countryside of productively employed people and depositing them in cities, particularly London, where they often became impoverished or resorted to criminal activity. Oglethorpe and a group of associates, many of whom served on the prison committee, considered that one solution to this problem was to remove this impoverished and criminal class from London by settling them elsewhere. They therefore petitioned in 1730 to form the *Trustees for the Establishment of the Colony of Georgia in America*. The petition was finally approved in 1732, and the first group of colonists, led by Oglethorpe, departed for the New World in November (Ettinger, 1936).

It should be noted that Oglethorpe's plan for the colonisation of Georgia was not the first such plan. In 1717, a Scottish laird, Sir Robert Montgomery, published a plan for a colony which he called the *Margravate of Azilia*. The initial settlement of Charles Town (now Charleston) in South Carolina, formed in 1670, had been threatened not just by the native Indians, but by the French colonists based in Louisiana and the Spanish from the South, who attacked Charles Town during the War of the Spanish Succession during the reign of Queen Anne. In his tract *A Discourse concerning the design'd establishment of a New Colony to the South of Carolina, in the most delightful country of the Universe*, Montgomery set out the principles for the new settlement.

The colony was to be 400 square miles. At the centre was to be a city three miles square, with the palace of the Margrave or ruler as the central focus. The city would be surrounded by a mile-wide void – effectively a green belt. Montgomery sought a grant from the proprietors of Carolina. The colony would pay a penny sterling for each acre of land – 400 square miles comprising 256,000 acres. Outside the green belt would be the homes of the gentry. Beyond the nobles' estates and four great parks – one in each quadrant – would live the commoners who would work the farms, who would obtain ownership of the farms after a number of years of indentured labour. The labourers would be indentured from England's poorer classes. They would be citizens and soldiers – a citizen army defending the perimeter wall against the French, the Spanish and the Indians (Montgomery, 1717; Reps, 1965, pp. 183–4).

Montgomery believed that

> Poor labouring Men, so secur'd of a fix'd future Settlement, will be thereby induced to go thither more willingly; and act, when there, with double Dilligence and Duty; And when their Time expirers, possessing just Land enough to pass their Lives as Ease, and bring their Children up honestly, the Familes they leave will prove a constant Seminary of sober Servants, of Both Sexes, for the Gentry of the Colony, whereby they will be under no necessity to use the Dangerous Help of Blackamoors, or Indians.

Montgomery's plan progressed no further than the publication of his pamphlet. According to Home, this was due to the collapse of business confidence in 1720 following the South Sea Bubble scandal. Oglethorpe's plan, though also aimed at providing farms for the destitute of London, was however to be based on slightly more egalitarian principles. There have been a number of studies of Oglethorpe and the colonisation of Georgia, a state which regards Oglethorpe as its founding father. Benjamin Martyn, biographer of the first Earl Shaftesbury who had founded Charles Town, and became secretary to the colony of Georgia, wrote a tract in 1733 justifying the settlement of the colony: *Reasons for establishing the colony of Georgia*, with the subheading *With regard to the Trade of Great Britain, the Increase of our People, and the Employment and Support it will afford to great Numbers of our own Poor, as well as foreign persecuted Protestants.*

The pamphlet was actually written before Oglethorpe and the first colonisers had arrived in the Americas, though it was first published together with a letter from Oglethorpe dated February 10th 1733, reporting on his arrival at the site on the Savannah river, the marking out of the town plan, the progress of clearing the site and the start of construction of the first house. Oglethorpe also reported that the local Indians were friendly – that they were

> desirous to be subjects to his Majesty King George, to have Lands given them among us, and to breed their Children in our Schools, and that Their Chief and his Beloved Man, who is the Second Man in the Nation, desire to be instructed in the Christian Religion

(Martyn, 1733, p. 44)

Oglethorpe's basic argument was that in England the 4000 debtors put in gaol each year made no contribution to society and that a third of the debt was never recovered, – 'For while they are in prison, they are absolutely lost, the Publick loses their Labour and their Knowledge' (Martyn, 1773, p. 18). The pamphlet then set out the economic argument:

Tho a Man, who has not been inur'd to the Labour of the Country, and has a Family, will not go to the Plough for so poor a Support for them, as a Labourer's Hire, and even this likewise precarious; yet he will not repine at any Fatigue, when it is on an Estate of his own, and his Gains from this Estate will rise in Proportion to his Labour, Add to this, the high Values of the commodities to be rais'd there, and the low Prices of Provisions will make it easy to conceive that the Man, who cannot do half the Work of an able Man here, may earn a sufficient Provision for himself and Family in Georgia, especially when he pays neither Rent nor Taxes for his Lands.

(ibid., pp. 17–18)

The Georgia settlement was funded by parliamentary grants amounting to £142,169 over the first twenty years. Over the period, there were 2122 colonists sponsored by the settlement trust, comprising a mix of the worthy poor recruited by the trustees, though few were people released from debtors prisons, soldiers and indentured servants – single people who after a fixed period of time were granted their own land; 3482 self-supporting colonists and 1026 foreign colonists, persecuted Protestants expelled from Salzburg in Austria ; Moravians who were descendants of the Hussites (most of whom relocated to Pennsylvania), Lutherans from the Palatine in Germany, Swabians from Bavaria and Protestants from the Vaud in Switzerland, and Sephardic and Ashkenazi Jews from Portugal, Germany and Italy. Land allocation was not entirely equitable – self-supporting colonists were granted 500-acre estates; trust sponsored colonists were granted only fifty acres. The self-supporting colonists were required to provide nine servants to help with the clearance of land for the wider settlement (Fries, 1904; Wilson 2012, pp. 103–6).

Savannah became famous for Oglethorpe's use of the grid square system. Writers have debated the extent to which this system derived from Vitruvian principles, channelled through Newcourt's unimplemented plan for London (Reps, 1975; Wilson, 2012), from Roman colonial/military settlements such as Timgad in North Africa, or from Renaissance cities such as Turin. It is interesting that Oglethorpe, according to Wilson (2012), took some of his governing principles from the Renaissance politician, Machiavelli, with recognition of the influence of British political theorists Henry Bolingbroke, James Harrington and George Berkeley as the basis for his governance arrangements. Thomas argues that Oglethorpe adopted from Machiavelli the principle that a settlement required a 'commodious Distribution of the People . . . living regularly and in Order'. One of the most contentious principles that there should be no slaves in the Georgia colony was however not derived from Machiavelli, but from Oglethorpe's own personal conviction.

By 1745, the settlement had grown to 250 homes. Public buildings included the trustees' storehouse, a court-house, a gaol, a guard house and a public wharf. Within each ward there was a public square. However, by then, there was a group known as the 'malcontents' who were challenging both Oglethorpe personally and the principles on which the settlement was based. Some 100 settlers had abandoned Savannah, the colony was only fifty per cent self-sufficient in food and the trustees' garden was unattended. The 'malcontents' argued that slaves were necessary if the colony was to be viable. This was resisted by Oglethorpe who was supported by the trustees. The trustees however reduced Oglethorpe's authority and in the latter years he focused on organising the military defence of the colony rather than the governance of the main settlement. When Oglethorpe returned to England in 1749, the trustees conceded to the 'malcontents' and petitioned the king to repeal the act prohibiting slavery in the colony. The principle of agrarian equality had also been abandoned and in 1752 the trustees surrendered the Georgian colony to the King, and Ogelthorpe's 'utopian' experiment was over. The physical plan of the town however largely survived and great efforts have been made to preserve the historic landmark district.

The debate over London's growth

The debate over planning in late 18th century and early 19th century England was not limited to the planning of new colonial settlements. Ever since the failure to implement the plans of Christopher Wren, Robert Hooke, John Evelyn and Richard Newcourt for the rebuilding of the City of London after the great fire of 1666, London's intellectuals had debated the need for planning the metropolis. In fact, the debate over the management of London's development had an even earlier origin with the first Mayor of London, Henry Fitz Ailwin establishing a building code in 1189, which regulated construction including party walls, rights of light, drainage and the location of privy pits and with Queen Elizabeth I issuing a proclamation against any new building within three miles of the City of London in 1580 – a proclamation widely ignored. Cromwell was later to promote a 10-mile limit. It was Evelyn who, having warned of the pollution arising from London's congestion, had in his polemic *Fumifugium* argued for more open space for London and who after the fire in his pamphlet *London Revived* put forward principles for the redevelopment of the city, which had led to King Charles II and parliament passing a series of rebuilding acts.

In 1766, John Gwynn published proposals for *London and Westminster Improved*.Gwynn was an architect and civil engineer and one of the founders of the Royal Academy. Gwynn had obtained Wren's original plan for London which he republished in 1749 with his own comments. These comments included the argument that Wren's work should not be left unfinished and that there should:

> be a general plan for the whole capital, improved and divided into proper districts, the execution of which improvements should be put under the direction of fit and able persons, who should be empowered by authority, to regulate the scattered and confused appearance they make, to restore the ruinated parts to beauty, and fix the proper mode of new improvements, by which means not only the value of private property would be considerably increased, but these improvements become conducive to health as well as publick convenience.

Gwynn's view was that:

> the magnificent, elegant and useful plan of the great Sir Christopher Wren was totally disregarded and sacrificed to the mean, interested and selfish views of private property, views which did irreparable injury to the citizens themselves, and to the nation in general, for had that great architect's plan been followed,

what has often been asserted must have been the result, the metropolis of this kingdom would inconceivably have been the most magnificent and elegant city in the universe.

(Gwynn, 1776, pp. 3–4)

Gwynn's plan, which covered Westminster, the City and the South Bank, put forward detailed proposals for a series of street widenings, extensions and new streets to create a network of boulevards. He also proposed that the cattle markets be moved away from the centre of the city to 'the back part of Islington', and to 'somewhere near the Borough of Southwark' (ibid., pp. 19–20).

Gwynn's main concern was that villages like Hampstead and Highgate would be incorporated into suburban London. He wanted London to be contained within the area south of the new road between Paddington and Islington (now the Marylebone and Euston Roads). He put forward proposals for formal layout of Hyde Park and also for the replacement of the jumbled network of roads south of St James Park into a grid system to reflect that north of the park.

Concluding his polemic, Gwynn urged that:

it must be allowed that publick works of real magnificence, taste. Elegance and utility, in a commercial city, are of the utmost consequence, they are not only of real use in point of splendour and convenience, but as necessary to the community as health and clothing to the human body.

(ibid., pp. 20–1)

Finishing with a patriotic challenge that if the British could beat the French in battle, they should also be able to compete in the splendour of their capital city.

There was a contrary argument put forward by James 'Athenian' Stuart, the architect, artist and pioneer of neo-classicism, in his 1771 pamphlet *Critical Observations on the Buildings and Improvements of London*. Stuart's pamphlet contrasts London with Louis XIV's Paris and puts forward proposals for road improvements, improvements to the main Belgravia and Westminster squares, the more effective use of the River Thames and for a new palace for the royal family – commenting 'how disgraceful to see the head of this mighty empire worse lodged than the Gonfalcionicre of San Marino or the chief magistrate of Glavis or Zug!' This is despite a comment that 'all public improvements must among us spring originally from the spirit of the people and not from the will of the prince' (Stuart, 1771, p. 2).

The conclusion to the polemic focuses on the need for London to grow:

On the whole I look upon the late increase of London as a natural consequence of the prosperity of the nation, and a sure token of its healthy and vigorous state, and cannot, with our gloomy politicians, foresee danger and calamity, from an evil, if it were one which naturally checks itself. At the same time, I ardently wish for every improvement, in a moral, political and economical sense, which the city is able to receive; and am convinced that the public works so much cherished at present will contribute in no small degree to those important ends. Canals, embankments, high roads, necessarily facilitate the transport of provisions and commodities, and the opening, paving, lighting, and removing nuisances from the streets and squares, certainly conduce to the health and security of the inhabitants.

(ibid., pp. 49–50)

Stuart also argued that physical improvements led to the populace becoming more civilised:

Nor are embellishments without their use. The refinement of taste in a nation never fails to be accompanied by a suitable refinement of manners; and people accustomed to behold order, decency, and elegance in public, soon acquire that urbanity in private, which forms at once the excellence and bond of society.

(ibid., p. 50)

For Stuart, the state of London is a symbol of the might of the British Empire:

It is the duty of every good man to join in promoting these designs; indeed if one may judge from the apparent spirit of the times, the period is not far distant, when Great Britain will possess a capital, worthy of a nation which stands foremost in reputation, and is at once the dread and envy of Europe.

(ibid. p. 50–1)

Jeremy Bentham, whose role will be discussed more fully in the next chapter, also contributed to this debate, though from a somewhat different perspective. In his *Manual of Political Economy* written in 1800, he referred to concerns about the growth of towns such as London as 'the most extravagant fears' of 'this imaginary evil'. 'Absurdity has been carried so far, as to make rules for limiting their bounds: they should rather have been made for extending them' (Bentham, 1848, quoted in Simo, 1988, p. 238).

Contagious disorders would thus have been prevented; the air would have been rendered more salubrious. The opposite regulations do not diminish the number of inhabitants, but oblige them to heap themselves up within close habitations, and to build one city upon another.

(Bentham, 1848, ch. 4)

John Gwynn and James Stuart's plans for improving London were only the first of a series of proposals. In 1789, William Pickett published *Public Improvement; or, a Plan for making a convenient and handsome communication between the Cities of London and Westminster*. Pickett was a silversmith and a member of the Corporation of London who in 1789 was Lord Mayor. His main concern was with increasing traffic congestion in the city. In 1787 he had proposed that the Corporation set up a committee to investigate how to make the entrance to the city at Temple Bar on the Strand more commodious for carriages. This generated little interest from his colleagues. His pamphlet proposed a plan for creating a new main street to the south of the Strand. The lack of support for the plan demonstrates the conservative nature of the city common councillors and aldermen and their unwillingness to interfere with the historic streets of the city, especially those which had survived the fire of 1666. In fact, there were to be no significant improvements to the streets of central London until the Kingsway project in 1898–1905 initiated by the London County Council.

The west end of London was, however, the centre of significant improvement activity and the development of the squares of Belgravia was followed by the creation of a major new highway in Regent Street developed by John Nash between 1811 and 1833 to connect the Marylebone Park, later named Regent's Park, with Trafalgar Square. This project should, however, be viewed as an 'embellishment' project as envisaged by James Stuart rather than aiming primarily to improve the passage of traffic through Westminster.

It is the landscape architect John Claudius Loudon, a friend of Bentham, who is generally credited for producing the first plan for London which explicitly proposed the notion of a Green Belt. Loudon was editor of the *Gardener's Magazine*. By the time he developed an interest in the planning of London, he had had an extensive career in both promoting landscape design and carrying out landscape projects. Loudon used his journal to argue the case against speculative building in Kensington Gardens and open sewers in Hyde Park. In 1803, he had written to the editor of the *Literary Journal* arguing for more evergreen shrubs to be planted in London's residential squares. Having an interest in wider reform issues, he also produced a design for a working men's college – a seven-storey apartment block for families, proposed as an alternative to the tenements of London's East End. In 1822, Loudon proposed a 'promenade', in fact an inner ring road for carriages, linking Regents Park to Vauxhall Bridge, Kennington, Blackheath, Greenwich, crossing the Thames on a new bridge, before joining City Road, the New Road (now Euston Road/ Marylebone Road) and completing the circle at Regent's Park (Simo, 1988, p. 216). Throughout the 1820s Loudon both criticised improvement projects and put forward his own proposals. In 1825 he was complaining about the dusty unpaved avenues that formed the approaches to London, which he referred to as a 'vast overgrown town' and proposed that old houses be demolished to create a grand western entrance to the metropolis at Hyde Park Corner (ibid., p. 217) Like Stuart, he argued that the King should get a new palace – his proposed location was at the eastern end of Hyde Park facing Park Lane.

It is, however, Loudon's plan for London *Hints for Breathing Places*, published in 1829, that stakes his claim to be London's first strategic planner. The plan is not a substantial work but a single diagram supported by three pages of text published in the *Gardener's Magazine*. As the first plan for Greater London with a green belt in concentric rings, it has obtained iconic status in both landscape architecture and strategic planning disciplines. Loudon states that his attention was drawn to 'the rapid extension of buildings on every side of London' by a recent attempt in parliament to enclose Hampstead Heath. He argues that it is the duty of government:

> to devise some plan by which the metropolis may be enlarged so as to cover any with perfect safety to the inhabitants, in respect to the supply of provisions, water, and fresh air, and to the removal of filth of every description, the maintenance of general cleanliness, and the despatch of business.

Loudon's key proposal was that London 'be extended in alternate mile wide zones of buildings with half mile zones of country or gardens, till one of the zones reached the sea', in effect a series of concentric circles. The aim was that:

> there could never be an inhabitant who would be farther than half a mile from an open airy situation. In which he was free to walk or ride, and in which he could find every mode of amusement, recreation, entertainment and instruction.
>
> (Loudon, 1829)

Loudon was aware that to bring the scheme into effect in London, homes would need to be demolished. He recognised that the plan might be more appropriate for a new town for example a capital for an Australian union, in which case all government buildings would be built in a central circle.

Loudon also proposed a street hierarchy, based on separating streets for public conveyances and streets for use of freight and cattle being brought to market. He suggested steam carriages running on railroads be established in all the main streets. Under every street there would be a sewer and subways for the mains of water and gas. He proposed a system for recycling human waste to generate manure, with filtered water piped out for use for irrigation in the country beyond the outer zone. There should be unrestricted development of leisure facilities in the country zones including water features – especially if there were no danger of them producing malaria. He concluded the article by hoping that the principles of his plan would be considered before any other enclosure bills were enacted.

Sidney Smirke, the architect, in his 1834 pamphlet of *Suggestions for the Architectural Improvement of the Western Part of London*, had a different perspective. Smirke was the architect of the British Museum Reading Room and the Bethlem Hospital in Kennington, now the Imperial War Museum. Smirke focused on the need for wider streets, clean air and better drainage and referring back to Gwynn's plan, proposed that a metropolitan commission be established which would introduce new planning regulations to replace the Building Acts. His pamphlet was a substantive work of over 100 pages with one picture – a grandiose proposal for a new parliament building which would be situated on the north bank of the Serpentine in what became Hyde Park, with the existing parliamentary buildings becoming a court of justice.

Like Gwynn, Smirke made a negative comparison with the achievements of the French but also pointed out that London had no monuments to compete with those of Berlin or Munich. On London's lack of grand avenues, he lamented that 'We look in vain for a Corso, a Strada nuova, a Canal grande, or a Herrengrasse' (Smirke, 1834). He then, like Gwynn, makes a series of detailed proposals for street improvements, though unlike Gwynn does not set these out on any plan.

Smirke also had plans for new developments of working class housing so people could move from the slums. He proposed that:

> portions of unoccupied ground should be taken on the skirts of the town and let a village, expressedly dedicated to the working classes be erected. The avenues should be laid out to be wide, clear and regular; and every means for securing cleanliness should be adopted. The houses should be arranged and constructed

upon a plan totally differing in every respect from the small, close, inconvenient tenements usually let out into lodgings and each should be built with a view to consult in every way the comfort of the inhabitants.

He suggested the wasteland beyond Vauxhall Road, the open fields west of the Edgware Road and those behind Euston Square. He stressed the importance of providing 'some open place for recreation, where healthy exercises and the innocent pleasures of society might be enjoyed during the hours of leisure and the days of rest.'

Smirke argued that:

> the ground should be purchased by the public money and appropriated for the use of the labouring classes; and a commission of some such permanent Board should assume the whole direction and superintendence of the works. If the requisite sum for the completion of this project be advanced by way of a loan, and entrusted to the management of the Board, there is every reason to hope that, even supposing these tenements to be let at a rate far lower than the usual rent which this class of people are accustomed to pay, an income would arise quite sufficient to pay reasonable interest on the money expended. And to yield a surplus that might form a sinking fund for the ultimate repayment of the principal.

Smirke pointed out that if the plan was left to be carried out by private speculators, the rents would be too high. He emphasised that it was necessary to house the poorest and most destitute classes as well as the various classes of mechanics (ibid., pp. 61–7).

Loudon responded to Smirke's pamphlet with an extended review in the *Architectural Magazine*. Loudon supported Smirke's overall approach. Loudon suggested that the whole developed area of London –

> say within a circle of five miles from St Paul's, with power of extension, ought to be formed into a representative municipal government; and this having been done, every thing connected with general improvement would come under the cognizance of a proper department, and discussed in public, and consequently open to the criticism of the press.
>
> (Loudon, 1834, p. 179)

Loudon did not however support Smirke's proposal for subsidised housing for working mechanics believing that 'These and every working class, must be put into a position to take care of themselves' (Loudon, 1834, p. 382).

Planning and anti-slavery: Granville Sharp and colonial planning

The first London radical to take a direct interest in the planning of new settlements was Granville Sharp. Sharp was a leading abolitionist, close friend of William Wilberforce, a member of the evangelical group known as 'the Clapham sect' and a political reformer and prolific pamphleteer. His role, through the 'Somerset case' in establishing the principle that any slave setting foot in England became a free man has detracted attention from his other significant achievements and he has not as yet been the subject of a full biography. Sharp was member of the Society for Constitutional Information. He published reform pamphlets, arguing the case for annual parliaments and for the liberty of the citizen. During the American war of independence, he advocated the representation of Americans in the British parliament. Sharp was a friend of General Oglethorpe, the planner of Savannah, now in his 90s, and collaborated with him against the enforced recruitment of sailors into the navy and therefore must have known about Oglethorpe's earlier work (Cooper, 1979; Watner, 1980).

In the 1780s Sharp helped to establish the Committee for the Relief of the Black Poor, which supported destitute negroes living in London. A botanist, Henry Smeatham, who travelled around the coasts of West Africa collecting specimens for Sir Joseph Banks at Kew Gardens, came up with the idea of a new agricultural settlement based on free labour. This idea was taken up by Sharp who proposed that the new colony on an island within what is now Sierra Leone, be settled by the London negroes. In 1786, Sharp published *A Short Sketch of Temporary Regulations (until better shall be proposed) for the intended settlement of the Grain Coast of Africa near Sierra Leone*. He also obtained a grant from the Treasury and in February 1787, 456 passengers of whom over 100 were white colonists, sailed from Portsmouth. Sharp named the colony the Province of Freedom as it was to be based on the prohibition of slavery and all settlers, irrespective of race, participating in its government. The first settlement was named Granville Town. The colony was to be based on groupings of ten families, with each grouping annually electing a leader who would represent them on the governing body. Land was to be divided equally. Taxation was to be direct in the form of sixty-two days' labour each year for the government. Labour was on the basis of an eight-hour day. The colonists, depleted by disease and desertion nevertheless tried to follow Sharp's intentions, though some of the settlers were sold into slavery by the local chief.

In December 1789, the settlement was burnt by a local chief known as 'King Jimmy' in retaliation for the burning of one of his towns by sailors from a British warship. The survivors with support from a newly founded Sierra Leone Company established a new settlement two miles further east at Fourah Bay. This settlement was then strengthened by the arrival of 1200 free negroes from Nova Scotia, who had to flee the newly independent America having fought for the British in the War of Independence. The settlement developed into Freetown, though had to be rebuilt after being destroyed by the French in September 1794. Sharp's friend, Zachary Macaulay, abolitionist, fellow Clapham sect member and father of the novelist, became governor in 1796. Sierra Leone became a crown colony in 1808. By then Sharp's principle of self-government had long been abandoned (Peterson, 1969).

In 1794, Sharp, not completely disillusioned by the difficulties in Granville Town, published *A General Plan for Laying out Towns and Townships on the new acquired lands in the East Indies, America or elsewhere*.

On the title page, Sharp set out the objective of the Plan:

> In order to promote Cultivation, and raise the Value of all the adjoining Land, at the Price of giving gratis the Town-lots. And in some cases (as in new Colonies) also the small Out-lots, to the first settlers and their Heirs, so long as they possess no other land; and on other equitable conditions.

The Plan included a sketch of the layout for a new settlement, together with detailed measurements.

> The town is contained in a square, each side of which is 4 furlongs, or half a mile; having a square furling, or 10 acres, in the centre, appropriated to public offices (viz, a church, town-hall, guard-house, separate penitentiary lots (or prisons) for males and females; also schools for each sex, and a public caravansera for strangers and travellers, under the control of the constable on guard by rotation). The Breadth of the streets and highways is proposed to be the 8th part of a furlong, or 82 feet 6 inches; which will allow room for aqueducts wherever streams of water can be introduced from superior levels, and also room for planting ranges of spreading trees to shelter the footpaths.
>
> (Sharp, 1794, p. 4)

The plan then gives detailed measurements of each type of lot and the width of streets. It then deals with the economics of settlement:

> In old settled countries, where land is already of considerable value, it is not to be supposed that the proprietors of land can be induced to give gratis more than the small town-lots of half an acre and a few poles each, which with the roads and streets will amount to about 120 acres to be given gratis out of 2560 acres, or less than 4 ¾ per cent; and the improved value of the remaining estat, most certainly, will amply repay the donation; as the value of land is generally doubled by the proximity of a town.
>
> (ibid., p. 5)

Sharp suggested that the minimum size for a new settlement was 100 householders 'which is a very respectable body of people for maintaining peace and good order according to the common law of England' (ibid., p. 6).

Sharp then went on to make a fairly obvious point:

> Whenever only one half of the plan is adopted, the side where the central line of division is made must be placed next to the water (whether the sea or river, creek or canal), and care must be taken that a sufficient strand, or space of common land, be reserved between town and the water, that all the inhabitants may have equal access to the waterside.
>
> (ibid., p. 6)

The plan sets out the conditions on which 'the proprietors of the land should give gratis to each male settler, of good moral character, and of ability to labour, one small town-lot' (ibid., p. 10).

The conditions include:

> For the safety and happiness of each community, the land should be granted on the farther especial condition, that the settlers shall promise to keep watch and ward by rotation of militia service, under their own elected chiefs, that they may duly maintain PEACE, JUSTICE and COMMON RIGHT, in their respective communities and folkmotes, according to the common law of England in

FRANKPLEDGE which is the only effectual mode of obtaining law, peace, and good government, without expence.

(ibid., p. 10)

Sharp then explains the notion of Frankpledge, which he had also used in his Sierra Leone regulations eight years earlier:

Frankpledge is an ancient patriarchal mode of arranging the families, or rather households, of a nation, in numerical divisions of TENS (or tythings), FIFTIES, HUNDREDS (or wappentacs) and THOUSANDS of householders, or masters of families ,including all that either rent a house by the year or live in their own houses, and pay their due proportion of public expenses. All such, by this most ancient and salutary system [a footnote explaining that the system was derived from Magna Charta which itself was derived from Moses governance arrangements as set out in Deuteronomy Ch 1] were required to pledge each other ; and to pledge (or be responsible) for every other individual living under their respective roofs; whereby all persons were rendered most completely, and readily amenable to JUST LAWS (an indispensable condition of LIBERTY; because , neither LIBERTY, nor JUSTICE, can walk upright and secure, unless they go hand in hand).

(ibid., pp. 10–13)

In a letter which accompanies the plan, Sharp emphasises that these governance arrangements, including the right to vote, should be applied among the Indian nations as well as among the colonists.

Oglethorpe and Sharp can both be seen as progressives, both seeking to establish the urban structure and governance of new settlements on enlightenment principles. Both colonial pioneers were actively engaged in domestic radical politics – Oglethorpe in campaigns for prison reform; Sharp in the anti-slavery campaign and a series of campaigns for constitutional reform. Both saw colonial settlement as an opportunity to apply their egalitarian principles in a new setting. Their writings and their practical application of their theories were to influence the colonial planners of the next phase of colonial settlement, in which the utilitarian followers of Jeremy Bentham were to play a significant role as will be discussed in the next chapter.

Primary sources

Gwynn, John (1766) *London and Westminster Improved, Illustrated by Plans* (London)
Hoare, Prince (1828) *Memoirs of Granville Sharp Esq*, 2 volumes (London: Henry Colburn)
Loudon, J C (1829) 'Hints for Breathing Spaces for the Metropolis' in *Gardener's Magazine* (London: Gardener's Magazine)
Loudon, J C (1834) 'Response to Sidney Smirke' in *Architecture Magazine*
Martyn, Benjamin (1733) *Reasons for Establishing the Colony of Georgia* (London: Meadows)
Montgomery, Sir Robert (1717) *A Discourse concerning the design'd establishment of a New Colony to the South of Carolina, in the most delightful country of the Universe.*
Pickett, William (1789) *Public improvement; or, a plan for making a convenient and handsome communication between the cities of London and Westminster* (Reprint of 1789)
Roebuck, J A (1835) *Pamphlets for the People* (London: Charles Ely)

Roebuck, J A (1849) *The Colonies of England: A Plan for the Government of Some Portion of our Colonial Possessions* (reprinted, London: Dawsons of Pall Mall, 1968)

Sharp, Granville (1782) *The Claims of the People of England* (London: J Stockdale)

Sharp, Granville (1784) *A Declaration of the People's Natural Right to a Share in the Legislature which is the Fundamental Principle of the British Constitution of State* (London: B White)

Sharp, Granville (1786) *A Short Sketch of Temporary Regulations for the Intended Settlement on the Grain Coast of Africa near Sierra Leone* (reprinted, New York: Negro Universities Press, 1970)

Sharp, Granville (1794) *A General Plan for laying out Towns and Townships on the new acquired lands in the East Indies, America or elsewhere* (reprinted, Utah, Repressed Press, 2013)

Smirke, Sidney (1834) 'Review and comment on Suggestions for the Architectural Improvement of the Western Part of London', *Architectural Magazine*. June 1834 and December 1834

Stuart, Charles (1836) *A Memoir of Granville Sharp* (New York: American Anti-Slavery Society)

Stuart, James (1771) *Critical Observations on the Buildings and Improvements of London* (London: J Dodsley)

Secondary sources

Cooper, R (1979) Entry for Granville Sharp in Baylen, J and Gossman, N (eds), *Biographical Dictionary of Modern British Radicals*, Vol 1, 1770–1830, pp. 433–6 (Sussex, UK: Harvester Press)

Ettinger, A A (1936) *James Edward Oglethorpe: Colonial Idealist* (Oxford: Oxford University Press)

Fries, A (1904) *The Moravians in Georgia 1735–1740* (reprinted, Clearfield, PA: Clearfield Books, 2009)

Hamer, D (1990) *New Towns in the New World* (New York: Columbia University Press)

Peterson, J (1969) *Province of Freedom: A History of Sierra Leone 1787–1870* (London: Faber and Faber)

Rich, E E (1956) 'The First Earl of Shaftesbury's Colonial Policy' in *Transactions of the Royal Historical Society*, Vol 7, Jan, pp. 47–70

Simo, M (1988) *Loudon and the Landscape* (New Haven, CT: Yale University Press)

Watner, C (1980) 'In Favorem Libertas: The Life and Work of Granville Sharp' in *The Journal of Libertarian Studies*, Vol 4, No 2 (Spring), pp. 215–32

Wilson, T D (2012) *The Oglethorpe Plan: Enlightenment Planning in Savannah and Beyond* (Charlottesville, VT: University of Virginia Press)

4 The Benthamites and utilitarian planning

The influence of Jeremy Bentham

Jeremy Bentham was a political theorist and self-appointed constitutional adviser to governments in Europe and the newly independent states of Latin America. He has key place in the historiography of the development of the theory and practice of government. He is known as the founder of the theory of utilitarianism, which is best summarised as: the doctrine that actions are right if they are useful or for the benefit of a majority; the doctrine that an action is right in so far as it promotes happiness, and that the greatest happiness of the greatest number should be the guiding principle of conduct. Bentham was the intellectual mentor of an extensive group of radical philosophers, politicians and civil servants, known as the utilitarians, with the political group becoming known as the philosophical radicals (Halevy, 1928; Thomas, 1979).

Bentham has achieved a place in the history of architectural theory for his development of the concept of the Panopticon – his design of an institutional building, which enabled the supervision of occupants from a single central point – a design which has been used as the basis of the design of prisons and therefore won prominence in theories of social control and the use of design for the suppression of dissidence and consequently a central role in the theories of Michel Foucault (Foucault, 1975).

For the history of planning, it is perhaps Bentham's *Manual of Political Economy*, originally written in 1800 but only published by Sir John Bowring in 1843, twelve years after Bentham's death, which is more useful as a concise summary of Bentham's writings on the economy and colonisation. The main purpose of this work was, having stated that 'According to the principle of utility in every branch of the art of legislation, the object or end in view should be the production of the maximum of happiness in a given time in the community in question' to answer the question 'how far the end in view is best promoted by individuals acting for themselves? and in what cases these ends may be best promoted by the hands of government?' (Bentham, 1848, ch. 1).

Bentham established the components of wellbeing as subsistence, security and enjoyment. These principles were to act as benchmarks for Bentham's followers.

Roebuck in a speech defined the utilitarian view of the role of government:

> The business of Government is not merely to prevent evil, but also, by the concentrated force of the social system, by all the means which its powers confer on it, the happiness and well-being of its subjects.
>
> (quoted in Roberts, 1979, p. 65)

Given Bentham's opposition to colonisation, which he argued was of no economic benefit to the home country and without legal or moral justification, it is perhaps curious that it was in the planning of new settlements overseas that his followers demonstrated how utilitarian principles could be applied.

John Arthur Roebuck – amenity and planning

J A Roebuck was the leading politician in the utilitarian group. A follower of Bentham and Joseph Hume, he worked closely with James Mill and Francis Place, the 'radical tailor of Charing Cross'. Born in India, and growing up in Canada, Roebuck returned to England in 1824 to study law. Joining the Utilitarian Society and active in the campaign for parliamentary reform, he was elected MP for Bath in 1833 in the first election after the passage of the Reform Bill of 1832. An advanced radical, he campaigned for the expropriation of the property of the Church of England, argued against coercion in Ireland and was one of the six MPs who sat on the committee which helped draft the People's Charter of 1838 (Leader, 1897; Beadle, 1984).

Hyde (1947) notes that in 1828, Roebuck put forward proposals for town development based on Benthamite principles to a meeting of the Utilitarian Society on the basis of a motion 'that this House views with concern the present state of the industrial towns'. He advocated boulevards and parks within towns and large tracts of common land around towns to be maintained by the state for the use of town dwellers:

> We must create a public trust and prevent by law if necessary the rights of the common people from being swept away at the hand of the proprietor who would enclose the land round our towns for his own future profit, and the pseudo-builder who would cover it with ugliness" The land was to be maintained from a tax on the increased value of land on the edge of towns which would be developed as the boundary of a town was extended.

In 1834, Roebuck led the Radical attack on an enclosure bill promoted by Lord Ellenborough. In 1835, in one of his series of political pamphlets, *Pamphlets for the People*, he published *On the Amusement of the Aristocracy and of the People*. He attacked the aristocratic obsession with hunting and racing and argued against the enclosure of the commons:

> A poor man must work during the week; hid only day of rest and recreation is the feast day of the olden church. His body and his mind both want rest and recreation – not mere idleness, and perfect inactivity, but such easy and pleasant exercise as sets the spirits in motion, and excites the mind to pleasurable feelings.
>
> (Roebuck, 1835, p. 4)

> Having driven the people from the commons, our legislators went another step in advance, and shut them out of the fields also . . . Now the grand delight of an English landowner is to have his pleasures to himself. He hates his park if the people walk through it; his fields lose their beauty if a path runs across them; so he goes to the Legislature, and there he passes an act by which any two justices can shut up a pathway . . .
>
> (ibid., p. 5)

In 1836 the Radicals, in an initiative led by Roebuck, amended the Common Field Enclosure Bill by protecting common land around towns:

Towns of 5,000 inhabitants to have no common lands enclosed within a radius of one mile

Towns of 15,000 inhabitants to have no commons enclosed within a radius of 1½ mile

Towns of 30,000 inhabitants to have no commons enclosed within a radius of 2 miles

Towns of 70,000 inhabitants to have no commons enclosed within a radius of 2½ miles

Towns of 100,000 inhabitants to have no commons enclosed within a radius of 3 miles

London was to have a radius of 10 miles.

Roebuck, with his Canadian background, had an interest in the governance of the colonies. The utilitarians were supporters of imperial expansion, believing that Great Britain had a responsibility to export civilisation and sound governance to other countries (Egbert, 1970; Shultz and Varouxakis, 2005). Roebuck provided advice to Lord Durham, who was sent to Canada in 1838 to deal with the secession of the French Canadians and to unite Lower and Upper Canada. Roebuck however reflected in 1849 that 'Lord Durham was about as capable of understanding these suggestions as I am of reading Cherokee, of which I do not know the letters; indeed I do not know whether there are any Cherokee letters' (Roebuck, 1849, p. 209 footnote).

In 1849 Roebuck published *The Colonies of England: A Plan for the Government of Some Portion of Our Colonial Possessions*. This book focused mainly on the structures of colonial governance. However, the book includes a chapter on the organisation and principles for colonial settlement. Roebuck's starting point is that 'the new colony should not cost the mother country anything', though this was caveated by the recognition that the home government would need to pay for the protection of a new settlement from foreign aggression (Roebuck, 1849, p. 123). It followed that a colony should tax itself and manage 'her own money concerns'. Whereas Sharp had argued for plots to be given free to the initial settlers, Roebuck argued that the colony should be financed from the sale of land. The assumption appears that this is wild land, with no payment to any aboriginal occupier being necessary. Roebuck does not consider the spatial arrangements for settlement but instead focuses on the cost. He notes that the original colonists of Virginia and Massachusetts 'began with having all things in common and could never advance – the right of private property was afterwards established, and from that moment the colonies began to prosper' (ibid. p. 131).

Roebuck recognises that initially a government should send out selected emigrants and fund the initial development – security must be established immediately, then roads, bridges, a wharf, a courthouse and a jail. It is interesting that for both Sharp and Roebuck, the Benthamite emphasis on social control is central. Roebuck sees these initial investments as critical to making a settlement attractive to voluntary migrants, at which point the government should stop providing subsidy and 'the application of the country's wealth ought to be left to the prudence of the people themselves' (ibid. pp. 132–3).

Roebuck also stresses the importance of concentrating new settlements rather than scattering a population. He points out that governments are mistaken in seeking to settle the largest area. He comments that:

> Philosophers are very apt to make terrible mistakes when they deal with men, on place of propositions. Locke failed egregiously when he attempted to frame a constitution for Carolina; but the settlers themselves devised one of great practical worth – one which has made the people of Carolina a very happy community.
>
> (ibid., p. 134).

Thomas Maslen

Maslen was a retired officer from the East India Company. His father had been an architect and he himself developed an interest in studying and drawing buildings on his travels in Europe, India and South Africa. In 1830 he published a plan for exploring and surveying the Australian Interior entitled *The Friend of Australia*. According to Graves and Rechniewski (2012), Maslen retired from the East India Company in 1821 because of ill health. Missing the warm climate of India and living in the 'Siberian Wilds' of Blackstone Edge in Yorkshire, he asked for his pension to be paid in Australia so he could emigrate there. When this was turned down, he decided to read everything he could find on Australia and put forward a plan for surveying the continent he was never able to visit himself. Most of the 400-page book is a detailed plan of how to prepare for and carry out a surveying expedition based on his experience in India. The book and a letter to introduce it addressed to the Friends of Australia, argue the case for supporting emigration to Australia –

> The expense of supporting the poor in Britain is at least equal to the cost of sending them abroad, leaving out of the question the increase of crime and the increase in misery . . . Good sense and prudence points out, that encouragement ought to be given to voluntary emigration; which encouragement should be in the shape of a free passage to the colony . . . There are in fact multitudes of our countrymen in a state of destitution, or at least gaining a bare livelihood; such being the case, the sooner means are devised to provide for their annual emigration, passage free, the better; for otherwise there will be an accumulation of discontent and wretchedness that must, apparently sooner or later, lead to some home calamity, in which case every class of society will suffer.
>
> (Maslen, 1830, pp. 199–201)

Maslen's case was very similar to the argument put forward nearly a century earlier by Oglethorpe. The emigration option could be made attractive to potential colonists:

> The promise of estates rent free, a free passage out, and assistance for the first twelve-month, would induce thousands to embark for the colonies, and it would

drain the United Kingdom of all who were in want of work, at the same time the emigrants would then only have to work on the land for their own families instead of slaving for poor wages and ending their days in a workhouse.

(ibid., pp. 202–3)

Maslen included a detailed description and plan for a new town, with details of streets, public buildings, open spaces and a canal. He pointed out as the territory of a newly discovered country was government property, the government could both plan and implement the development on a systematic basis – there was no risk of grievances by private individuals, which applied where improvements to an existing town were proposed – there was no recognition that there may be an indigenous community. Like previous colonial planners, Maslen assumed a *tabula rasa*. He recognised that his system was only applicable to 'rising states, where towns have to be planned and marked out from the beginning'. He then criticised Governor Darling of New South Wales for proposing that main streets should be only 100 feet wide. Giving the example of the French colonial settlement of Pondicherry in India, Maslen proposed that the main streets should be tree lined avenues 150 yards wide, with the second order streets 100 yards wide (ibid., pp. 260, 269–70). He commented on Darling's proposal – 'Such narrow streets, in a warm and dry climate, will neither admit of a current of air nor prevent conflagrations from spreading'. Maslen gave very detailed plans for individual houses:

> All houses, both of rich and poor, should have a piazza, alias verandah, round at least three sides; for in winter, during the heavy torrents of rain, it is a great comfort; and in the summer, the glare of light is almost intolerable to the eyes unless softened by this delightful shade. The roofs of verandahs should certainly be flat or terraced, so that the roof of the lower one might serve as an open balcony or gallery round the upper rooms.
>
> (ibid., p. 273)

Maslen also proposed a minimum space standard for individual rooms as fifteen feet square, before setting out proposals for establishing a building society to finance development and specific annual rents for different types of dwelling, pointing out that rents needed to be lower than those in England if colonists were to be attracted, noting that with the use of convict labour, the costs of building homes would be lower than in the home country (ibid., pp. 280–2). The book contained other advice to colonists – on what food to eat to stop your teeth rotting; how to build water tanks, with diagrams of three different types of tank; proposals for establishing an Australian nobility, a proposal for an Australian flag, and proposals for introducing simple musical instruments among the aboriginal population.

Maslen also argued against discontinuing sending convicts to Australia as having a cheap labour force was essential to the viability of settlements and otherwise wealthy Australians would have to import 'men on their own account of all colours and all religions from the various islands where men are easily procured and willing to work, such as the New Zealanders, Tahitians, Sandwich Islanders, Malays, Chinese and even Americans!' (ibid., pp. 310–11). Maslen did recognise that there were a few black tribes at present in existence in Australia but considered that they 'will be so amalgamated (if I may be allowed the expression) in the course of time, as to entirely disappear, at the rate they are known to diminish'. The 'amalgamation' was to be achieved by the aboriginal women being 'trained' to be the wives of the white convicts. Maslen believed that

> Eastern Australia will be the same to an Englishman as the British islands, but with the additional advantages of a serene sky, a milder temperature, and a country of romantic grandeur ... So that Eastern Australia is, without any exaggeration or stretch of truth, the Paradise of the southern hemisphere.
>
> (ibid., pp. 312–13)

Having completed his monumental tome, and his idea for a Society for the Promotion of Free Emigration to the Colonies of Australia not being taken up by the Noble and Wealthy Friends of Australia, Friends of the Poor and Friends of Emigration, Maslen turned to other interests, writing first a proposal for a *New Decimal System of Money, Weights, Measures and Time*, and then *Suggestions for the Improvement of Our Towns and Houses*, the latter published in 1843. This work applied his idea of long straight streets as put forward in his Australian work, to London and other towns in England, with detailed proposals, described without maps, for street widening in York, Leeds, Halifax, Manchester, Chester, Liverpool, Colchester and Hull as well as following Gwynn, Smirke and Stuart with proposals for the capital city. He rounded off the book with detailed proposals for the construction of private dwelling-houses, house ventilation and the construction of chimneys, comments on bridges and sewers, the need for post offices and public swimming baths, a Building Regulations Bill, the window tax and suggestions for ten new cities in England, including one next to his own home at Blackstone Edge on the Rishworth Moors near Oldham. He concluded rather pessimistically that 'professional men and tradespeople, are so wedded to their old rules and customs, especially architects and builders, that I do not expect any of these classes will adopt my recommendations' (Maslen, 1843, p. 249).

The utilitarians and the South Australian experiment

Maslen's idea for a systematic colonisation programme was, however, to be pursued separately by Edward Gibbon Wakefield. Wakefield was a diplomatic courier, who while in Newgate prison in 1829 for abducting an heiress in an attempt to finance a parliamentary candidacy, wrote a series of letters promoting colonisation (Garnett, 1897; Bloomfield, 1961; Radzevicius, 2011). These letters, purporting to be written by a colonist in Australia, were published anonymously but as edited by Robert Gouger. Gouger was a radical and friend of Robert Owen who in 1833 established the South Australia Association to promote the founding of a colony.

The *Letter from Sydney* mainly comprised a description of the purported experiences of the author as a colonist in Sydney. The letter however concluded with a set of articles outlining arrangements for a planned system of colonisation.

In 1833 Gouger published a pamphlet – *Emigration for the Relief of Parishes Practically Considered*. This argued that to date emigration had not been conducted on sound principles and therefore Gouger had set up an agency for the reception of poor migrants in Canada, South Africa and Australia. He considered that indiscriminate emigration was a mistake. His proposal was that a parish would pay for the migrant's initial costs (in order to relieve the parish of any long term liabilities) and that the agency would ensure that a person of standing resident in the port of arrival would take care of them on arrival and transport them to wherever labour was needed. The pamphlet also set out the provisions needed for each group of six migrants during the passage and listed appropriate clothes for migrants to Canada, including a great coat at a cost of £3 per pauper migrant.

Gouger was to emigrate to Adelaide where he acted as colonial secretary from 1835 to 1837, publishing a series of letters in *South Australia 1837*, though he was suspended after a fight only to be reinstated by the Colonization Commission. He then acted as colonial treasurer under Governor George Grey from 1841 to 1844. Gouger's journals of his time in the colony were later published.

Gouger's South Australian Association was established with a committee comprising most of the radical Members of Parliament, with Wolryche Whitmore as chair, but including more familiar names – George Grote, William Molesworth, Charles Buller and Colonel Torrens. Joseph Parkes, the Birmingham radical, was the committee solicitor. It was Parkes who had edited Bentham's pamphlet against colonisation (Buckley, 1926). The committee also included other leading radicals such as Dr Southwood Smith, the postal reformer Rowland Hill and his brother, the Birmingham recorder and penal reformer, Mathew Davenport Hill, who was a friend of Bentham. The committee promoted a Bill for South Australian colonisation and held a public meeting in Exeter Hall on 30th June 1834 (Hey, 1989; Escott, 2009).

Wakefield then published a pamphlet – *A Sketch of a Project for Colonising Australia*. Wakefield's pamphlet was an explanation of the financial arrangements for the proposed colony. Land was to be taxed at 10 per cent of the rent and an initial payment of £2 per acre was required. This revenue would be used to establish an Emigration Fund to pay for the free conveyance of labourers to the colony. The demand for and supply of labour would be balanced to ensure there was no labour shortage and no surplus labour. There would be a balance of sexes in emigrants selected and preference would be given to applicants between 18 and 24. The basic argument was that it was more cost effective to send childless young couples than to send an existing family. A migrant reaching a settlement without sponsorship would be granted land. Any surplus would be used for general purposes by the colonial government. Wakefield's financial proposals were supported by long extracts from Adam Smith's *Inquiry into the Causes of the Prosperity of New Colonies* within his 1776 classic work on the *Wealth of Nations*. Wakefield uses the term 'capitalist' for those who employ labour. The proposed plan contrasts with the more egalitarian arrangements advocated by Oglethorpe, Sharp and those to be later promoted by J S Buckingham, which are discussed below.

In 1834, parliament passed the South Australian Colonization Act, promoted by Whitmore and Torrens. Torrens became chair of the Colonisation Commission, with Gouger being appointed colonial secretary to the Commission, meeting at the Adelphi in the Strand to set out the principles and appoint the personnel for the settlement. In his role as chair of the Commission, Torrens published a pamphlet on the *Colonization of South Australia*.

The development of Adelaide in South Australia was the most positive output from the involvement of British utilitarians in the planning of new settlements.

The development of the Adelaide plan and the narrative of the initial years of the settlement, named after the wife of the new king, William IV, have been studied in detail by a number of planning and political historians (Mills, 1915; Pike, 1957; Dutton, 1960; Cheesman, 1986; Bunker, 1988, 1998; Home, 1997; Freestone, 2008). The South Australian Commissioners set a number of criteria for the identification of the first settlement:

1st A commodious harbour, safe and accessible at all seasons of the year

2nd A considerable tract of fertile land immediately adjoining

3rd An abundant supply of fresh water

4th Facilities for internal communication

5th Facilities for communication with other ports

6th Distance from the limits of the colony, as a means of avoiding interference from without in the principle of colonisation

7th The neighbour of extensive sheep-walks

The above of primary importance, the following of secondary value:

8th A supply of building materials, as timber, stone, or brick, earth and lime

9th Facilities for drainage

10th Coal

(cited in Dutton, 1960, p. 162)

The plan was the product of the surveyor general of the new colony, Colonel William Light. The plan however was far from uncontentious. Light identified a suitable site before the arrival of the first Governor, Captain John Hindmarsh, who being a seaman wanted the settlement on the sea. Light only won the argument by demonstrating that Hindmarsh's chosen site was subject to flooding. Light was also aware that keeping port and future capital separate had the advantage of insulating the seat of government separate from the transient population of a port.

Light's plan is however recognised for bringing into effect the utilitarian radicals' concept of a green belt or parkland. Home notes that Light may have been influenced by the plans of both Montgomery and Maslen (Home, 1997, p. 29), though it should be recognised that neither plan was translated from vision to reality. Home also notes that the role of Light in Adelaide as a government employee rather than freelance planner, established a tradition of government promoted land use planning.

The governance of Adelaide proved to be even more contentious than the planning of the town. There was a dual system of government with a governor and a resident commissioner, with a continuous conflict between the two. Robert Gouger also alternated between the position of colonial secretary, acting Governor in the interregnum between second and third governors and colonial treasurer. Light had himself initially thought he was going to be appointed governor. Other officials found themselves taking sides in the disputes, with many officials confusing their private business with their official roles. There were numerous petty disputes as well as legal cases and occasional scuffles. Hindmarsh was recalled though he continued to argue to the end that Adelaide should be moved to an alternative site. Gouger was sacked then re-instated. In 1838, Light resigned in frustration. It needed the third Governor, George Grey, to impose some stability. Light's deputy, G S Kingston, went on to become speaker of the colony's House of Representatives and to be awarded a knighthood.

The utilitarian theorists had designed South Australia as a 'radical utopia' or 'paradise of dissent' (Pike, 1957) but the lack of clarity over governance and the distance from the Commission in London led to such factionalism that it is surprising that the town was built at all. The colony was designed to be slave-free and convict-free, unlike the penal settlements at Swan River (later Perth), Sydney and Van Diemen's Land (later Tasmania). The colony was also designed to be secular in the sense of allowing freedom of religion. Light even proposed that a cathedral should be shared by all denominations. Yet Adelaide did prove to be a success, despite the tension between autocratic governors and the free spirited colonists, between the 'Adelphi theorists' and the 'practical men' to the extent it was the first colonial settlement to be granted its own municipal charter and a degree of urban self-government (Pike, 1957).

As demonstrated by Williams (1966), Adelaide was itself to be a prototype for the development of other 'parkland towns' in Australia and New Zealand, many promoted by Wakefield's New Zealand Company, including Wellington, Nelson, New Plymouth and Canterbury. It is however noticeable that these plans move away from the standard grid arrangement to more flexible arrangements which reflect the topography of the specific locations (Graves and Rechniewski, 2012).

Wakefield later published his most famous work, *A View of the Art of Colonization* in 1848. This work set out his theory of systematic colonisation based both on his earlier pamphlets and on his own experience in Canada, Australia and New Zealand. It is perhaps not surprising that one biography of Wakefield is subtitled *'Builder of the British Commonwealth'* (Bloomfield, 1961). The book promotes colonisation but points to the low morality of early migrants (including transported convicts) and argues for planned migration based on the selection of respectable persons. Most of the book is an argument for reform of colonial government. There is a detailed analysis of land allocation and the means of financing of settlement but no comment on the planning or design of the settlement. Appended to the main text is a speech by the Benthamite MP Charles Buller in parliament in April 1843.

Buller had in 1840 published a book of his own on *Responsible Government for the Colonies*, based on his experience as secretary to Lord Durham's Commission in Canada and which constituted a strong critique of the role of the colonial office.

The speech however, despite being forty pages long, did not put forward a specific programme of colonisation but called on her Majesty, Queen Victoria, to consider 'the means by which extensive and systematic colonization may be the most effectively rendered available for augmenting the resources of Her Majesty's empire, giving additional employment to capital and labour, and thereby bettering the condition of her people' (Wakefield, 1849, p. 500).

John Silk Buckingham and 'Victoria'

Buckingham was the most important of the utilitarian planners. Ebenezer Howard acknowledged Buckingham's contribution to his concept of a garden city (Howard,

1898, p. 112). This has generated some interest amongst planning historians, but Buckingham's role is often reduced to a historical footnote, even in the most detailed studies of early planning (Ashworth, 1954, pp. 124–5; Home, 1997, p. 29). Benovolo does however give Buckingham more substantial treatment (Benovolo, 1971).

Buckingham was a leading radical MP, representing the new constituency of Sheffield in the reform parliament between 1832 and 1837. Before becoming an MP, Buckingham was a journalist and traveller. He travelled in Europe, India, the Middle East and North America, in 1840 visiting the slave states, including the town of Savannah. Each journey produced a volume of travelogue. Buckingham edited a series of journals: the *Calcutta Journal*, the *Oriental Herald and Quarterly Review,* the *Sphynx* and launched the *Athenaeum.* On entering parliament, he edited the *Parliamentary Review* which provided a detailed commentary on parliamentary debates. He was active in the temperance movement, of which he published a history in 1850. He campaigned vigorously for political reform and published a series of political tracts, including *Outlines of a New Budget* in 1831, *Evils and Remedies of the Present System of Popular Elections* and an *Address on the Proposed Reforms in the Commerce and Finance of the Country* in 1841, *Plan of an Improved Income Tax* in 1845 and *National Evils and Practical Remedies* in 1849 (Turner, 1934; Mackey, 1984).

Like Sharp and Oglethorpe, Buckingham opposed the impressment of sailors into the navy and like Roebuck, he argued for the provision of public walks and play-grounds as well as for the provision of Literary and Scientific Institutes and Museums. Following his experience in Calcutta, where his paper was closed down by officials, he campaigned for the replacement of the East India Company by a colonial administration accountable to parliament (Maccoby, 1935, p. 77). Buckingham published two volumes of autobiography focusing on his travels (Buckingham, 1855) and the volumes covering his later political career were never completed. The only full biography of Buckingham was published in 1934 by an American historian, Ralph Turner, and a more detailed study is long overdue.

Buckingham's 1849 work was largely a summary of his previous pamphlets. It includes an extensive analysis of the existing evils of society, proposals for financial reform, proposals for a new reform bill and the purification of the electoral system and for the regeneration of Ireland. The book however also included proposals for a model town and associated community and a section promoting emigration and colonisation. It is however the plan and drawing included in the volume, which drew the attention of Ebenezer Howard.

In the introduction to his book, subheaded '*Evils of Communism – Benefits of Association*', Buckingham explained that he had studied a range of proposals for social systems and co-operative associations as well as having visited the co-operative communities of the Shakers and Rappites in America and presented a paper at a conference in Paris in December 1846 on '*Considerations sur quelques REFORMES SOCIALES qui restent encore a accomplir, avant que la CIVILIZATION ait attaint son dernier perfectionement.*' Curiously, there is no specific mention of Robert Owen, though as we shall see both his analysis and proposals had similarities to Owen's. There is however evidence in his earlier writings in the *Calcutta Journal* in 1820 and 1821, that he was aware of Owen's New Lanark project (Turner, 1934, p. 199). Buckingham instead acknowledged the influence of a pamphlet written by Rev

Shergold Boone, curate of St John's, Paddington, poet, critic and colleague of John Henry Newman, entitled *One, Manifold, or System*, from which he quotes extensively. Boone had argued that a model town was necessary to correct social evils:

> We must have a just system; and we can only arrive at it by a well-appointed concert of tasks and labourers; we must endeavour to provide for the mass of mankind, space, food, employment; to better their habitations and their habits; to elevate and refine their tastes; to raise the standard of comfort; to foster in them both self-development and self-denial; to inform not only their senses and their minds, but their immortal spirits.
>
> (Boone, 1848, quoted in Buckingham, 1849, p. 29)

Buckingham's objective was to consider:

> whether it be not possible, by a New Organization of Society, among the labouring portion of the community, at least, to devise means by which continuous employment may be secured to all who are able and willing to work, independently of reliance on foreign demand, and profitable to all parties engaged in it, by a System of Co-operative Association.
>
> (Buckingham, 1849, p. 104)

Buckingham, in true utilitarian fashion, first defined the elements of happiness as:

1   Perfect health of body.
2   Perfect serenity of mind.
3   Competency of means to procure the enjoyment of sufficient food, raiment, shelter, and repose.
4   Labour in a moderate degree.
5   The expectation and belief of progressive advancement.
6   The love and esteem of those by whom we are surrounded.

He then analysed how these elements were impeded by the existing arrangements within society – 'scarcely any state of things can be imagined more unfavourable to their perfect development than that under which we at present live' (ibid., p. 110).

Buckingham set out the principles for the new settlement, which should be developed by a company incorporated by Royal Charter. He called the town 'Victoria', in honour of the Queen but also to celebrate the victory over social evils.

He established a set of principles for the new settlement. The town was to be about a mile square with 10,000 inhabitants. It was to be surrounded by 10,000 acres of farmland. Manufactures and handicraft trades were to be located at the edge of the town, while establishments unsuited to the town should be placed at a sufficiently remote distance – the examples given were abattoirs, collections of sewage for manure, depots of coal and lime, cattle-markets, stables, gasworks, tan-pits, chemical laboratories – 'and every other kind of manufacture producing effluvia of an unhealthy or disagreeable nature' (ibid., p. 151).

All land, houses, factories and materials were to be the property of the company. No alcohol or opium or tobacco was to be allowed in the town, which was also to be free of weaponry. Perfect freedom of religion was to be allowed with each congregation able to administer its own affairs. No labour was to be permitted on the Sabbath which was to be free for recreation. An eight hour working day applied to all men; women were disbarred from heavy labour; with restrictions on child labour relating to the age of the child – children under ten were to be limited to four hours' labour a day. Marriage was to be protected and men and women penalised equally for illicit intercourse by expulsion from the Association.

Every home was to have a water closet. Each single person was to have his own room; couples were to get two rooms; families with children at least three rooms. Rents would be controlled. Public baths were to be provided. Common restaurants would be provided, but households could eat in their own homes if they chose to. Nurseries would be provided for children. Education would be free with children taught up to the age of fifteen. Medical facilities would also be free. Beyond the town, there was to be a park with fountains, a botanical garden, a gymnasium and a public cemetery – 'rendered as beautiful as they are usually gloomy, to assist in making associations of death more cheerful.' It was also proposed that where the population grew beyond the 10,000, the town would sponsor new settlements (ibid., pp. 142–53).

Buckingham then provided an explanation of how the settlement would be financed. He estimated the development cost at £3 million with a further £1 million necessary to stock the farms, factories and workshops. He proposed to raise this capital through 200,000 shares of £20 each, paid in monthly instalments of £1 per share for twenty months. Interest would only be paid when the settlement became profitable. All adult male residents had to be shareholding members, holding at least one share of £20. The section included estimates of likely profit including arrangements for distributing profit. Buckingham pointed out that not wasting money on alcohol would make the settlement much more economically viable – he referred to an estimate that the financial loss arising from alcohol consumption in England in 1847 was £154 million, including cost of purchase, labour lost and the cost of pauperism, crime, disease and drunken sailors drowning (ibid., pp. 154–81).

In designing the layout of the town, Buckingham's object was

> to unite the greatest degree of order, symmetry, space and healthfulness, in the largest supply of air and light, and in the most perfect system of drainage, with the comfort and convenience of all classes; the due proportion of accommodation to the probable numbers and circumstances of various ranks; ready accessibility to all parts of the town, under continuous shelter from sun and rain, when necessary; with the disposition of public buildings in such localities as to make them easy of approach from all quarters, and surrounded with space for numerous avenues of entrance and exit. And, in addition to all these, a large intermixture of grass lawn, garden ground, and flowers, and an abundant supply of water – the whole to be united with as much elegance and economy as may be found practicable.
>
> (ibid., p. 183)

This was followed by a detailed explanation of the arrangements for the town as given in the plan below.

This section of the book – sections on financial reform, emigration and colonisation, electoral reform and the regeneration of Ireland follow – concluded with a detailed analysis of how his plan would meet the six objectives of happiness he defined at the start. This section included extensive extracts from other writers including Charles Babbage and Mill's *Principles of Political Economy*, notably the section reviewing the systems of Owen, Saint-Simon, Cabet and Louis Blanc, though none of these authors were quoted directly. There is also extensive commentary on the American co-operative communities, with extracts from Buckingham's American travelogues as well as those of Harriet Martineau.

It is perhaps surprising, given the comprehensiveness of Buckingham's plan, that it has been studied so little by planning historians. Most commentaries focus on the diagram of the proposed urban form, comparing its symmetry with examples from other plans. The most detailed commentary in Sennett (1905, Vol 1, pp. 125–36) presents substantive extracts from the design description from Buckingham's volume, which he refers to as an 'interestingly comprehensive plan of a city for a community – most thoughtfully to consist of all grades – of 10,000 inhabitants'. Sennett also contrasts Buckingham's rectangular proposal with Ebenezer Howard's 'circular suggestion'.

The Savannah plan was clearly one of the sources for Buckingham, but a reading of Buckingham's work shows that he drew on a wide range of material. Buckingham was an active politician, an experienced social reformer involved in a wide range of reform movements, someone who had probably travelled to more parts of the world than any of his contemporaries and someone who was committed to democratic governance. His 1849 book is in many ways his magnum opus – it brings together his previous works and focuses on how his principles as well as those of more philosophical writers can be implemented in practice. Like Mill twenty years later, his conclusion was that associationism was the only basis for urban development and governance. He was far from being a Utopian but he proposed a more egalitarian and less autocratic form of governance than that his more famous contemporary, Robert Owen, who will be discussed in the next chapter.

Primary sources

Bentham, J (1787) *Panopticon Letters* (republished Edinburgh, UK: William Tait, 1843)

Bentham, J (1793) *Emancipate your Colonies*. Addressed to the National Convention of France (London: Robert Heward)

Bentham, J (1843) *A Plan for an Universal and Perpetual Peace* (reprinted Peace Book Company, Bristol, Newark, 1939)

Bentham, J (1848) *Manual of Political Economy* (Edinburgh, UK: William Tait):

Boone, Rev Shergold (1848) *One Manifold or System* (London: John W Parker)

Buckingham, J S (1831) *Outlines of a New Budget* (London: Bradbury and Evans)

Buckingham, J S (1841) *Evils and Remedies of the Present System of Popular Elections* (London: Simpkin and Marshall)

Buckingham, J S (1842) *A Journey through the Slave States of North America* (abridged edition Charleston: History Press 2006)

Buckingham, J S (1845) *Plan of an Improved Income Tax* (London: J Ridgway)

Buckingham, J S (1849) *National Evils and Practical Remedies with The Plan of a Model Town* (London: Peter Jackson, late Fisher, son and co)

Buckingham, J S (1855) *Autobiography of James Silk Buckingham including his Voyages, Travels, Adventures, Speculations, Successes and Failures*. Volumes 1 and 2 (London: Longman, Brown, Green and Longman)

Buller, Charles (1840) *Responsible Government for the Colonies* (London: James Ridgway)

Gouger, Robert (1833) *Emigration for the Relief of Parishes Practically Considered* (London: Ridgway and Sons; Effingham Wilson)

Gouger, Robert (1837) South Australia in 1837 in a series of letters with a postscript as to 1838

Hodder, E, ed. (1898) *The Founding of South Australia as Recorded in the Journals of Robert Gouger* (London)

Howard, E (1898) *Tomorrow: A Peaceful Path to Real Reform*

Maslen, Thomas J (1836) *The Friend of Australia: Or, a Plan for Exploring the Interior and for Carrying On a Survey of the Whole Continent of Australia* (reprint by Ulan Press)

Maslen, Thomas J (1843) *Suggestions for the Improvement of our Towns and Houses* (London: Smith Elder and Co; reprinted by Kissinger Publishing 2012)

Torrens, Robert (1835) *Colonization of South Australia* (London: Longman)

Wakefield, Edward Gibbon (1829) *A Letter from Sydney, the Principal Town of Australasia together with the outline of a system of colonization edited by Robert Gouger* (London)

Wakefield, Edward Gibbon (1829) *Sketch of a Proposal for Colonizing Australia*

Wakefield, Edward Gibbon (1849) *A View of the Art of Colonization* (London: John W Parker, reprinted New York: Augustus M Kelley 1969)

Secondary sources

Ashworth, W (1954) *The Genesis of Modern British Town Planning* (London: Routledge and Kegan Paul)

Beadle, G (1984) Entry for J A Roebuck in Baylen, J and Gossman, N (eds), *Biographical Dictionary of Modern British Radicals*, Vol 2, 1830–1870, pp. 436–41(Sussex, UK: Harvester Press)

Beevers, R (1988) *The Garden City Utopia: A Critical Biography of Ebenezer Howard* (London: Macmillan)

Benovolo, L (1971) *The Origins of Modern Town Planning* (Cambridge, MA: MIT Press)

Bloomfield, P (1961) *Edward Gibbon Wakefield: Builder of the British Commonwealth* (London: Longmans)

Buckley, J (1926) *Joseph Parkes of Birmingham* (London: Methuen)

Bunker, R (1988) 'Systematic colonisation and town planning in Australia and New Zealand' in *Planning Perspectives* 3, pp. 59–80

Bunker, R (1998) 'Process and form in the foundation and laying out of Adelaide' in *Planning Perspectives* 13, pp. 243–56

Bunker, R (2008) 'Why and How did Adelaide come about?' in *Planning Perspectives* 23, pp. 233–40

Cheesman, R (1986) *Patterns in Perpetuity* (Adelaide: Thornton House)

Dutton, G (1960) *Founder of a City: The Life of Colonel William Light* (Adelaide: Rigby)

Egbert, D D (1970) *Social Radicalism and the Arts: Western Europe* (New York: Knopf)

Escott, M (2009) Biography of Wolryche Whitmore in D R Fisher (ed.), *History of Parliament 1820–1832* (Cambridge: Cambridge University Press)

Foucault, M (1975) *Discipline and Punish* (London: Allen Lane)

Freestone, R (2008) 'The Adelaide Wars' in *Planning Perspectives*, Vol 23, No 2, pp. 221–4

Garnett, R (1897) *Edward Gibbon Wakefield. The Colonisation of South Australia and New Zealand* (London)

Graves, M and Rechniewski, E (2012) 'Mapping Utopia: Cartography and Social Reform in 19th century Australia' in *PORTAL Journal of Multidisciplinary International Studies*, Vol 8, No 2 (Sidney UTSe Press)

Halevy, E (1928) *The Growth of Philosophical Radicalism* (London: Faber and Faber)

Hey, C (1989) *Rowland Hill: Genius and Benefactor 1793–1879* (London: Quiller Press)

Home, R (1997) *Of Planting and Planning. The Making of Colonial Cities* (London: Spon, 2nd edn, Routledge 2013)

Howard, E (2003) *Tomorrow: A Peaceful Path to Real Reform*. Original edition with commentary by Peter Hall, Dennis Hardy and Colin Ward (London: Routledge)

Hyde, F E (1946) 'Utility and Radicalism' in *Economic History Review*, Vol XVI, No 1, pp. 38–44

Hyde, F E (1947) 'Utilitarian Town Planning 1825–1845' in *Town Planning Review*, Vol 19, pp. 153–9

Journal of Libertarian Studies (Spring 1980) Vol 4, No 2, pp. 215–32

Leader, R E (1897) *Life and Letters of John Arthur Roebuck with chapters of autobiography* (London: Edward Arnold)

Maccoby, S (1935) *English Radicalism 1832–1852* (London: Allen and Unwin)

Mackey, H (1984) James Silk Buckingham. Entry in Baylen and Gossman (eds), *Biographical Dictionary of Modern British Radicals*, Vol 2, 1830–1870 (Sussex, UK: Harvester Press)

Martin, D (1981) *John Stuart Mill and the Land Question: Occasional Papers in Economic and Social History*, No 9 (Hull, UK: University of Hull)

Mills, R C (1915) *The Colonization of Australia 1829–1842: The Wakefield Experiment in Empire Building* (London: Sidgwick and Jackson)

Pike, D (1957) *Paradise of Dissent* (Melbourne: Melbourne University Press)

Radzevicius, M (2011) *England Elsewhere: Edward Gibbon Wakefield and an Imperial Utopian Dream* (PhD thesis, University of Adelaide)

Roberts, D (1979) 'The Utilitarian Conscience' in Marsh, P (ed.), *The Conscience of the Victorian State* (New York: Syracuse University)

Roebuck, J A (1835) *Pamphlets for the People* (London: Charles Ely)

Roebuck, J A (1849) *The Colonies of England* (London: John W Parker)

Sennett, A R (1905) *Garden Cities in Theory and Practice* (London: Belrose and Sons)

Schultz, B and Varouxakis, G (2005) *Utilitarianism and Empire* (Lanham, MD: Lexington Books)

Thomas, W (1979) *The Philosophical Radicals: Nine Studies in Theory and Practice, 1817–1841* (Oxford: Clarendon Press)

Turner, R (1934) *James Silk Buckingham* (London: Williams and Norton)

Williams, M (1966) 'The Parkland Towns of Australia and New Zealand' in *Geographical Review*, Vol 56, No 1, pp. 67–89

5 Owenite co-operation and plans for new communities

18th century Utopian experiments

Before discussing the new communities established by Robert Owen and his followers, it is important to acknowledge that there was an earlier tradition of communitarianism both in England and in the United Sates. Armytage in his comprehensive study of Utopian experiments in England between 1560 and 1660 (Armytage, 1961) traces the tradition of communitarianism from the Diggers of the mid-17th century, through the Quakers, the Philadephians, the Camisards or French Prophets and the Moravians. While the Diggers were later to be taken up by late-19th century reformers such as Hyndman and Morrison Davidson, the Moravians were to be referenced by the Spencean, Thomas Evans; mid-19th century reformers such as Goodwyn Barmby, John Minter Morgan, James Silk Buckingham; and even by the Christian socialist, Charles Kingsley. As mentioned earlier, the Moravians were also involved in Oglethorpe's settlement of Savannah in Georgia.

The Moravian church was a form of primitive Christianity, descended from a sect that had followed the Bohemian Protestant, Jan Hus. A group of Moravians settled at Fulneck near Halifax in the early 1740s. In the 1750s the group established another community in London, actually in Beaufort House, which had once been owned by none other than the author of *Utopia*, Sir Thomas More. The Moravian settlements operated on a communal basis, with sexes segregated, managed by a congregational council and elected elders. A third community was established in Duckinfield, near Manchester. The settlements also had an educational focus, following a curriculum set by the Moravian educationalist Comenius – the school at the Fulneck settlement producing the factory reformer Richard Oastler and the American architect Benjamin La Trobe. The Moravians were not an exclusive or millenarian sect. Their manager in the mid-to late-18th century, Benjamin La Trobe, was a friend of luminaries such as Charles Wesley, Rowland Hill and Hannah More. The Moravian communities proved to be successful commercial enterprises and survived into the 19th century (Armytage, 1961, pp. 47–57). They can be contrasted with religious groups of a more millenarian disposition, such as the various groups of followers of Joanna Southcott or the Anglo-Israelite community set up by Richard Brothers who sought to establish a 'New Jerusalem' (Armytage, 1961, pp. 69–72; Harrison, 1979; Podmore, 1998; Mason, 2001; Madden, 2010; Lockley, 2014).

Robert Owen's *New View of Society*

Robert Owen finds a place in the standard histories of British planning (for example Ashworth, 1954, pp. 119–25; Bell and Bell, 1969, pp. 240–9). Owen's categorisation varies – for Ashworth he is included in a chapter on the creation of new model villages and towns; for Bell and Bell, Owen is included in a chapter on tied towns. Works on political theory tend to view Owen as the founder of socialism, or more specifically of utopian socialism in Britain. Studies of the labour movement view Owen as a founder of British trade unionism while studies of co-operation tend to view Owen as the father of the British co-operative movement. It is not the purpose of this study to challenge these attributions, though it is relevant to comment that some of these attributions are based on an approach to historiography which focuses too much on the role of individuals, without sufficient consideration of the context and the myriad of organisational inter-relationships, influences and interdependencies. Recent research, especially the works of John Harrison, Greg Claeys and Noel Thompson (Harrison, 1969; Thompson, 1984; Claeys, 1986, 1987, 1989), has done much to correct this oversimplification and to situate Owen within his historical context and to recognise the roles played by Owen's collaborators and followers, many of whom rejected Owen's paternalistic and autocratic approach.

Owen was an industrialist, who having managed a cotton mill in Manchester, entered into a partnership with David Dale, the owner of a mill in New Lanark near Glasgow. Owen bought the mill in 1799 and married Dale's daughter. While he made improvements to the mill and millworkers' accommodation, he was not the original designer or builder of the complex, which included some low rent housing and separate accommodation for the 500 children Dale had recruited from the Glasgow workhouse. Owen did however provide a school, a grocery store, a communal washhouse and an Institute for the Formation of Character. Owen also improved the existing houses and built rows of new houses. Owen seems to have had some inspiration from the proposal of the Quaker, John Bellars, for a College of Industry, which had been published in 1695, a copy of which was given to Owen by the radical Francis Place.

As Bell and Bell point out, Owen's activity as a philanthropic factory owner was not unique. Samuel Oldknow had initiated a similar project for his mill at Mellor in Cheshire in 1787. Titus Salt was to develop Saltaire in Yorkshire between 1853 and 1863. James and George Wilson relocated their candle company from Battersea to a new industrial village at Bromborough on the Wirral in 1853 (Bell and Bell, 1969, pp. 241–62). Plans for new industrial villages were quite common in the early Victorian period. A London architect, Mr Moffat, proposed a series of new villages around London to house 350,000 people at a cost of £10 million, while in 1848, the *Edinburgh* magazine referred to a scheme for a new village for 5,000 people near Ilford station on the eastern edge of London, requiring capital investment of £250,000 (Bell and Bell, 1969, pp. 262–5). The initiatives of Owen, Oldknow and Salt were later to be followed by the Cadbury family's development of housing linked to their chocolate factory at Bournville in Birmingham, the development of Port Sunlight in Cheshire by the palm oil importer and soapmaker, W H Lever (the plan apparently being based on Versailles), and the development of New Earswick in York by the Rowntree family, who were, like the Cadburys, Quakers and chocolate manufacturers.

Owen's role in the history of radical planning does not however derive primarily from his role at New Lanark but from his overall vision of a new social system and his proposals for other communitarian settlements. Despite his own role as an industrialist, Owen was an advocate of agricultural settlements. In contrast with the settlements of the Puritans, William Penn and Granville Sharp, which were all inspired by religion, Owen was a rationalist, who sought to devise a new social system based on a communitarianism which was independent of religion (Lloyd Jones, 1900; Podmore, 1906; Harrison 1969; Garnett 1971).

His rationalism has led to Owen sometimes being viewed as a utilitarian. Owen was no follower of Bentham and although Bentham was one of the celebrities he managed to persuade to take shares in his enterprise, he was not one of Bentham's circle and Owen's own account of their one recorded meeting leaves the image of competing egos rather than collaboration (Owen, 1857, p. 132). While Owen was a friend of James Mill, in his autobiography Owen is scathing of Bentham:

> who spent a long life in an endeavour to amend laws, all based on a fundamental error, without discovering this error; and therefore was his life, although a life of incessant well-intended industry, occupied in showing and attempting to remedy the evils of individual laws, but never attempting to dive to the foundation of all laws, and this ascertaining the cause of the errors and evils of them.
>
> (ibid.)

Owen does however seem to have been influenced by Patrick Colquhoun, the Scots merchant and Lord Provost of Glasgow who was a Benthamite and in 1814 wrote a *Treatise on the Wealth, Power and Resources of the British Empire* (Harrison, 1969, p. 17). Colquhoun had earlier written *A Treatise on Indigence* which had put forward 'propositions for ameliorating the condition of the poor and increasing the comforts of labouring people'.

Owen was a utilitarian in that he accepted the principle of the 'greatest good'. The fourth essay in his *New View of Society*, his first major work published in 1813, commences with the statement 'The end of government is to make the governed and the governors happy. That government then is the best, which in practice produces the greatest happiness to the greatest number' (Owen, 1813, p. 163). This work, subtitled *Essays on the principle of the Formation of the Human Character and the application of the principle in Practice* is primarily a treatise on Owen's educational experiment at New Lanark.

Owen's basic principle for the formation of character was that the 'happiness of self, clearly understood and uniformly practised, which can only be attained by conduct that must promote the happiness of the community' (Owen, 1830, p. 103). Owen argued that it was the responsibility of governments to establish 'rational plans for the education and general formulation of the characters of their subjects' (ibid., p. 106). Owen explains how when he took over the New Lanark mill, he stopped the previous practice of employing children between the ages of six and ten, and instead ensured that children under ten were taught reading, writing and arithmetic before starting work. Owen claimed that being taught rationally, the children then acted rationally – those employed became industrious, temperate, healthy, faithful to their employers and kind to each other. He then asserted that the improved behaviour of the children had a positive impact on the behaviour of the adults – 'The community exhibits the general appearance of industry, temperance, comfort, health and happiness' (ibid., p. 127).

Owen also stressed that the proprietors benefited from improved performance of the workforce (ibid., p. 124). Owen argued that his principles should be applied on a national basis, with the establishment of a national network of free schools. He also argued that the government should introduce religious toleration and remove all religious tests on individuals, abolish the national lottery, reform the poor laws and guarantee full employment, though this was to be achieved 'through training and education of the poor and lower orders ... so that they will all find employment sufficient to support themselves' rather than through direct employment by the government. He argued that in periods of depression, the government could provide direct employment for national works, but at a rate lower than private employers would provide – there is nevertheless an indication here of the Keynesian principle of the government providing a counter-cyclical stimulus (ibid., pp. 168–96).

In 1817 Owen drew up a plan for a new manufacturing town for the Association for the Relief of the Manufacturing and Labouring Poor. Each village – the drawing appears to show at least three – would accommodate 1200 people with 1000 to 1500 acres of land. The public buildings divide the squares into parallelograms. The central building has a public kitchen and communal dining room. There is an infant school, lecture room and place of worship. A separate building has a school for older children, a committee room and a library. There are enclosed grounds for exercise and recreation which should have trees. Three sides of the square were for lodging houses for families. The fourth side was for dormitories for children over three years old (and any surplus younger children who could not fit into the family homes). There is also an infirmary and accommodation for visitors. The buildings for manufacturing and mechanical purposes, including the slaughter house and stables are separated from the village by plantations (Owen, 1817).

There seems little relationship between Owen's focus on education in his *New View of Society*, derived from his experience of the industrial community at New Lanark, and his proposal for agricultural settlements in his 1820 *Report to the County of Lanark*. The report starts by stating that 'manual labour, properly directed, is the source of all wealth, and of national prosperity ', a precept derived from Adam Smith and shared with Owen's own contemporary, David Ricardo, rather than from the utilitarians. Owen however went on to argue that lack of employment was caused from a want of wealth or capital and that the distribution of wealth would generate beneficial employment for all who were unemployed. Owen's solution is not however the communalisation of the means of production as later advocated by Marx but the establishment of agricultural communities based on tilling the soil by spade rather than by plough. He proposes communities of 300 to 2000 people. These communities would be self-sufficient. He suggests that a community of 1200 persons would require 600 to 1800 acres, before for the first time setting out the spatial arrangements for the new settlement:

> It being always most convenient for the workman to reside near his employment, the site for the dwellings of the cultivators will be chosen as near to the centre of the land as water, proper levels, dry situation etc may admit ; and as courts, alleys, lanes and streets create many unnecessary inconveniences, are injurious to health, and destructive to almost all the natural comforts of human life, they will be excluded, and a disposition of the buildings free from these objections and greatly more economical will be adopted.
>
> (Owen, 1820, p. 230)

This leads on to Owen's proposal for a large square or parallelogram, as it would provide communal cooking and eating and supervision and teaching of children:

> The four sides of the figure may be adapted to contain all the private apartments of sleeping and sitting rooms for the adult part of the population; general sleeping apartments for the children while under tuition; store rooms, or warehouses in which to deposit various products; an inn or house for the accommodation of strangers, an infirmary etc ... In a line across the centre of the parallelogram, leaving free space for air and light and easy communication, might be erected the church or places of worship; the schools; kitchen and apartments for eating; all in the most convenient situation for the whole population, and under the best possible public superintendence, without trouble, expense, or inconvenience to any party.
>
> (ibid.)

The focus on supervision bears some similarity with the concept of design for social control in Bentham's panopticon.

Owen then goes to put the case for communal living. He attacks the principle of individual interest advocated by 'celebrated political economists to be the cornerstone to the social system and without which society could not subsist.' Owen argues that

> From this principle of individual interest have arisen all the divisions of mankind, the endless errors and mischiefs of class, sect, party and of national antipathies, creating the angry and malevolent passions, and all the crimes and misery with which the human race have been hitherto afflicted.
>
> (ibid., pp. 231–2)

Towards the end of his Report, having considered in some detail the arrangements for providing the residents with access to gardens, schooling, cooking and even for the style of clothing they should wear, Owen turns to the issue of the governance of the parallelograms. He recognises that those founded by landowners and capitalists will be governed by superintendents appointed by the founder and under rules laid down by them. In contrast,

> Those formed by the middle and working classes, upon a reciprocity of interests, should be governed by themselves, upon principles that will prevent divisions, opposition of interests, jealousies, or any of the common or vulgar passions which a contention for power is certain to generate. Their affairs should be conducted by a committee, composed of all the members of the association between certain ages – for instance of those between thirty-five and forty-five, or between forty and fifty. In a short time the ease with which these associations will proceed in all their operations will be such as to render the business of government a mere recreation; and as the parties who govern will in a few years again become the governed, they must always be conscious that at a future period they will experience the good or evil effects of the measures of their administration.
>
> (ibid., p. 256)

Owen did not however include in his *Report to the County of Lanark* or any other publication any diagram or image for his proposed parallelogram. However, in 1819, he commissioned the architect Thomas Stedman Whitwell to prepare a design for his proposed new communitarian settlement in America to be called New Harmony.

Whitwell had worked as an architect in the London Docks before moving to Birmingham and Coventry. His most memorable building was the Birmingham Pantechnetheca, now demolished, which was on New Street and was a building for the display of Birmingham's industrial products. He also designed the Brunswick Theatre in Whitechapel, London, which unfortunately collapsed within days of opening. It was no doubt the former project rather than the latter which led to Owen commissioning Whitwell to draw a design for his project. In 1830 a description of the design was published in London.

New Lanark had been managed by Owen and his superintendents under rules he devised. Garnett has an interesting footnote at the beginning of his 1971 paper – 'This paper is restricted to an investigation of the Owenite communities in Britain. Robert Owen's experience at New Lanark is not here considered relevant as New Lanark was really a capitalist enterprise with an infusion of business ethics and paternalism' (Garnett, 1971, p. 39). Owen was to be involved in the establishment a range of communitarian settlements which were to be self-governing – the Orbiston Community near Motherwell in Scotland (1825–7), Harmony Hall, Queenswood in Hampshire (1839–45), and New Harmony in Indiana (1825–7). The Owenite E T Craig also established a communitarian settlement at Ralahine in County Clare, Ireland which was operational between 1831 and 1833.

These projects have been subject to detailed study – Alexander Cullen's *Adventures in Socialism* (1910) presents a detailed narrative of both New Lanark and Orbiston, Garnett's *Co-operation and the Owenite socialist communities in Britain* (1972), an expanded version of a 1971 paper, considers Orbiston, Ralahine and Queenswood. Royle's *Robert Owen and the Commencement of the Millennium* (1998) focuses on the Queenwood experiment, while Bestor's *Backwoods Utopias* (1971) and Taylor's *Visions of Harmony* (1987) cover the American projects. Armytage's *Heavens Below* (1961) includes shorter studies of Orbiston, Ralahine and New Harmony, together with a much more extensive range of other utopian experiments, as does Hardy's study of *Alternative Communities in Nineteenth Century England* (1979). Ralahine is the subject of a detailed memoir by its founder, E T Craig whose *The Irish Land and Labour Question, Illustrated in the History of Ralahine* was published in 1893, the year before his death at the age of ninety as the only surviving Owenite to be a member of William Morris's Socialist League, which will be discussed in Chapter 9.

The literature on the Owenite settlements is so extensive that it would be superfluous to seek to provide a new assessment of their achievements. It is sufficient to state that the chronology above is sufficiently explicit to make it clear that none of the projects were viable in the medium term. A reading of Cullen on Orbiston demonstrates the optimism of Owen's 1830 statement given above was somewhat unfounded. The Ralahine project, the scheme with the least involvement of Owen, was perhaps the most successful of the initiatives and would have continued beyond 1833 had the landowner, John Scott Vandaleur, not bankrupted himself on the gaming tables of the Dublin clubs (Garnett, 1971, p. 49).

The difficulties his practical experiments and those of his followers faced, did not stop Owen from continuing to advocate the principle of agricultural communitarian settlements, for in 1841 he published through the Home Colonization Society he had established, *A Development of the Principles and Plans on which to establish Self-Supporting Home Colonies*. Owen was not the first writer to promote home colonies. His colleague, the Quaker William Allen, had in 1827 published a pamphlet on *Colonies at Home*, which provide detailed guidance on growing vegetables, targeted at Irish peasants with their over-dependence on potatoes. Allen was to establish a charity school at Lindfield in Sussex, where the children operated a commercial printing press. Also in 1832 land surveyor, E J Lance published a pamphlet whose full title was *The Cottage Garden or Farmers' Friend: Pointing out the means of making the Earth serviceable to the Rich and Poor, by giving Employment to Capital and Labour on all sorts of Land*. Rowland Hill, the Benthamite advocate of emigration to South Australia and postal reformer, published in the same year *Home Colonies: Sketch of a Plan for the Gradual Extinction of Pauperism and for the Diminution of Crime*. Hill proposed settlements of paupers on the Dutch and Belgian model, based on a grant of land and loan from government, with the settlement being exempt from taxation. It was suggested that the first settlement should be near London so that the government could watch its progress. Hill included financial details of a Dutch pauper colony to demonstrate that the proposal was viable and that a loan could be repaid at 5 1/2 per cent interest (Hill, 1832).

The Home Colonization Society was established in 1840 by Owen, William Galpin and Frederick Bate, primarily to raise funds for the Queenswood community. The brochure issued under the name of A C Cuddon, secretary, stated the Society's objects:

1   To submit the plans for the Colonies, in all their details, to the most scientific and experienced men in every department of life;
2   To make these plans extensively known to the public; and to demonstrate their efficiency for the purposes designed;
3   To demonstrate that these Colonies, in consequence of their very superior economical arrangements, will afford a safe and profitable investment for capital;
4   To arrange the preliminaries for Joint-Stock Companies to carry the same gradually into extensive execution; and
5   To publish the most useful authentic works, explanatory of the principles of the system of Home Colonization, in order to convey to the public correct information on this most important subject.

The full title of Owen's pamphlet gives an indication of his ambitions:

A Development of the Principles and Plans on which to establish Self-Supporting Home Colonies as a most secure and profitable investment for capital, and an effectual means of permanently to remove the causes of ignorance, poverty and crime; and most materially to benefit all classes of society; by giving a right application to the now greatly misdirected powers of the human faculties and of physical and moral science.

The pamphlet is dedicated to the governments of Great Britain, Austria, Russia, France, Prussia and the United States of America, with a dedication asserting that

The SUPREME POWER OF THE UNIVERSE has, now, placed the Sovereignty of the Earth for a time, at your united disposal. To you, is given the High and Mighty Trust, in this your day of power, to effect, by your union, wisely directed, the greatest good that human agency has ever attained for man. You have now, at your control, the means, in the most abundant superfluity, to give such direction to the industry, skill, and mental faculties of the human race, that they shall, speedily, fertilize and beautify the earth; and greatly to improve the character and condition of the present generation; and form all its inhabitants of the succeeding generations, to be highly useful, healthy, intelligent, essentially good, wise and happy.

(Owen, 1841, p. v)

This is followed by *20 Questions to the Human Race* and signed by *The Friend to all Governments and People, Robert Owen*. The pamphlet is an expansion of the proposals set out in the *Report to the County of Lanark*. There are, however, significant changes. Owen is no longer focusing on the 'spade husbandry' of the earlier work. He now breaks down the business of the colony into agriculture and gardening, manufactures and trades, commercial transactions, as well as what he refers to as domestic economy (maintaining the homes and public kitchens and dormitories), health, police and education (ibid., pp. 66–7). Owen is also more explicit about the type of residents. He had always equivocated on the issues of communal ownership of property and equality of status and incomes of all residents. He now sets out four categories of colonist – a first class of hired servants and labourers; a second class of 'candidates for membership' who would have superior lodging rooms, food and clothes, a third class of Full Members of the Colony who 'will possess these advantages in a still higher degree', and a fourth class – the Family Club. This will consist of 'families and of single persons, with independent incomes, of good education, manners and habits'. These club members would live in private apartments and could take their meals in their own apartments, but would have free use of all the public institutions – 'their children will be educated, from birth, to become far superior, physically, morally, intellectually, and practically, to the past and present race of men'. There is an indication here of the notion of a governing elite similar to that of the 'samurai' later to be promoted by H G Wells in his 1905 *Modern Utopia* – Owen can be seen as a precursor to the social Darwinist and eugenicist thinking which was to become widespread amongst a group of socialist intellectuals in the pre-First World War period.

The pamphlet also includes a 'synoptic table' showing the numbers and in each class by gender (an equal division between males and females in the first three classes, clearly assuming no intermarriage across class boundaries) and their costs. In a colony in its first stage of 3708 colonists, there were to be 864 hired servants and labourers, 324 candidates for membership, 360 members (of which 288 were to be married and 72 single), 432 family club members with 1728 children (no assumption about gender split here). There was no provision for persons in the first three classes to have children, even though there were assumed to be 144 married couples in the third class (ibid., pp. 44–51).

The pamphlet also sets out detailed instructions on the management of the colony, and an estimate of the cost of one of the superior home colonies or family clubs at £700,000. This includes £440,000 for 2000 acres of land and £252,000 for seventy-two houses and four colleges of education at £4,000 each. The pamphlet also includes a site plan for the development, with some drawings of the main building with a detailed description of layout in the text. Unlike in Whitwell's earlier plan, no authorship for the design is given.

There are also numerous appendices – extracts from George Combe's *Moral Philosophy*, studies of co-operative colonies in America including extracts from Harriet Martineau and J S Buckingham, and a number of Owen's previous works including an *Outline of the Rational System of Society* which includes a General Constitution of Government and Universal Code of Laws, his 1837 Manchester lectures, and a new pamphlet entitled *The Signs of the Times or the Approach of the Millennium: Address to the Tories, Whigs, Radicals and Chartists, Churchmen, Catholics, Dissenters and Infidels, to all Producers of Wealth and Non-Producers in Great Britain and Ireland*.

Ambrose Cuddon, the secretary of the Home Colonisation Committee which published Owen's pamphlet was later a supporter of Bronterre O'Brien and was chairman of the committee which published the *Working Man* journal in the 1860s.

Robert Owen was to live until 1858. Despite his involvement in trade unionism and co-operation, it is difficult from reading the increasingly autocratic and millenarian tone of his writings to see Owen as a radical when his views on the planning of new settlements are considered. Despite the fact that at the time of the Orbiston initiative he advocated equality and common property, he was not a consistent egalitarian. While his earlier work attracted criticism by William Cobbett for proposing 'parallelograms of paupers', his later work proposes a highly regulated hierarchical community, with no semblance of equality between residents or co-operative ownership or management. Garnett is fairly damning in his appraisal – Owen:

> believed that a paternalistic system of management was all that was necessary to organise resources and distribute the real surplus created by labour. He never really emancipated himself from the idea of poor-law colonies. Owen was not really interested in community development, nor was he at heart capable of co-operation.
>
> (Garnett, 1971, p. 60)

Owen saw himself as a prophet. As Garnett comments:

> When faced with intolerable situations which he himself had largely brought about through imbuing his followers with grandiloquent images of community life, Owen could always evade responsibility and action by pointing out that his disciples had not followed his precepts. In the last resort he could claim that only he could visualise the new society, and on these almost logical positivist terms no one could prove him wrong.
>
> (ibid., p. 55)

While Owen is often categorised incorrectly as one of the utopians criticised in Engels' *Socialism: Utopian and Scientific*, Engels had considerable respect for Owen. In May 1871, the International Working Men's Association (IWMA) received an invitation to a celebration of the centenary of Owen's birth. At the meeting of the General Council, the O'Brienite, George E Harris, reminisced that he had known

Owen personally and worked with him. The trade unionist Thomas Mottershead commented that he 'bows to no one in his estimation for Robert Owen' and that the middle class Christian Socialists had put Owen down as they saw him as a challenge to their own power. Engels said that:

> there was no doubt about Robert Owen. There were things to be found in his writings that had not been superseded yet. He had started from his own ideas, had been originally a manufacturer himself and the first that had stood up against his class . . .

The carpenter John Weston commented that the IWMA 'embraced to a larger extent the principles of Robert Owen than any other association' (First International, 1870–1, pp. 190–3). Engels was actually consistent in his positive view of Owen. In *Socialism: Utopian and Scientific*, published in 1880, Engels commented that:

> Every social movement, every real advance in England on behalf of the workers is linked with Owen's name . . . He introduced as transition measures to the complete communist organisation of society . . . cooperative societies which have since at least given practical proof that the merchant and the manufacturer are quite superfluous personages.
>
> (ibid., pp. 60–1)

The next sections will examine how Owen's ideas were adapted and radicalised by some of his contemporaries and followers.

William Thompson

It could be argued that Thompson is as important in the history of socialism and co-operation as Owen. He also made a significant contribution to the early literature on settlement planning. As compared with extensive literature on Owen, little attention has been paid to Thompson despite his significant output. The only biography was published by Richard Pankhurst in 1954 (Pankhurst, 1954). His role is however considered by Lowenthal in her work on the Ricardian socialists (1911), in Harrison (1969) and Claeys (1987, 1989).

Thompson was an Irish landowner who in the 1820s reorganised his family estate at Glandore on a co-operative basis. He built a school and tried to develop small industries. He read the works of Bentham and William Godwin and travelled to France and the Low Countries where he made contact with the Saint-Simonians. He then initiated a correspondence with Bentham and in fact stayed at Bentham's home in London for four months at the end of 1822 where he met the leading utilitarians. Thompson also met Owen in 1822. He disapproved of the social system outlined in Owen's *Report to the County of Lanark*, which he, in comments similar to those of Cobbett, considered to be 'an improved system of pauper management'. He disliked Owen's focus on trying to convert the rich and famous – 'No high sounding moral maxims influence or can influence the rich as a body'.

Much of Thompson's first major work – *An Inquiry into the Principles of the Distribution of Wealth*, was written while he lodged with Bentham, Bentham's influence is reflected in the work's full title *An Inquiry into the Principles of the*

Distribution of Wealth most conducive to Human Happiness, applied to the newly proposed System of Voluntary Equality of Wealth. It is however the last phrase of the title that takes Thompson beyond Bentham and Owen and supports a case for him to be regarded as the first British socialist, noting that he was Irish rather than English. As the Webbs pointed out in their *History of Trade Unionism*, Owen derived much of his economic analysis from Thompson rather than vice versa (Webb and Webb, 1920, pp. 162–3). In fact, Thompson's economic analysis is much clearer than that of Owen, who, as mentioned earlier, was often ambivalent on key issues such as collective ownership and equality of wealth and income.

Thompson's position was unequivocal. The first section of the first chapter of his *Inquiry* is headed 'Wealth is produced by labor: no other ingredient but labor makes any object of desire an object of wealth. Labor is the sole universal measure, as well as the characteristic distinction, of wealth'. The fifth chapter is headed 'Of the present state of the distribution of wealth, as resulting from the institutions of insecurity; and of the means of reducing the existing forced expedients of unequal distribution to the voluntary mode of equality limited by security'. Chapter 6 is summarised as 'Of voluntary equality in the distribution of wealth. Labor by co-operation opposed to labor by individual competition'. His final section is summarised as 'equality of wealth must be established by reason alone'. In his conclusion after nearly 600 pages of analysis, Thompson makes the link between utilitarianism and egalitarianism explicit:

> Of all the causes which operate on the human character and human happiness, none is of such importance as the distribution of wealth; because on that depend almost all those circumstances, those relations, on which the development of character and happiness depends . . . . No existing distribution ought to be upheld further than it ca be shown to promote preponderant good. In order to produce the greatest happiness deliverable from wealth, the greatest equality reconcileable with security, every producer, whether agricultural, manufacturing or in any other way affording a satisfactory equivalent for wealth, ought to possess the faculty of freely directing his labor, with capital sufficient to secure to himself the whole products of his labor, whether producing on his own account alone, or co-operating in company with others.
>
> (Thompson, 1834, pp. 597–600)

His *Labor Rewarded*, published three years later (Thompson, 1827), which is written in response to Thomas Hodgkin's *Labour Defended against the Claims of Capital*, restates his previous argument that equality of remuneration was most productive of happiness, skill and improvement, before setting out the political and economic reforms necessary to improve the situation of the 'industrious classes' and then setting out proposals for mutual co-operation. It is this section that he is critical of Owen's projects, insistent on his own attachment to 'the system of industry by the voluntary association of large numbers and the equal distribution of the products of their labour' (ibid., p. 99). He refers to various co-operative initiatives including the London Co-operative Society, whose membership includes 'Mr Owen, late of New Lanark, now of New Harmony and The World'. The book concludes with an exhortation to Men and Women of the Industrious Classes to 'UNITE IN LARGE NUMBERS' to establish cooperative communities (ibid., pp. 108–14).

It should be noted that between writing these two books, Thompson in collaboration with his friend Anna Wheeler, also managed to produce one of the earliest feminist works: *Appeal of One Half of the Human Race. Women, against the Pretensions of the Other Half, Men, to restrain them in Political and thence in Civil and Domestic Slavery* (1825). This work denounced the unbreakable bonds of marriage, the double standard of morality and the subservient position of women. It was written as a riposte to the utilitarian James Mill's essay on *Government* which had grouped women with children as being adequately represented through the male head of the household.

In 1830, Thompson published another substantive volume – *Practical Directions for the Speedy and Economical Establishment of Communities*. This book first reviews the recent development of co-operative societies – referring to 300 established in England, Scotland and Ireland before explaining that it is intended as a practical guide for societies to set up co-operative communities. The practical guide starts with a set of definitions – Labour, wealth, necessaries, conveniences, superfluities and extravagances. 'Community' is defined as 'an association of persons, in sufficient numbers, and living on a space of land of sufficient extent, to supply by their own exertions all of each other's wants' (Thompson, 1830, p. 7). Mutual co-operation implies:

> that every individual entering a community is willing to direct his or her labor, mental or physical, or as is most frequently the case, both combined, to whatever objects may be deemed by the general voice, most conducive to the general good.
> (ibid., p. 8)

Equal distribution is 'that which affords to every individual exerting, or equally willing to exert, his or her faculties for the common good, equal means of physical, intellectual, and social enjoyments' (ibid.). Thompson emphasises that community of property does not mean that no person shall possess anything but no adult person should own more than another. Thompson also refers to equality of enjoyments – 'that equal advantages should be secured to all, as far as may be in the power of the community to effect it, by equal exertions of each for the benefit of all' (ibid., p. 14).

Thompson then gives detailed guidance on raising funds for new settlements and for acquiring and managing land. Thompson is critical of the proposal for a large communal dormitory of 1000 people put forward by T R Edmunds in his *Practical, Moral and Political Economy*. Thompson argues instead for individual independence and privacy. He proposes a community of 2000 people, comprising 1400 adults and 600 children on a site of 2000 acres. He then examines the implications of a community of this size for economy of labour, health, social and intellectual enjoyment and individual independence (ibid., pp. 24–43). He also comments that a community of 2000 is the maximum size which would allow full participation of all members in the governance of the community (ibid., p. 43). Adults and children are to live separately.

Thompson then sets appropriate arrangements for buildings within the context of a general plan. Domestic buildings were to have a ground floor, two stories and an attic (ibid., p. 49). Detailed internal arrangements are provided, including arrangements for water supply, heating, ventilation, sewerage and the phasing of the construction of the different buildings. This detailed specification is then followed by details of the division of the agricultural labour force between different agricultural products, with details of how many man hours for so many bushels of grain or so many tons of potatoes or vegetables (ibid., pp. 90–1). He then estimates how much of each product would be eaten and the surplus generated for sale. This is followed by a monthly schedule of sowing, planting and harvesting (ibid., pp. 108–17), the machinery required for different forms of production – flax, cotton, iron and brass, and flour (ibid., pp. 141–76). There is a guide to budget management (ibid., pp. 188–213), preservation of health (ibid., pp. 213–25), and education and mental pleasures (ibid., pp. 225–43). This comprehensive work concludes with arrangements for governing the community and a warning of the evils which arise if the overall population of the country grows too quickly. This includes a commentary on the sexual behaviour of different classes in different countries. Thompson's conclusion is that the co-operative arrangements proposed would stabilise the population of a community, 'which would be conducive to the improvement and happiness of both sexes' (ibid., p. 268).

It should be noted that throughout the book, possibly with the exception of the last section, Thompson's guidance is supported by the experience, positive and negative, of existing settlements. In this regard Thompson was very different from Owen, who had a tendency to avoid analysing the problems of pre-existing communities before promoting new ones. Thompson had proposed to use his own directions as the basis for setting up a new co-operative community and issued a prospectus for it. Thompson nevertheless continued to promote his practical proposals which contrasted with Owen's increasingly impractical millenarianism, before dying in March 1833. It is Thompson, rather than Owen, who should be considered to be the theorist of co-operation and co-operative settlements. In contrast with Owen, he was a much more consistent proponent of egalitarianism and the potential for co-operation to replace the capitalist state, rather than as an alternative form of management within capitalism.

John Thimbleby

Little is known about John Thimbleby, other than that he was an artisan, who lived in Barnet, at that time a village north of London, and at one time traded as a pawnbroker with his son. He wrote a pamphlet entitled *Man's Birthright: Time. The Only Real Wealth* (1849). He was also to publish in 1863 *The Dreams of a Dreamer*, which is best described as a Christian meditation on obedience to the Holy Ghost. His relevance to this study is that in 1832 he published a pamphlet – *Monodelphia*, subtitled *The Formation of a New System of Society without the intervention of a circulating medium*. The circulating medium to which Thimbleby was opposed was money. He quoted the Letter to Timothy in the *New Testament*: 'The love of money is the root of all evil'. Unlike his later pamphlet, this pamphlet sought to put forward practical proposals. His starting point was that :

> All the misery to which man is subjected under the existing system, is to be attributed to Individual property, or the Circulation of Money. To abolish these evils, must, therefore, be the first step towards effecting a change for the better: and the second, to substitute a new system, in place of the present one, pure and

efficacious in its principle, simple in its construction, and replete with all that is requisite to combine the real and permanent happiness of individuals, with the best interests of society at large. The basis of this system must be BROTHERLY LOVE. Individual Property must be succeeded by equal participation in the general stock; and the use of a Circulating Medium by a reciprocal exchange of the necessaries and conveniences of life.

(Thimbleby, 1832, p. 17)

Thimbleby drew up a systematic plan. His town would comprise 6000 people, three times the size of Thompson's settlement. All exchange within the town and with external merchants was to be through barter. In contrast with Thompson's recognition of the need for gender equality, Thimbleby's community was to be governed by men over forty, with the younger men doing the work, the women looking after their husbands and children. Unmarried women were to care for the elderly, while unmarried girls over fourteen would be required to help married couples without children. Any couple could marry and divorce, at which point the divorced woman would rejoin the unmarried women in caring for the elderly in the 'Temple of Happiness'.

The pamphlet focused mainly on arrangements for education and religion. The concluding section reads like Morris's *News From Nowhere*, with a visitor being given a tour by a 'courteous youth with modern grace' from the workshops to the Garden of Pleasure, the Dancing Hall, the Reading Rooms, the Conversation Hall, the Garden of Praise, the Hymeneal Altar, to which an eager youth is leading a willing maid, the Government Hall, the Schools, finishing the tour at the Temple of Happiness (ibid., pp. 64–70). Thimbleby's vision was a community – in fact a world – 'in the undisturbed possession of perfect freedom and unalloyed happiness' (ibid., p. 76).

John Minter Morgan

Thimbleby was not the only Owenite who produced a utopian plan for a Christian co-operative settlement. Morgan was a Christian philanthropist who in 1819 published a book which effectively endorsed Owen's *New View of Society*, while rejecting the anti-Christian basis – *Remarks on the Practicality of Mr Owen's Plan to improve the condition of the Working Classes*. He then published a further article entitled *Mr Owen's proposed Villages for the Poor shown as highly favourable to Christianity* and in 1827 *An Inquiry Respecting Private Property and the authority and perpetuity of the apostolic institution of a community of goods*. As can be ascertained from the title, this work was a polemic using biblical quotations and other theological works to support his argument against private property.

Morgan's most famous work is his *Revolt of the Bees*, published in 1826. The title intentionally reflected Bernard Mandeville's 1705 poem *Fable of the Bees: Private Vices; Public Benefits*. The book is in the form of a Socratic dialogue with different characters discussing different forms of social system, with the final sections focusing on the works of Owen and Thompson. Part of the dialogue is in effect auto-biographical with one character, Henry Neville, explaining how he was converted to the Owenite principles (ibid., pp. 252–3) The following section presents a vision of a new community run on co-operative principles:

The stranger on his first arrival is struck with the solidity and splendour of the edifices, the luxuriance of the fields, gardens and parks, the profusion of the products of foreign commerce, and of domestic industry; at the same time remarking the small portion of time in which the occupants are productively occupied. In a few days, however, he discovers the secret, in the judicious appliance of every talent or power, physical or mental, both individually and collectively . . . For the more stupendous results of their combination, they are indebted to the mutual aid of several communities, alternatively assisting each other . . .

(ibid., p. 254)

In 1842, Morgan petitioned the House of Commons to support his plan for the employment and support of 300 poor families and for the establishment of superior normal schools in every diocese in the Empire.

In 1846, he established a Society to promote The Establishment of Self Supporting Institutions for People Destitute of Employment. This was launched at a public meeting in Exeter Hall on 27th May. Morgan subsequently issued a prospectus for *The Church of England Self Supporting Village for Promoting the Religious, Moral and General Improvement of the Working Classes by forming establishments of three hundred families on the land, and combining agricultural with manufacturing employment for their own benefit.* This included a proposal for establishing a model self supporting village requiring capital of £50,000. The village was to be called Victoria, as in Buckingham's proposal the previous year. The prospectus listed three bishops and five MPs as vice presidents, with the committee including Lord John Manners and Richard Monckton Milnes. The scheme however met with little support and Morgan died in 1854. He did however manage to establish the National Orphan Home near his own home on Ham Common.

Morgan's most detailed proposal for establishing new settlements is in his *Christian Commonwealth*, published in 1850. The book comprises a critique of contemporary political economy and a prospectus for the Self Supporting Institution for 300 families, which Morgan had been promoting for several years. This time he costs the proposal at a total of £60,000. He then calculates the value of labour – it being assumed that the main pursuit is agriculture. He does however allow for handicraft work, such as that of wheelwrights, coach and cart building, tanning, printing and bookbinding. Morgan has a strong opposition to large manufacturing enterprises. The residents, referred to as 'inmates' would enjoy 'the best of food (in their own cottages if preferred) comfortable clothing and habitations, good education for their children with leisure for rational recreation and improvement, either in the Institute or elsewhere.' There is a strong focus on moral and religious improvement – there are proposals for Sunday schools and normal schools – and lectures for the adults. Selected boys (not girls) would be taught natural philosophy and the sciences and mathematics, and at the age of thirteen, Latin and Greek. Morgan is keen to emphasise that the self supporting institution 'neither interferes with the distinctions of class nor of wealth' (ibid., p. 90). Clearly in seeking to raise funds from the clergy, Morgan could not risk his project being viewed as in any way revolutionary.

The plans of Thimbleby and Morgan were not the only plans for new settlements circulating in the 1840s and 1850s. Other plans emerged from Owenite circles. Owen's Orbiston partner, James Hamilton, published in 1825 A *Mode of forming societies for mutual benefit on rational and practical principles, without the assistance of the rich, or the necessity of borrowing one shilling* – addressed to the working classes. *Rules and regulations of the Association for the internal colonisation of artisans and the poor by means of a new system of manual labour,* was published anonymously in 1837. In 1842, a pamphlet was published in Cheltenham by the Christian cooperative community society – *Elements of the principles calculated to heal the wounds of mankind.* In 1843, Thomas Hunt published a report of a meeting of intending emigrants, *comprehending a practical plan for founding co-operative colonies of united interests in the north-western territories of the United States* (Co-operative Communities, 1972).

Two earlier Owenite pamphlets advocated the purchase of land by workers to establish self-governed settlements, for example Samuel Bower's 1838 pamphlet *A Sequel to the Peopling of Utopia or the Sufficiency of Socialism for Human Happiness,* published in Bradford, and the Salford teacher Robert Cooper's *A Contrast between the New Moral World and the Old Immoral World,* also published in 1838. Bower argued that founding new communities was more important than universal suffrage. Cooper proposed that:

> the working classes should subscribe all the money they possibly can ... and with this money purchase land and upon this land should erect suitable buildings, such as houses to live in, and manufactures to work in ... then commence to work and produce for themselves, to enjoy and distribute equally all the profits of their labour and to establish a system of united interests and commonality of property.
>
> ...
>
> mankind would soon establish other communities; and thus in the course of time, this miserable and irrational state of society would be gradually removed, and be substituted by the happy and rational, communiol, or social basis of Society.
>
> ...
>
> how much more consistent it is with the laws of human nature, how much more conservative it is of human happiness, how much more it tended to cultivate and invigorate all those social, charitable and amiable feelings which bind man to man, and how much more conducive it is to the enlightenment and advancement of the human race.
>
> (Cooper, 1838)

Another of Owen's associates, George Mudie, had founded a cooperative community in Spa Fields in London in 1821, later founding the *Economist* journal and in 1849 publishing a pamphlet proposing the organisation of labour in self-supporting communities – *A Solution of the Portentous Enigma of Modern Civilization now Perplexing Republicans as well as Monarchs with Fear of Change* – the pamphlet was addressed to Prince Louis Napoleon, President of France and soon to become Emperor Napoleon III (Armytage, 1961; Harrison, 1969; Claeys, 1987, 1989).

In Brighton, the co-operator William King established a c-operative institution and published the *Co-operator* journal between 1828 and 1830. King also became in 1826 a commissioner for the 'better regulation, paving and managing the town and the poor ther of' until the town of Brighton was incorporated in 1854. In this role he was involved in buying the Royal Pavilion to provide a leisure facility for the town's residents (Mercer, 1922; Armytage, 1961). In 1840, King published *Four Letters on the working of money capital; showing its present inefficient and limited agency for commercial and social purposes*, a profound critique of the capitalist system, which included the following polemic:

> A Political Economist is a thorough going money juggler, a being dead to all the best feelings of our nature, a being that is ever on the scent for cheap goods and dear money, a being that promotes the competition of wood, iron and steam, against human labour, for the exclusive use of capitalists.

Robert Pemberton's *Happy Colony*

Robert Pemberton was an Owenite and friend of Morgan. In the late 1840s and early 1850s he wrote a number of pamphlets on education for nursery and infant schools.

In 1854 he wrote a pamphlet entitled *The Happy Colony* which set out a framework for development of colonial towns in New Zealand. He was later to publish a further pamphlet explaining that his proposals were in harmony with Owen's philosophy. The original pamphlet was dedicated to the 'working men of Great Britain' and was in three parts – a philosophical dialogue, an address and a description of the 'Elysian Academy or Natural University'. Pemberton's starting point was that every child was born into slavery and that only in the new world could a new society be built. Labour was to be the basis of the economic system – 'All truths must emanate from the people – the emancipating power must proceed from the labour kingdom . . . . Wealth is the tyrant of labour and the destroying angel of the happiness of the human race'. Whereas Buckingham's plan assumed ownership of land through a joint stock company, Pemberton assumed occupiers would collectively own their plots.

Whereas Owen's plan and Buckingham's plan, like many of their predecessors', were based on a rectangular arrangement for development, Pemberton proposed a series of concentric rings – an inner ring with four colleges; a middle ring with factories and hospitals, and an outer ring as a park to be three miles in circumference. His justification for the design was that:

> Every workman must have seen that all the grand forms in nature are round – the sun, moon, star, planets, our world, the human form, animals, trees, and perhaps everything in the animate creation. Consequently, the round, or circle, is the most natural, the most convenient, and the most scientific plan you can adopt.

Pemberton had strong views on urban design:

> Right angles are opposed to the harmony of motion, and in a town there must be motion; therefore, the best method for the free circulation of man and beast must be adopted. You must make up your minds to abandon the system of the old countries in everything relating to the bad formation of towns as well as the bad formation of minds, and discard, and for ever renounced, all crooked lanes, angles, narrow streets, filthy alleys, and nasty courts and impasses.

He also saw a link between collective ownership and co-operative behaviour:

> All must be public property. That is to say: must belong conjointly to the Happy
> Colonists. By adopting this system you can never have a nuisance, and all
> contention about individual property will be for ever done away with. Your ideas
> will be expanded and you will commence acting upon universal systems, the same
> as those observed in the divine creation.

Pemberton was also a believer in the compact city principle:

> Concentration will be the grand feature in the Happy Colony, so that the divine
> creative principle, economy of time, labour and space will be acted upon; yes,
> concentration is the grand principle to be acted upon in the Happy Colony, in
> training man, from birth, in love, science and labour . . .

The contribution of Owenite communitarianism

Socialist communitarianism in England was generally escapist. Proposals put forward
tended to be for new settlements either in the colonies, based on the notion of starting
afresh on a *tabula rasa*, in a new world free from the evils and corruptions and slavery
of English society, or the idea of a self-contained community within England, as a
retreat where a select group could live in a community isolated from the evils of the
modern world. Neither Owen nor most of his followers fundamentally challenged
the existing social and political structure. Most initiatives either relied on aristocratic
or business philanthropists. A few initiatives could be seen as self-reliant in the sense
of being independent working class led propositions. Owen's proposals developed
from the New Lanark project, the paternalistic and highly regulated management of
an industrial enterprise in his ownership and under his direct control, to a series of
proposals for small self-contained communities, including the projects at Orbiston
and Queenwood, together with E T Craig's Ralahine commune, to the idea of a new
community in the new world, the New Harmony project.

With the failure of both Orbiston and Queenswood, Owen abandoned the idea
of communitarian settlements within England and in effect became an escapist, both
in terms of the geographical location of his projects, and in moving towards millenarianism, effectively seeking to escape the realities of the contemporary world by
advocating a new spiritual world that transcended the realities of the real world.
Minter Morgan's schemes were largely based on the concept of a community of the
select, in his case with an explicit Christian basis. In contrast, Robert Pemberton's
scheme focused on the New World, based on a highly idealised version of the nature
of a new settlement and a new beginning, with no consideration of practical details
of how either the migration or the new settlement would be funded. Thimbleby's
proposals were similarly lacking in practical details and based on millenarian concepts.
Other contemporaries of Owen, such as James Pierrepoint Greaves, sought to set up
new communities on the basis of seeking to recreate Eden in its state before original
sin and the surrender to the temptations of the world.

What all these initiatives have in common is a failure to challenge in any practical
sense the contemporary domestic political and economic structures. The focus of the
communitarians was on transcendence rather than reform – there was no attempt to

take power within the existing society and state, only to escape from it. This explains why Owen could win support from the aristocratic and political elite because he offered an option for containing the working class through education and discipline. To the governing classes this was preferable to conceding either political or social reform to the Chartists and other radical working class movements. Owen was no democrat – he was a snob and inveterate name-dropper. He ran all his organisational creations in an autocratic manner and would resign his position if he was unable to do this. He was also impractical. Harrison points out that he was always somewhere else when something went wrong. He saw his involvement in settlements such as Orbiston and Queenswood as inspirer and law maker and considered that any failure was not due to any fault of his own but due to his followers not sufficiently bringing his precepts into effect.

Primary sources

Allen, W (1827) *Colonisation at Home* (London: Longman)

Bower, Samuel (1838) *A Sequel to the Peopling of Utopia or the Sufficiency of Socialism for Human Happiness* (Bradford: C Wilkinson)

Colquhoun, Patrick (1806) *A Treatise on Indigence* (London: Hatchard)

Colquhoun, Patrick (1814) *A Treatise on the Wealth, Power and Resources of the British Empire* (London: J Mawman)

Cooper, Robert (1838) *A Contrast between the New Moral World and the Old Immoral World* (Hulme, UK: A Heywood)

Cooperative Communities: Plans and Descriptions. Eleven Pamphlets 1825–1847 (Arno Press, New York, 1972)

Craig, E T (1893) *The Irish Land and Labour Question: Illustrated in the History of Ralahine*

Engels F (1880) *Socialism: Utopian and Scientific* (Peking: Foreign Languages Press 1975)

Hill, Rowland (1832) *Home Colonies: Sketch of a Plan for the Gradual Extinction of Pauperism and for the Diminution of Crime* (London)

King, William (1840) *Four Letters on the Workings of Capital: Showing its Present Inefficient se and Limited Agency for Commercial and Social Purposes* (London: W King)

Lance, E J (1832) *The Cottage Garden or Farmers' Friend: Pointing out the means of making the Earth serviceable to the Rich and Poor, by giving Employment to Capital and Labour on all sorts of Land* (London: J Ridgway)

Morgan, John Minter (1817) *Remarks on the Practicability of Mr Owen's Plan to improve the Condition of the Lower Classes* (London: Samuel Leigh)

Morgan, John Minter (1826) *Revolt of the Bees* (London: Longman, Rees, Orme, Brown and Green)

Morgan, John Minter (1827) *An Enquiry Respecting Private Property*

Morgan, John Minter (1850) *The Christian Commonwealth* (London: Charles Gilpin)

Morgan, John Minter (1850) *The Church of England Self-Supporting Villages*

Mudie, George (1849) *A Solution of the Portentous Enigma of Modern Civilization Now Perplexing Republicans as well as Monarchs with Fear of Change* (London: C Cox)

Owen, Robert (1813) *A New View of Society* (London: Cadell and Davies)

Owen, Robert (1817) *Report to the Committee of the Association for the Relief of the Manufacturing and Labouring Poor* (London: Robert Owen)

Owen, Robert (1820) *Report to the County of Lanark of a Plan for Relieving Public Distress* (Glasgow, Edinburgh)

Owen, Robert (1841) *A Development of the Principles and Plans on which to establish Self Supporting Home Colonies* (London: Home Colonization Society)

Owen, Robert (1842) *The Book of the New Moral World* (London: Home Colonization Society)

Owen, Robert (1857) *Autobiography* (edited Max Beer London 1920 G Bell and Sons)

Owen, Robert (ed.) (1832–3) *The Crisis*, Vols 1–2 (reprint by Greenword Reprint Corporation, New York 1868)

Owen Robert (ed.) (1835) *The New Moral World*, Vol 1 (London: Association of All Classes of All Nations)

Pemberton, Robert (1854) *The Happy Colony* (London: Saunders and Otley)

Thimbleby, John (1832) *Monadelphia or the Formation of a New System of Society* (Barnet)

Thimbleby, John (1849?) *What is Money Man's Birthright, Time, the only Real Wealth* (London, E Wilson)

Thimbleby, John (1863) *The Dreams of a Dreamer* (London: Wertheim, Macintosh and Hunt)

Thompson, William (1824) *An Inquiry into the Principles of the Distribution of Wealth* (London: Longman, Hurst, Orme, Brown and Green)

Thompson, William (1827) *Labour Rewarded: The Claims of Labor and Capital Conciliated or How to Secure to Labor the Whole Products of its Exertions* (London: Hunt and Clarke)

Thompson, William (1830) *Practical Directions for the Speedy and Economical Establishment of Communities* (London: Strange)

Thompson, William and Wheeler, Anna (1825) *Appeal of One Half of the Human Race. Women, against the Pretensions of the Other Half, Men, to restrain them in Political and thence in Civil and Domestic Slavery.* (London: Longman)

Whitwell, Thomas Stedman (1830) *Description of an Architectural Model for a Community upon a Principle of United Interests as Advocated by Robert Owen Esq* (London: Chance and Co.)

Secondary sources

Armytage, W H G (1961) *Heavens Below: Utopian Experiments in England 1560–1960* (London: Routledge and Kegan Paul)

Ashworth, W (1954) *The Genesis of Modern British Town Planning* (London: Routledge and Kegan Paul)

Bell, C and Bell R (1969) *City Fathers: The Early History of Town Planning in Britain* (London: Cresset Press)

Bestor, A (1971) *Backwoods Utopias* (Philadelphia, PA: University of Pennsylvania Press)

Claeys, G (1986) '"Individualism", "Socialism" and "Social Science": Further Notes on a Problem of Conceptual Formation 1800–1850' in *Journal of the History of Ideas*, Vol 47, No 1, pp. 81–93

Claeys, G (1987) *Machinery, Money and the Millennium: From Moral Economy to Socialism 1815–1860* (Cambridge: Polity Press)

Claeys, G (1989) *Citizens and Saints: Politics and anti-politics in early British Socialism* (Cambridge: Cambridge University Press)

Cole, G D H (1925) *The Life of Robert Owen* (London: Macmillan)

Cole, G D H (1953) *A History of Socialist Thought: The Forerunners 1789–1950* (London: Macmillan)

Cullen, A (1910) *Adventures in Socialism: New Lanark Establishment and the Orbiston Community* (London: John Smith and Son; A C Black)

Evans, A (2008) 'E T Craig: proto-socialist, phrenologist and public health engineer' in *International Journal of Epidemiology*, Vol 37, No 3, pp. 490–505

Galgano, M (1979) Entry on William Thompson in *Biographical Dictionary of British Radicals*, Baylen and Gossman (eds), Vol 1, pp. 475–84 (Hassocks, UK: Harvester)

Garnett, R G (1971) 'Robert Owen and the Community Experiments' in Pollard, S and Salt, J (eds), *Robert Owen: Prophet of the Poor* (London: Macmillan)

Garnett, R G (1972) *Co-operation and the Owenite socialist communities in Britain 1825–45* (Manchester, UK: Manchester University Press)

Hardy, D (1979) *Alternative Communities in Nineteenth Century England* (London: Longman)

Harrison, J (1969) *Robert Owen and the Owenites in Britain and America: The Quest for the New Moral World* (London: Routledge and Kegan Paul)

Harrison, J (1979) *The Second Coming: Popular Millenarianism 1780–1850* (London: Routledge and Kegan Paul)

Kaswan, M (2008) *Happiness, Well-being and William Thompson's Social(ist) Utilitarianism.* Paper presented to the 10th Conference of the International Society for Utilitarian Studies, Berkeley, California, CA

Lloyd-Jones, P (1900) *Life, Times and Labours of Robert Owen* (London: Swan Sonnenshein)

Lockley, P (2014) *Visionary Religion and Radicalism in Early Industrial England* (Oxford: Oxford University Press)

Lowenthal, E (1911) *The Ricardian Socialists* (New York: Columbia University Press)

Madden, D (2010) *The Paddington Prophet. Richard Brothers' Journey to Jerusalem* (Manchester, UK: Manchester University Press)

Mason, J (2001) *The Moravian Church and the Missionary Awakening in England 1760–1800* (Woodbridge, UK: Boydell Press)

Mercer, T W (ed.) (1922) *Dr William King and the Co-operator* (Manchester, UK: The Co-operative Union)

Pankhurst, R (1954) *William Thompson: Pioneer Socialist* (London: Watts)

Podmore, C (1998) *The Moravian Church in England 1728–1760* (Oxford: Clarendon Press)

Podmore, F (1906) *Robert Owen: A Biography* (London: George, Allen and Unwin)

Royle, E (1998) *Robert Owen and the Commencement of the Millennium: A Study of the Harmony community* (Manchester, UK: Manchester University Press)

Taylor, A (1987) *Visions of Harmony* (Oxford: Clarendon Press)

Thompson, N (1984) *The People's Science: The popular political economy of exploitation and crisis 1816–1834* (Cambridge: Cambridge University Press)

Webb, S and Webb, B (1920) *The History of Trade Unionism* (London: Longmans)

6   The influence of the French utopian socialists in England

The Saint-Simonian missions to England

Robert Owen and his collaborators were not the only utopian socialists who had an interest in the planning of new settlements. Many Owenites were aware of the somewhat different forms of socialism which had emerged across the Channel in France. Three distinct traditions had impacts on the early development of socialism in England – the Saint-Simonians, the followers of Etienne Cabet known as Icarians, and the followers of Charles Fourier. The exchange was two-way and French socialists were also aware of the work of Robert Owen (Moret, 1997). The Saint-Simonians' activity in England has been covered in some depth by Richard Pankhurst (Pankhurst, 1957) who has also carried out a study of the Fourierists in England (Pankhurst, 1956). Less is known about the British Icarians.

Saint-Simon himself appears to have taken little interest in England, other than seeing England as France's main national rival. He only visited England once. While recognising that England was superior to France in its industrial development and that France needed industrial organisation to catch up, he argued that the French were superior in 'organic conception' (Carlisle, 1987, p. 37). However, the leading Saint-Simonians, Gustave D'Eichthal and Charles Duveyrier visited England in 1831 on a mission to convert Britain on the instructions of Saint-Simon's successor, Barthelemy Prosper Enfantin (referred to as Pere Enfantin), Saint-Simon having died in 1825. Before arriving in London, D'Eichthal had had an extensive correspondence with both Thomas Carlyle and John Stuart Mill. He was also a friend of the utilitarian MP, Charles Buller. Whereas Saint-Simon like Owen sought to create a new social system, by the time of the visit to England, the Saint-Simonians had become more of a religious cult. Mill acted as a guide for the missionaries, introducing them to Thomas Carlyle and other radicals. The missionaries were also supported by Anna Wheeler who had been a member of a Saint-Simonian circle in Caen, and by James Elishama Smith, the Owenite universalist pastor.

Very little of Saint-Simon's writing was available in English. The Saint-Simonians therefore circulated *An Address to the British Public*, sending copies to potential supporters such as Thomas Carlyle, W J Fox, Thomas Attwood, the *Co-operator* and the Russian ambassador.

The pamphlet stated that:

> We have come to London for the purpose of ourselves in communication with all persons in England who, being desirous of ameliorating the present state of

society, by means of religion, politics or philosophy, may feel interested in the efforts of a like kind now making in France. Our society, at once religious, political and philosophical, is now so widely spread and so influential in France, that it may legitimately claim the first rank among political parties, by its power of rallying round it, the most earnest and active members of every party.

Saint-Simon's pamphlet *Nouveau Christianisme* was published in 1834 as *New Christianity: Dialogues between a Conservative and an Innovator* by J E Smith, who had by then succeeded Owen as editor of *The Crisis*. Mill, who read French, was familiar with Saint-Simon's earlier works on industrial organisation. Many of the utlilitarians and Owenite co-operators, however, objected to the virulent attack on established religion, both Catholic and Protestant, in the Saint-Simonian propaganda. The publication of Saint-Simon's pamphlet by Smith, whose millenarian tendencies were of a more religious dimension than those of the secularist Owen, would only have reinforced this impression. While the missionaries had some contact with the London based Central Co-operative committee, the Owenites were of the view that there was insufficient agreement for collaboration. In 1833 two Italian Saint-Simonians, Fontana and Prati, ran a lecture series in the Burton Lecture rooms in London. They were however not an official mission from the Saint-Simonian Society in Paris which had been wound up. Gregorio Fontana styled himself as chair of the St Simonian Religion in England; Gioacetto Prati as their preacher. They also published a pamphlet *St Simonism in London: Community of Goods or the Organisation of Industry; Community of Women or Matrimony or Divorce*. *The Crisis* commented that attendees at the lectures were unsure whether the Saint-Simonians were Christian fanatics or disguised atheists. The Owenite Rowland Detroisier continued to attend Saint-Simonian meetings but stressed that he was an inquirer not an advocate (Pankhurst, 1957). It would appear that any theories that Saint-Simon might have propounded as to the organisation of industry and principles of community development became lost in a superfluity of pseudo religious mumbo jumbo. The editor of the *Poor Man's Guardian* commented after a lecture by Prati that Saint-Simonianism would 'make no progress in England' (quoted by Pankhurst,1956, p. 125).

The pamphlet generated a lengthy and generally supportive article by Mill in the *Examiner*. However, although Mill soon distanced himself from the missionaries' meetings, he remained sympathetic, remarking in his *Principles of Political Economy* that Saint-Simonism 'sowed the seeds of nearly all the Socialistic tendencies' (p. 204 quoted by Pankhurst, 1957, p. 147). In his autobiography he added 'the writings by which more than by any others, a new mode of political thinking was brought home to me were those of the Saint-Simonian school in France' (cited Pankhurst, 1957, pp. 147–8).

Etienne Cabet and the Icarians

Cabet was influenced more by Thomas More's *Utopia* than he was by Robert Owen's writings (Prudhommeaux, 1907). He nevertheless was in contact with Robert Owen, visited New Lanark and may have taken his advice on the location for his first settlement in America, in Texas. The Icarians' promotional activities focused on emigration to the Americas rather than establishing new settlements in Europe. Cabet was elected in 1830 as a member of the French National assembly but he lived in exile in London between 1834 and 1839, and in fact wrote most of his historical work on the French revolution and his classic utopian work *Voyage en Icarie* in the British Museum, with the latter book being published in Paris after his return there in 1840. It should be noted that *Voyage en Icarie* was not translated into English until 2003 (and his historical works remain untranslated), so that English radicals without a knowledge of French would have needed to rely on the Icarian brochures. Cabet, while in exile in London, did however meet Owen and collaborated with the Chartist, Peter McDouall, who had himself spent some time in Paris (Prothero, 2003; Bensimon, 2013).

In France, Cabet organised a political movement based on the principle of pacific communism, with his ideas being disseminated through his newspaper, *Le Populaire*. By 1847, Cabet, frustrated with his failure to achieve political reform in France, and criticised by other radicals for his pacifism and passivity, decided to lead the Icarians to the new world. A pamphlet by Cabet calling for his disciples to go to Icarie was published in English by the Icarian committee, based in Newman Street in Soho. The British section of the Icarian communists also published in November 1848 an *Address to the proletarians and others of Great Britain and Ireland*. This was inviting recruits to join the Icarian settlement and follow on from the first group – 'men tried and proved by dangers and persecutions – men, not merely communists from the fears of the present, but Communists from a faith in the principles which are to guide, animate and restrain them in the future'.

Neither Johnson nor Prudhommeaux refer to the Icarian group in London and it is not known how many Britons heeded the call and migrated to the settlements in Texas and Illinois. It appears that the Icarians had little impact on either British socialism or the planning of communistic settlements in England.

It should however be recognised that *Voyage en Icarie* did actually include an outline for the model city, with Cabet focusing on both practical aspects of urban infrastructure and the design of public spaces. He was less interested in theoretical urban form, whether grid squares or parallelograms or concentric circles, than his predecessors and contemporaries. Cabet first focused on the need for clean air to promote the health of the residents – the cemeteries, hospitals, factories, slaughter houses, butchers and stables would all be on the outskirts in open places near swift flowing streams. The sidewalks would be swept every morning and the streets would be paved, with rainwater and mud draining out into subterranean canals and with fountains. Each street was to have iron tracks for coaches, with engines on railroad tracks. There would be separate streets near the canal and railroads for freight from workshops and warehouses. Horses would not be allowed on sidewalks. To avoid accidents, pedestrians and vehicles should keep to the right of the sidewalk or road. Freight should not travel while people are on their way to work or on their way home. The streets would be well lit and the gas lamps would be odourless. Everywhere there would be privies – some for men some for women – 'where modesty may enter for a moment without fear for itself of public decency'.

Cabet was enthusiastic about having monuments, squares and promenades, with paintings, sculptures and statues (but no voluptuous nudes). Art should be directed toward the goal of utility – 'Nothing favouring despotism and Aristocracy, fanaticism and superstition, but everything favouring the People and their benefactors, liberty and its martyrs, or opposing the old system and their minions'. Recreation was important to Cabet –

Thousands of youths and maidens of every age, all neatly and attractively clad, run, skip, dance, and play at a thousand games, always in groups and under the eyes of their parents. Only joy and pleasure are evident, only laughing, happy shouts, songs and music are heard.

It was some time before the American Icarian settlements at Nauvoo and Cheltenham fully reflected this idealised vision (Nordhoff, 1875).

The Fourierists

The Fourierists had a significant role within French socialism (Beecher, 1986, 2001; Pilbeam, 2000a, 2000b, 2005) but also appear to have had greater impact on British socialism and communitarianism than Cabet's followers. Charles Fourier had met Anna Wheeler in France. Owen was also initially supportive of Fourier and it was the London Cooperative Society which effectively launched Fourierism in England, by publishing Fourier's pamphlet *Political Economy Made Easy* in 1828, translated by William Thompson. Fourier's leading promoter in London was the Owenite Irishman, Hugh Doherty, who had worked with Fourier in Paris in 1837. In May 1840, Doherty presented a Fourierist address to the Owenite Universal Society of Rational Religionists conference in Leeds, arguing that there was no inconsistency between the Owenite and Fourierist proposals. Settling in London, he established a journal, the *Morning Star* or *Phalansterean Gazette*, the name of which was changed the following year to the *London Phalanx,* which continued to 1843. Docherty published a series of pamphlets promoting Fourier – *A Memoir of Charles Fourier* in 1841, *Organic Philosophy* in 1864 and *The Philosophy of Reason* in 1865. He published an English translation Fourier's *The Passions of the Human Soul* in 1851, with an extensive introduction (Pankhurst, 1956).

Fourier's work was also promoted by Sophia Chichester, who in 1841 translated the Belgian Fourierist Gatti de Gamond's *Le Phalanstere* and published the work as *The Phalanstery or Attractive Industry and Moral Harmony.* Chichester and her sister Georgiana Fletcher Welch were philanthropists and supporters of a number of radicals including James Pierrepoint Greaves, whose Ham Common Concordia was near where they lived, James E Smith, John Zion Ward, the atheist Richard Carlile and the secularist Owenite and co-operator George Jacob Holyoake. The sisters were also acquainted with Owen though may not have funded his projects. Chichester collaborated with the Owenite Alexander Campbell to promote vegetarianism and was also president of the Universal Concordia Society in which capacity she published a statement in the *New Moral World* in July 1844 – supporting Greaves' spiritual vision in opposition to Owen's materialism (Latham, 1999).

Chichester's introduction to Gamond's book reflects the somewhat mystical and millenarian approach she shared with Greaves, Smith and Ward. She repeatedly referred to 'Unity' and the 'Unifier'. All attempts at political, social and economic reform will fail 'unless Man himself is firmly and permanently established in Unity'.

The Fourierist group in London was joined in 1840 by the German Fourierist Jacob Etzler. Four years earlier in 1836, Etzler had published in Pittsburgh his own vision of a new society in his work *The Paradise within the Reach of All Men.* This was a futuristic work which in many ways pre-empted the writing of H G Wells. Etzler's main argument was that the advances in mechanical technology and the use of the power generated by nature would dramatically reduce the need to work. His references to wind power, tidal power, and solar power (with sunlight reflected by giant mirrors) no doubt appeared fantastical at the time, but now appear prescient. Land clearance and agriculture were to be mechanised, Etzler also put forward detailed proposals for the construction of his settlement, using materials from nature including crushed and liquidised vegetation, as well as detailed arrangements for ensuring homes were sufficiently spacious. He proposed machines for transporting people both up and down and along galleries – effectively lifts and travelators. The pamphlet also set out a detailed governance structure for the new community with five committees – for provisions, health, instruction, pleasures and police, each committee appointed by the general meeting of the whole community. This was to have weekly meetings with every person having a vote and decisions on a majority basis. A state assembly would comprise deputies from each community, and would appoint five national committees to parallel those at communal level. Men and women would have equal status. The pamphlet also envisages four stages in the development of the new society, contending that 'this ultimate happy state can and will be attained within five to ten years'.

Etzler originally submitted his plan to the American president, Andrew Jackson. In England, Etzler's scheme was promoted by Doherty and his editor, Elishuma Smith, in the *London Phalanx*. Etzler also undertook some experiments with new machines including helping Docherty build a boat which was supposed to be powered by the waves. Unfortunately, the boat sank and nearly drowned Etzler's partner, Stollmeyer. Doherty quarrelled with Smith, who was less attached to Fourierist principles than himself, which led to the closure of the *London Phalanx*, and Doherty never seemed to recover from the boat incident which Smith teased him about. Etzler and Stollmeyer therefore transferred their affiliation to James Pierrepoint Greaves, the Christian communitarian mystic and friend of Sophia Chichester, who had established his 'Concordium' at Ham Common. Etzler then used the Concordium press to print a new pamphlet, this time suggesting emigration to Venezuela. Another supporter of the concordium was the Christian communist poet, Goodwyn Barmby and his wife Catherine, who had previously written a column in Owen's *Crisis*. Barmby established his own community at Hanwell in Middlesex, publishing a paper called *The Promethean or Communitarian Apostle* under the auspices of his Universal Communitarian Association. Another supporter of Etzler, J E Duncan published a Fourierist journal called the *Sun Ray or Rising Sun* (Gregory, 2014). Etzler and Stollmeyer, after approaching the Venezuelan ambassador in London to support their Tropical Emigration Society, embarked for Latin America. Etzler is never heard of again though Stollmeyer was reported to have been seen at a Fourierist meeting in New York in 1844 (Armytage, 1955). This appears to have been the end of Fourierism in Britain. Barnby's colleague Thomas Frost survived to participate in the Reform League in the 1860s and to publish his memoirs *Forty Years' Recollections* in 1880.

This discussion of the role of Fourierists in London has so far somewhat ignored the issue of what Fourier and his promoters were actually promoting in terms of new settlements and whether this impacted on the development of actual settlements in Britain. Fourier's work can be quite difficult to read in that it is necessary to separate the principles and practical proposals from the more surreal output of his creative imagination. Fourier is often mocked for his more bizarre suggestions, for example that the sea will become pink lemonade, but these suggestions could be perhaps best viewed as the way Fourier wished to keep his readers entertained rather than as serious propositions.

It should be noted that Fourier's perspective was libertarian in that he wished to maximise the liberty of the individual which contrasted with the authoritarian regulation perceived as essential by Owen. Fourier also rejected the collectivist tendencies and religious pretensions of the Saint-Simonians. He believed that pain, either physical or mental, was the sign of error; pleasure the sign of truth. His analysis was that human desires or 'passions' were the motivation for all human behaviour. He identified five sensual passions – taste, touch, sight, hearing and smell; four affective passions – friendship, love, family and ambition; three distributive or mechanising passions – the passion for intrigue, the passion for change and contrast and the passion for enjoyment combining physical and mental pleasure. There was a thirteenth collective passion – for harmony or unity – the inclination to relate one's own happiness to that of others. Fourier therefore presented an optimistic view of human nature. Believing in the principle of self-direction and liberation, Fourier argued against a social, political and economic system which suppressed the ability of the majority to be self-directed and liberated by concentrating wealth and power in a small minority – the parasitic classes.

Fourier believed that the way to transform society was to establish small associations – communities which he called 'phalanxes'. Each phalanx would have a population between 1500 and 1800. Residents would live in a communal building known as a 'phalanstery'. However, Fourier recognised that the family was the key unit of association. Residents of each phalanx were to be varied in terms of 'wealth, age, personality and theoretical and practical knowledge'. The phalanx was to be both economically productive and harmonious. However, manufacturing industry was to be subordinate to agricultural production. An innovative suggestion was that persons undertaking more unpleasant work should be paid more than those in more pleasant jobs. A somewhat more questionable suggestion was that as children liked getting dirty, they could clean out the sewers, look after the dung heaps and supervise the slaughter houses. Fourier did not aim for absolute equality within the community but recognised that there was a need to guarantee a minimum standard of living to avoid absolute poverty. The majority of the phalanx's income would be used to reward labour – a profit sharing scheme would mean that individuals would want the whole community to prosper. Fourier's objective was to establish a network of phalanxes across the country – in effect across the whole world.

Phalanxes would co-operate to carry out major projects which were in their mutual interest – he gave as examples the cultivation of the Sahara Desert or construction of a canal between the Caspian and Aral seas. Stripped of his more surreal propositions, there is a basic logic to Fourier's argument that a society can be economically successful and still enjoyable, and that a degree of individual freedom, in an uncompetitive environment, actually encourages rather than constrains collaboration both within and between communities. Compared with the rigid authoritarianism, regulation and cultism of Owen and Saint-Simon, Fourier's vision had considerable appeal. His theories also have clear implications for how a new community is planned, with a mechanism for balancing individual freedom and collective interests.

The views of Fourier were given detailed and sympathetic consideration in Mary Hennell's *Outline of the Various Social Systems and Communities founded on the principles of Cooperation*, published in 1844. Hennell lived in Hackney, and was sister in law of the Owenite philosopher Charles Bray, author of the *Philosophy of Necessity*, and a member of a progressive intellectual circle which included Mary Ann Evans, also known as George Eliott, who was also influenced by Comte's positivism. Hennell's book is a comprehensive and sophisticated review of utopian and cooperative systems from ancient times to her own period, including the Jesuit missions in Paraguay, the anabaptists, Rappites, the Metayer system of cultivation, William Godwin, the Owenite experiments and the English co-operative movement.

Hennell's treatment of Fourier is extensive and takes thirty pages, and is the penultimate section of the book, with the final section considering earlier utopian writings such those of Plato, More, Bacon, Campanella, Gaudentia de Lucca, Thomas Spence, Condorcet and her contemporaries William Thompson and John Minter Morgan. Hennell also repudiates Malthus's objections to 'systems of equal and united interests' and in fact uses that miserabilist's own words against him 'The system of equality ... is the most beautiful and engaging of any that has yet appeared. A melioration of society to be produced merely by reason and conviction, gives more promise of permanence than any change effected and maintained by force'. Presenting herself as Fourier's disciple, Hennell responds:

> We who wish to adore and bless God, the sovereign creator of heaven and earth, of man and his passions, the dispenser of universal life, the Father of love, of happiness, and harmony; we shall not conclude with saying – That is impossible because it is too beautiful; we shall conclude on the contrary, religiously – That is too beautiful not to be possible.
>
> (Hennell, 1844, p. 252)

Fourier's ideas had relatively little impact in terms of the direct development of new communities in Britain. They certainly did provide support to those Owenites who rejected Owen's authoritarianism, in a similar manner to the Fourierists in France drawing in disillusioned Saint-Simonians. The French Fourierists undertook two attempts at community settlement – one at Citeaux in Burgundy in a Cistercian monastery, led by the Franco-British Arthur Young and funded by the Belgian Gatti de Gamond, the second at St Denis du Sig in Algeria, led by two Lyons doctors, Imbert and Barrier. Neither project was successful. It is significant that the leading French Fourierist, Victor Considerant, publisher of *La Phalange*, did not support either project as he thought they diverted funds and attention from the political and promotional work. Considerant was a Paris deputy in the National Assembly and was focusing on the politics and social reform of the city rather than on communal retreats. Together with his colleague Cesar Daly, he had a significant influence on the planning of the city of Paris (Beecher, 2001, pp. 118–24; Papayanis, 2004, 2006). However, it should be recognised that a number of new communities were established in America on Fourierist principles and that some proved to be more successful than the Icarian and Owenite settlements. Fourierist principles influenced the views of later American socialist activists such as Horace Greeley and Edward Bellamy. It is perhaps somewhat ironic that Considerant, who had rejected the communitarian schemes in the 1840s, after political defeat in Paris and exile in Belgium, in December

1852, joined the American Fourierist, Albert Brisbane in Texas (Beecher, 2001; Guarneri, 1991).

The influence of the French utopians

It is interesting that Owen appeared indifferent to the activities of the French utopians. *The Crisis* and the *New Moral World* edited by Owen have no references to Saint-Simon or Cabet, though from 1841, there was some coverage of Fourier in the *New Moral World*. To Owen, the French utopian socialists were competitors who were best ignored. The feeling appears to have been mutual. The fact that Owen could not read French clearly did not help. Beecher tells the story of how in 1822 Fourier approached Owen with a proposal for cross-channel collaboration (Beecher, 1986, pp. 367–71). This was not taken up by Owen, but in 1823 after reading the *Report to New Lanark*, which he referred to as 'monastic statutes' and meeting Owen's amanuensis and translator, Philip Skene, Fourier commented that Owen 'is imbued with all the prejudices most contrary to the system of industrial attraction and the equilibrium of the passions. He is quite simply a moralist.' By1827. Fourier had concluded that 'the Owenites whom I have seen . . . have convinced me by the obstination in their philosophy that there is no hope of getting them to undertake an experiment in true association' (cited in Beecher, 1986, p. 371). In 1831, Fourier published a pamphlet accusing both Owen and Saint-Simon of being charlatans. It is not therefore surprising that when Owen and Fourier attended the same banquet in Paris in 1847, they ignored each other (Desbazeille, 2006).

The four utopian socialists can be seen as competing egos, each trying to hold on to their own following, while pursuing their individualist vision and reluctant to adapt to either incorporate different perspectives of their less hero-worshipping followers or in response to external realities. All four movements developed millenarian tendencies, although in the case of Fourier, this represented a technological rather than religious imagery. Some of their followers were of course more flexible. For example, James Elishama Smith was prepared at different times in his career to edit Owenite and Fourierist journals. The Owenite and co-operator, Lloyd Jones, biographer of Owen, was to become an active participant in the Christian Socialist movement which we will consider later. There is a case for paying more attention to the foot-soldiers of the movement.

There is a contrast between the Owenites and the French utopian socialists. As demonstrated in the studies by Carlisle and the recent comparative study by Moret, the original Saint-Simonians were practical and often highly technical professionals. They engaged with politics and governance and despite the millenarian diversion of Pere D'Enfantin, engaged in practical projects within France and beyond with their engagement in colonisation and schemes such as the building of the Suez Canal. As Moret and Papanyanis have shown, the second generation of Fourierists moved on from some of the more surreal propositions of their founder to engage directly in governance, with the Fourierist leader Considerant becoming an active politician and colleagues, such as Cesar Daly, becoming directly involved in urban governance, in Daly's case in the planning of Paris. While the Fourierists, like the Icarians, set up colonies in America, they did not ignore the necessity of domestic political, economic and social reform. It is not insignificant that of the utopian socialist tendencies prevalent in England, it is that of Saint-Simon, as modified by August Comte, that produced through the development of the positivist movement a cohort of reformist intellectuals including Frederic Harrison, E S Beesly, F J Gould, J H Bridges, J K Ingram and Godfrey and Vernon Lushington, and that the proto-positivist John Morley directly engaged in contemporary politics, governance and education, despite what can be seen as growth of an increasingly separate religious orientation under Richard Congreve. We will return to the role of the English positivists in the development of social policy and planning in Britain in a later chapter.

Primary sources

British Section of Icarian Communists (1848) *Address to the Proletarians and Others of Great Britain and Ireland*

Cabet, Etienne (1842) *Voyage en Icarie* (2nd ed., Paris: J Mallet et cie)

Cabet, Etienne (1847 or 1848) *Community of Icarie* (London: J Watson)

Etzler, John (1836) *The Paradise within the Reach of All Men* (London: John Brooks)

Fourier, Charles (1851) *The Passions of the Human Soul*. Translated by Rev J R Morell and edited with introduction in 2 volumes by Hugh Docherty (London: Hippolyte Bailliere)

Frost, Thomas (1880) *Forty Years Recollections* (London: Sampson Low)

Gamond, Gatti de (1841) *The Phalanstery or Attractive Industry and Moral Harmony*. Translated with an introduction by an English Lady (Sophia Chichester) (London: Whittaker and Co)

Hennell, Mary (1844) *An Outline of the Various Social Systems and Communities which have been founded on the Principle of Cooperation* (London: Longman, Brown, Green and Longmans)

Hill, Rowland (1832) *Home Colonies: Sketch of a Plan for the Gradual Extinction of Pauperism and for the Diminution of Crime* (London: Simpkin and Marshall)

Mill, J S (1834) 'Fontana and Prati's St Simonism in London' in *Examiner*, 2nd February 1834, pp. 68–9

Saint-Simon, Henri de (1834) *New Christianity*. Translated by Rev J E Smith (London: B D Cousins, Crisis Office and Effingham Wilson)

Saint-Simonian missionaries (1832) *An Address to the British Public* (London: Effingham Wilson)

The Crisis (1832–1833) Vols 1–2 (London: Eamson, reprinted New York: Greenwood 1968)

The New Moral World (1835) Vol 1 (London: Rowland Hunter for Association of All Classes of All Nations)

Secondary sources

Armytage, W H G (1955) 'Technology and Utopianism: J A Etzler in England 1840–44' in *Annals of Science*, Vol 11, No2, pp. 129–36

Armytage, W H G (1958) 'John Minter Morgan's Schemes 1841–1855' in *International Review of Social History*, Vol 3, No 1, pp. 26–42

Beecher, J (1986) *Charles Fourier: The Visionary and his World* (Berkeley, CA: University of California Press)

Beecher, J (2001) *Victor Considerant and the Rise and Fall of French Romantic Socialism* (Berkeley, CA: University of California Press)

Beer, M (1920) *History of British Socialism* (London: G Bell and Sons)

Bensimon, Fabrice (2013) 'French Republicans and Communists in Exile to 1848' in Kelly, D and Cornick, M (eds), *A History of the French in London* (London: Institute of Historical Research)

Carlisle, R (1987) *The Proffered Crown: Saint-Simonianism and the Doctrine of Hope* (Baltimore, MD: John Hopkins University Press)

Desbazeille, M M (2006) 'Owen and Fourier: Collusion and Collision' in *Spaces of Utopia*, No 2 (electronic journal) retrieved from http://ler.letras.up. pt/uploads/ficheiros/1636.pdf

Gans, J (1964) 'Les relations entre socialistes de France et d'Angleterre au debut de XIX sciecle' in *Mouvement Social*, Vol 46, pp. 105–18

Gide, C (1930) *Communist and Co-operative Colonies* (London: Harrap)

Gregory, J (2014) *Poetry and Politics. Radical Reform in Victorian England* (London: I B Tauris)

Guarneri, C J (1991) *The Utopian Alternative. Fourierism in Nineteenth Century America* (Ithaca, NY: Cornell University Press)

Hardy, D (1979) *Alternative Communities in Nineteenth Century England* (London: Longman)

Johnson, C (1974) *Utopian Communism in France. Cabet and the Icarians 1839–1851* (Ithaca, NY: Cornell University Press)

Jones, Lloyd (1889) *Life, Times and Labours of Robert Owen* (London: Swan Sonnenshein)

Latham, J (1999) 'The political and the personal: the radicalism of Sophia Chichester and Georgina Fletcher Welch' in *Womens History Review*, Vol 8, No 3, pp. 469–87

Latham, J (1999) *Search for a New Eden. James Pierrepoint Greaves. The Sacred Socialist and his Followers* (Cranbury, NJ: Associated University Presses)

Moret, F (1997) *Les Socialistes et La Ville: Grande Bretagne , France 1820–1850* (Lyons: ENS editions)

Nordhoff, C (1875) *The Communistic Societies of the United States* (reprinted New York 1961)

Pankhurst, R (1954) *William Thompson: Pioneer Socialist* (1991 edition, London: Pluto)

Pankhurst, R (1956) 'Fourierism in Britain' in *International Review of Social History*, Vol 1, No 3, pp. 398–432

Pankhurst, R (1957) *The Saint Simonians, Mill and Carlyle* (London: Lalibela Books/Sidgwick and Jackson)

Papayanis, N (2004) *Planning Paris before Haussmann* (Baltimore, MD: John Hopkins University Press)

Papayanis, N (2006) 'Cesar Daly, Paris and the emergence of modern urban planning' in *Planning Perspectives*, Vol 21, No 4, pp. 325–46

Pilbeam, P (2000a) *French Socialists before Marx* (Teddington, UK: Acumen)

Pilbeam, P (2000b) 'Dream Worlds? Religion and the early Socialists in France' in *The Historical Journal*, Vol 43, No 2, pp. 499–515

Pilbeam, P (2005) Fourier and the Fourierists. A Case of Mistaken Identity? Retrieved from www.h-france.net/rude/2005conference/Pilbeam2.pdf

Prothero, I (1997) *Radical Artisans in England and France 1830–1870* (Cambridge: Cambridge University Press)

Prothero, I (2003) 'Chartists and political refugees' in Freitag, S, *Exiles from European Revolutions: Refugees in mid-Victorian England* (New York: Bergahn Books)

Proudhommeaux, J (1907) *Icarie et Son Fondateur Etienne Cabet* (Paris: Edouard Cornely)

Sanchez de Juan (2001) The City in Transition: Engineering, freemasonry and liberalism in the planning of the modern city. Retrieved from www.academia.edu/1066336/The_City_in_Transition_Engineering_freemasonry_and_liberalism_in_the_planning_of_the_modern_city

Sargent, W L (1850) *Robert Owen and his social philosophy* (London: Smith Elder)

Shirai, A (1970) 'William Godwin and Robert Owen' in *Keio Economic Studies*, Vol 7, pp. 64–7 (Tokyo)

Swain, E S (1989) *Brotherly Tomorrows* (New York: Columbia Press)

Taylor, B (1983) *Eve and the New Jerusalem* (London: Virago)

Taylor, K (1982) *The Political Ideas of the Utopian Socialists* (London: Frank Cass)

Varouxakis, G (2004) 'French radicalism through the eyes of John Stuart Mill' in *History of European Ideas*, Vol 30, pp. 433–61

Webb, S and Webb, B (1920) *The History of Trade Unionism* (London: Longmans)

7   Working class radicals and the land

The historiography and the radical heritage

Most of the historiography on 19th and early-20th century reform campaigns relating to land, housing and planning focuses on the philanthropists and middle class, and often aristocratic reformers. Reform is generally viewed as something gifted by altruistic businessmen and reform politicians in parliament and in government. While some historians have pointed out that reform was on occasions granted in response to perceived threat from the mob (notably in the reform debates after Chartist unrest) or to concerns as to the physical and moral health of the nation and its fitness to defend the Empire (for example during the Crimean, Boer and First World Wars), few writers however focus on the active role of the working classes themselves in pursuing social reform. The works of Thompson and Hobsbawm, which are exceptions to the general trend, tend to focus on the pre-Chartist period.

There are however three notable exceptions. Barry (1965) includes a chapter on the land nationalisation campaigns of the late-19th century including the role of the Land and Labour League; Englander (1977, 1983) includes material on the Workman's National Housing Council (WNHC) as well as local housing struggles, though unfortunately the edited diary of Fred Knee, later to become the WNHC secretary, ends before the establishment of the WNHC. Wohl (1977) also gives some consideration to the WNHC. Chase (1988, 1991, 2003) and Howkins (2002) have also examined elements of the working class radical tradition and land reform in the 19th century, but as yet no study has sought to examine the continuity of working class radical thought across the period.

Any narrative of working class reform movements in the 19th and early-20th centuries must acknowledge the inheritance from the Digger and Jacobin traditions – from the writings of Gerrard Winstanley in the 1650s, from Thomas Spence's *The Real Rights of Man* of 1775, William Ogilvie's *Right of Property in Land* of 1792, and Thomas Paine's *Agrarian Justice* of 1797 (Beer, 1920). The belief that land was a gift of God (or of nature, if, like Paine, you were an atheist) was a fundamental component of late-18th century and early-19th century radicalism. After Spence's death the agitation was carried forward by the members of the Society of Spencean Philanthropists, who were active from Spence's death in 1814 to 1820, when a number of the group's leaders were arrested in the Cato Street conspiracy – a plot to assassinate the Prime Minister and the cabinet (Chase, 1988). The belief in the common ownership of land was also held by more progressive economic philosophers such as Charles Hall. In Hall's *The Effects of Civilization on the People in European States* of 1805, he wrote 'The land being in the first instance common, no person could have any exclusive right to any part of it.' Hall argued that ownership of land was the basis of political power and was the root of many social ills (Hall, 1805).

Chartists and the land

Given this heritage, it is therefore not surprising that within the Chartist movement there was a strong advocacy of land rights, even though it was not one of the six points of their Charter which focused on political reform. It should also be remembered, as discussed above, that the paternalistic socialism of the philanthropist Robert Owen generated a strong working class movement, which not only focused on the establishment of trade unions and retail cooperatives but also led to the establishment of a number of shortlived utopian settlements, of which the most significant were Harmony Hall in Hampshire, New Harmony in Indiana and Ralahine in Ireland, the last active between 1831 and 1833 under the leadership of E T Craig. Feargus O'Connor established the Chartist Land Company in 1846. The Company established a number of settlements including O'Connorville near Rickmansworth, Charterville at Minster Lovell, Lowbands and Snigs End near Worcester and Great Dodford near Bromsgrove. It should be stressed that whereas Spence and his followers argued for the common ownership of land, the Chartist Land Company operated a system of household occupation of smallholdings, let by the company which was financed by subscriptions, with properties allocated through a ballot system. O'Connor wrote a guide for the management of the Chartist settlements: *A Practical Work on the Management of Small Farms* (O'Connor, 1847). The company was wound up in 1851, with most of the properties on the five estates sold off within three years of O'Connor's death in 1855 (Hadfield, 1970; Epstein, 1982).

With the disintegration of the Chartist political reform movement after the failure of the Kennington Common demonstration of 1848, leading Chartists such as Ernest Jones, George Julian Harney and Bronterre O'Brien turned to broader issues of social policy – the Charter and something more (Saville, 1952; Schoyen, 1958; Plummer, 1971; Bronstein, 1999; Maw, 2005). Bronterre O'Brien advocated the nationalisation of land in the mid-1830s and 1840s, based on a system of government purchase and redistribution of the land by rental, criticising O'Connor's smallholding based approach as 'conservative'.

> What a chain of evil follows upon the usurpation of the soil! What a rapid striking off of the links of the chain would follow upon the nationalisation of landed property! Only prevent one set of men from making God's 'gift to all' their private property, and that moment you open the door to unlimited improvement.

O'Brien argued that 'Every man who joins these Land Societies is practically enlisting himself on behalf of the Government' and that O'Connor's scheme was 'a government plot to stifle in embryo our movement for the nationalisation of land' (*National Reformer* 9 Jan 1847 and 14 May 1847 cited in Armytage, 1961).

In January 1847 O'Brien published in the *National Reformer*, a programme, the first three points of which focused on the land issue:

> 1st The land of the United Kingdom must be made the public property of the whole people of the United Kingdom;

2nd That the only rational way of doing that is to abolish the private ownership of land altogether, make all the rents payable to and for the state, make the tenant right, or right of occupancy, equal to all, and secure to every leaseholder full value for all bona fide improvements made by him on the soil during his occupancy.

3rd That the only safe, peaceable, and humane way of effecting such settlement is, to restore the land gradually to the public, as the land lords die off, so as not to disturb any proprietor existing at the time of passing the law, during his or her life; and on the lapse of their estates to the nation, at their death, to secure to their heirs, assigns, or representatives, the full money value of each estate, so that even the remotest appearance of confiscation or spoliation may be avoided, and the aristocracy left without a shadow of pretext for rebelling against the law.

(cited in Cole and Filson, 1965, p. 407)

O'Brien's approach was supported by John Francis Bray in his *Labour's Wrongs and Labour's Remedy* (Bray, 1839) and by the Scottish agriculturalist Patrick Dove in his *Theory of Human Progression* and his *Elements of Political Science* (Dove, 1851, 1854). O'Brien set out further details of his mechanism for achieving his objective in his *The Rise, Progress and Phases of Human Slavery*, not published until 1885 by the O'Brienite, Martin James Boon, but based on articles he had written in the 1840s and 1850s (O'Brien, 1885).

George Julian Harney also supported land nationalisation and included land nationalisation in the principles of the Society of Fraternal Democrats, founded in 1845: 'We declare that the earth with all its natural productions is the common property of all; we therefore denounce all infractions of this evidently just and natural law, as robbery and usurpation' (cited in Cole and Filson, 1965, p. 402).

The Chartist, Thomas Cooper, published a pamphlet on *Land for the Labourers* in 1848, based on Louis Blanc's scheme for the Paris National Assembly.

Let the state buy up at once all the land of the country, and all the public funds of the nation, and pay them by instalments without interest, the amounts of instalment to be reckoned in fair proportion to the wants of each family and the amount of individual riches. That being done, labour could be organised immediately in every agricultural and individual parish, where all interest would centre in one common stock.

(Cooper, 1848)

The Islington Chartist poet, Ebenezer Jones, author of *Studies of Sensation and Event*, published a small book in 1849 on *The Land Monopoly: The Suffering and Demoralisation Caused by it*, which can be considered to be a precursor of Henry George's *Progress and Property* of 1879. This is an important work which has not been given due consideration by historians, and justifies an extensive quotation.

To terminate the land monopoly would be to extinguish the source of those evils which have been shown to spring from it – the physical evils being at once prevented, and the moral evils rendered possible of cure. If every man had his interest in the land acknowledged, and the occupation of the land were arranged for the benefit of all, every man would be at least secured from want – that is, unless there became universal, that kind of lunacy which prevents men from taking care of their property; every man would enjoy the independence and respect which attach to the possession of property, every man would have his share of natural capital renewed to him yearly. There would be no slave class, with its consequent abominations. Forced, and therefore untrue and unjust inequality would be prevented; and every man would be able to obtain a position in society accordant with his morality and intelligence. No man could be born poor; and competency and independence would be enjoyed by all, save the idle and extravagant. They who regard as good so complete a change, would of course allow it to be expedient in the highest degree to terminate the land monopoly.

To terminate the land monopoly would be to establish property on an immovable, because just, basis. That is justly the property of an individual, which is the result of his labour, or intelligence; or has been given to him by any one who acquired it by the same means. Limit property to possessions thus acquired, and scarcely any man will dream of attacking it. The outcry against property raised by communists, results not from an enquiry into the justice of the institution, but from an observation that as it now exists, including within its sacred name that gigantic robbery which is the land monopoly, it renders impossible liberty, fraternity, and that just gradation of position which would result from the only equality possible or desirable – the equality of rights. Prove to the mistaken, but not unconscientious communists, that property is no enemy to happiness and freedom, by separating from it that land monopoly which is; present them with their fair share of property themselves; and communism will be but a tale of the past.

Besides, to terminate the land monopoly would be not only to ensure the labouring classes plenteous and certain subsistence, but would produce infinitely worthier consequences – it would terminate the moral evils which their present slavish dependence necessitates, not only for themselves, but for all other members of society, – a result that cannot possibly by any other means be arrived at.

(Jones 1849)

Jones's polemics are more significant perhaps than his poetry, which is widely derided. He has been called England's worst poet (Lindsay, 1978).

The engraver and Mazzinian republican William Linton, at that time based in London (he later moved to Brantwood in Cumbria before emigrating to America), published a pamphlet in 1850 on *The People's Land and an Easy Way to Recover It*. Rather than arguing for the nationalisation of land, Linton proposed a tax on land. He proposed that a tax on land should be in place of all other taxes. He in fact referred to it as a 'single tax' a term later adopted by Henry George and his followers. He argued that so long as a landowner paid the tax they should not be dispossessed and suggested that proof of payment should be sufficient proof of legal title. He believed that landlords would give up unused land to the state rather than pay tax on it, and that this land could then be used to settle able-bodied paupers (Linton, 1850; Smith, 1973).

The 1851 Chartist convention which agreed the social programme adopted a commitment to land nationalisation. The issue had originally been left out of the draft programme and was only included at the insistence of O'Brien.

This Convention believes that the land is the inalienable inheritance of all mankind; monopoly is therefore repugnant to the laws of God and nature. The nationalisation of land is the only true basis of national prosperity.

With the view of arriving at this ultimatum, it is Resolved that the following measures be successively urged upon the public.

1st The establishment of a Board of agriculture.

2nd The restoration of poor, common, church and crown lands to the people. Such lands to be divided in suitable proportions. Those located to be tenants of the state, paying a proportionate rent-charge for their holdings.

3rd Compensation to outgoing tenants for improvements. Tenants not to be tied down to any old covenants of rotation of crops. The repeal of the game laws. All rents to be commuted into corn-rents.

4th The state to be empowered to purchase land, for the purpose of locating thereon the population, as tenants, individually or in association, paying a rent-charge to the state. The funds for each purpose to arise from the rent-charge payable on the common, poor and crown lands above mentioned, and such other sources as may hereafter be determined.

5th Government purchasing land as above, not to be permitted to sell again, but to hold such lands as national property for ever, letting to the tenants in such quantities, and under such conditions, as may secure freedom to the tenant, and safety to the state.

6th The state to have priority of purchase at fair current prices.

7th To provide for the final and complete Nationalisation of the land the state shall resume possession of the soil as rapidly as existing interests can be extinguished by law, by death, by surrender, or by any other means accordant with justice and a generous treatment of all classes.

(cited in Saville, 1952, pp. 259–60)

The Chartist Ernest Jones had also been critical of O'Connor arguing that 'There is nothing more reactionary than the freehold system. It is increasing the strength of landlordism' (cited in Saville, 1952, appendix 3). Jones promoted the common ownership of land, though he was less specific about the means of achieving this. In his 1856 address on *The Hereditary Landed Aristocracy* in his *Evenings with the People* series, he appealed to his audience to

Join with me for the re-conquest of the land. It is the task f the age – the mission of the century. You talk of unchaining yourselves: unchain the land, and your own chains will fall. The franchise is the bond that binds your hands; but land monopoly is the dungeon that surrounds your bodies.

(Jones, 1856)

In the same year, Robert Dick, a Kensington physiologist and poet, published a pamphlet – *On the Evils, Impolicy and Anomaly of Individuals Being Landlords and Nations Tenants*. This polemic, based on a series of biblical references, argued that private ownership of land and by implication of property, was contrary to Christian principles. Dick concluded that

> The power of accumulating masses of land and sums of money, thereby exempting individuals and their heirs from their intransferable obligation to labour and doubling the labour of some other men inevitably causes monstrous inequalities in society; and heaps inordinate labour on landless and moneyless men.
>
> (Dick, 1856)

The Chartists had focused largely on the issue of land reform and not on housing conditions, partly because they saw poor housing as one of the outcomes of the land monopoly. Having turned to the land issue, they focused less on the issue of the preconditions for new settlements, and with the failure of the Chartist rural settlement programme, they also turned away from Owenite utopianism.

It should however be noted that two members of O'Brien's National Reform League, George Murray (brother of Charles and James) and John Days in 1854 attempted to establish a new settlement in America, based on O'Brien's principles. Murray died of cholera in New Orleans while Days abandoned the initiative to become a member of the Californian legislature. Days however returned to London in 1868, and the London O'Brienites established a Mutual Land, Emancipation and Cooperative Colonization Company. A group of colonists bought a plot of land in northeast Kansas. The company was based at the O'Brienites' Eclectic Hall in Denmark Street, Soho. The colonists' leader was Edward Grainger Smith. In London, the scheme was promoted by John Radford, who reported in the *National Reformer* in July 1869 that

> The O'Brienite principles are eagerly sought after, and inquired into, and the people generally speak approvingly of the aims and objects of the new colonists. Labour is recognised as the only true dignity, and there are no merchant millionaires nor aristocratic blockhead princes in the locality to devour the people's industry.

In 1870, after Smith's death, Charles Murray, as president of the colonising company, visited Kansas. The colony however struggled, though received an injection of funds from Frederick Wilson, publisher of a labour journal – *The Comprehensionist*. In 1874, Radford travelled to Kansas to take over the colony's leadership. However, in 1878, Wilson withdrew his investment, and the surviving settlers, including Radford, bought plots within the colony to operate as private farms. Radford then became active in the Kansas Populist Party, still pursuing his O'Brienite anti-capitalist agenda (Entz and Whitehead, 2005).

While other Chartists, such as Linton, moved to America, it was not to found utopian or socialistic settlements. Jones and Harney, following Marx and Engels, focused on a national political and social reform agenda, rather than seeking to support new settlements, with Owenites, Icarians and Fourierists, all of course criticised by Marx and Engels, transferring their initiatives to the New World. While London's working class radicals and republicans mixed with European socialists in the 1850s and 1860s and with the exiled communards after 1871, it was the lessons of the 1848–50 republic and the 1871 commune which drew their attention, rather than the experiments in Illinois or Paraguay.

The discovery of the housing problem

The housing crisis in London was caused first by the massive increase in population and then by clearance both to remove slums and therefore reduce health hazards and to make way for the new railway lines and railway stations. A series of philanthropists initiated programmes to provide new homes for the industrious working classes – Lord Shaftesbury established the Society for Improving the Condition of the Labouring Classes. The American philanthropist George Peabody was building his first tenements for working Londoners as was the Metropolitan Association for Improving the Dwellings of the Industrious Classes. Angela Burdett Coutts, daughter of the Radical MP, Sir Francis Burdett, also initiated a housing scheme in Highgate as well as founding with Charles Dickens a hostel in Shepherd's Bush for rescued prostitutes called Urania Lodge. The Christian Socialists, led by Charles Kingsley, were also writing about health and housing issues and supporting a number of cooperative ventures, including considering the possibility of co-operative building.

A group of working men, based at the Southwark Working Men's Club in 1866 agreed that philanthropy was unequal to the task of solving London's housing problems and decided to take their own initiative. The committee they established published a report and held a public meeting at the Lambeth baths with the intention of setting up their own company to build houses. The chair of the committee was E Dresser Rogers who was a member of the Metropolitan Board of Works between 1886 and 1889 and stood unsuccessfully as an Independent Liberal for the Camberwell parliamentary seat in 1885. The secretary was W H Robinson. It included Robert Hartwell, the editor of the *Beehive*. The committee had commissioned plans and drawings from Thomas Twining of the Twickenham Economic Museum, and had also put their proposals to an architect, Samuel Sharp. The committee also proposed that noxious industries should be closed with the sites to be used for working class housing and that landlords with unfit buildings should be required to either replace them with better buildings or sell the properties 'at a fair price to others who will undertake the work'.

The London Trades Council was established in 1860. There is no evidence that despite the Council's involvement in a builders' strike, they gave any priority to housing issues in its early years. As will be discussed below, the Trades Council's secretary George Shipton was to give evidence to the Royal Commission on Housing of the Working Classes in 1885, during which he stated that London's trade unionists did not have the resources to deal with housing issues. There does not appear to have been any initiative in London to compare with the work of James Hole in Leeds or of Charles Rowley in Manchester. London trade unionists were to play an active role in the International Working Men's Association, also known as the First International, which was founded in London in 1864. Despite Engels' previous study of housing conditions in Manchester, the First International did not focus on housing issues, though the issue of land ownership was discussed on a number of occasions. The Brussels Congress in 1868 had agreed that arable land should be the common property of society, and should then be leased by the state to agricultural companies. In June 1869, on the initiative of the O'Brienite tailor, George Milner, the General Council discussed whether this policy should be strengthened (Harrison, 1964)'

Milner argued that land should be common property not as a matter of expediency but as a natural right. The London trade unionists, Martin Boon, John Weston and

George E Harris, supported Milner, while Marx attacked the concept of 'natural right' arguing that 'the animal had a natural right to the soil since it cannot live without it'. He argued against the idea that every individual should cultivate their own share of land. Boon replied that he was actually in favour of the nationalisation of land and co-operative farming. The French anarchist Elisée Reclus, who was also present at the meeting as a visitor, gave his opinion that while there had been a number of individualists at the IWMA's Brussels conference, most working men were for collective property. Marx commented that the Brussels resolution originated with the French Proudhonists, led by Henri Tolain. In fact, the resolution supporting collective ownership of land had been promoted by the Belgian, Cesar de Paepe, and opposed by the Proudhonists, who preferred peasant proprietorship. Marx believed that

> the small man is only a nominal proprietor, but he is more dangerous because he still fancies that he is a proprietor. In England the land could be transformed into common property by act of Parliament in the course of a fortnight.
>
> (First International, 1868–70)

The O'Brienites, the First International and land reform

In 1865, the Unitarian minister, essayist and author of *Elements of Individualism* and O'Brienite, William Maccall, published a pamphlet, *The Land and the People: An Argument for an English Land League*. The League's objects were to be 'I: The abolition of the law of primogeniture; II: The abolition of the law of entail, and III: The promotion of every measure to facilitate land sales, to render them inexpensive and to establish on a firm basis the validity of titles'. The League went on to state that it 'disclaims all socialistic and revolutionary projects; all schemes of confiscation, all wish to interfere with the freedom of bequest.'

Maccall insisted on distancing himself from Feargus O'Connor:

> Feargus O'Connor was a singularly successful demagogue, but demagogues are seldom reformers, and reformer assuredly Feargus O'Connor was not. I am no demagogue – permit me to believe I am a reformer. To be a reformer, however, in politics, is to seek not merely for what is desirable, but what is possible. Into whatever else Utopias may be admitted, they are sternly excluded from politics. The politician deals with the tangible, with the definite.
>
> . . .
>
> I should complicate the action of the Land League with no socialistic theories: I should utter no threats: I should indulge in no violent demonstrations; I should take the same determined attitude, pursue the same pertinacious course which the agitators for free trade in food so conspicuously and so victoriously took.
>
> . . .
>
> We are very sure that this is the solid earth, and that God did not give it to be the everlasting possession of the idlest, most foolish, and often most infamous class ... We demand rather more of the soil than just suffices for our grave ...we ask no favour; we ask only fair play- we ask only justice.
>
> (Maccall, 1865)

In October 1869, the O'Brienite members of the IWMA set up the Land and Labour League. The secretaries were Martin James Boon and John Weston, and the treasurer was the naturalised German tailor and friend of Marx, G J Eccarius. After a dispute as to whether Odger or Bradlaugh be appointed president, the Irish trade unionist, Patrick Hennessey, was appointed to the post, thus avoiding a split in the radical ranks. The initiative was also supported by radicals such as Alfred Walton, William Maccall and John Hales (Harrison, 1964; Barry, 1965).

The League immediately challenged the more moderate position of John Stuart Mill's Land Tenure Reform Association (LTRA). Mill's organisation, established in 1870, mainly comprised radical Liberals, and included the economists Henry Fawcett and Thorold Rogers. It also had support from Charles Dilke, Captain (later Admiral) Maxse, John Morley and the naturalist, Alfred Russell Wallace. Peter Taylor MP was one of the treasurers and Howard Evans and Andrew Reid were secretaries. Membership also included some IWMA members – Benjamin Lucraft, George Odger, William Randal Cremer, Thomas Mottershead and John Weston (Peacock, 1961, p. 15).

Mill's original position included reform of primogeniture, entail and the freedom of transfer of land, extension of facilities for workmen to acquire land and preservation of the commons. The first draft of the LTRA manifesto did not include any proposal to tax the 'unearned increment' (Mill, 1871). However, in order to obtain support of the working class radicals, the LTRA extended its position to include that the value land acquired from the increase of population and the growth of industry should belong to the nation and not to a few individuals. Mill proposed that land should be periodically valued and that all increase of value not directly traceable as resulting from the application of labour or capital should be paid into the public exchequer. Mill however resisted the pressure for the LTRA to adopt a commitment to land nationalisation, deploring the 'violence' of the resolutions of the 'rival society formed by working men who thought the programme ought to be much bolder' (Packe, 1954). Howard Evans later remembered that most LTRA members did not support taxing the 'unearned increment' and deferred to Mill's judgement on the issue (Evans, 1913).

The Land and Labour League published its own a nine-point programme, of which the first two points were the nationalisation of land and home colonisation. The programme also included: National, Secular, Gratuitous and Compulsory Education; Suppression of Private Banks of Issue; The State only to issue Paper Money; A direct and progressive Property Tax, in lieu of all other Taxes; Liquidation of the National Debt; Abolition of the Standing Army; Reduction of the Number of Hours of Labour, and Equal Electoral Rights, with Payment of Members. The manifesto included the following peroration:

> You are swindled out of the fruits of your toil by land laws, money laws and all sorts of laws. Out of the paltry pittance that is left you, you have to pay the interest of a debt that was incurred to keep your predecessors in subjection; you have to maintain a standing army that serves no purpose in your generation, and you are systematically overworked when employed, and underfed at all times. Nothing but a series of such radical reforms as indicated on our programme will ever lift you out of the slough of despond in which you are at present sunk. The difficulty can be overcome by unity of purpose and action. We are many;

our opponents are few. Then working men and women of all creeds and occupations claim your rights as with one voice, and rally round, and unite your forces under the banner of the 'LAND AND LABOUR LEAGUE' to conquer your own emancipation!

(Land and Labour League, 1869)

The years 1867 to 1871 saw a vigorous debate between the leaders of the Land Tenure Reform Association and the O'Brienites and other radicals on approaches to land reform. Alfred Walton in 1865 had published a *History of Landed Tenures*, which concluded

Let us face the whole question like men desirous of dealing with it in a clear, straightforward, honest manner, by redeeming the land, and making it national property, and the reduction and levying of taxes, the adjustment of the public debt. And the reduction of our naval and military expenditure will speedily follow.

(Walton, 1865)

In 1867 and 1868 Walton wrote a number of articles in the *Beehive* on land reform, to be followed by a contribution from the trade unionist T J Dunning, who opposed land nationalisation as 'a nightmare, leading to an economically inefficient and politically dangerous government monopoly'. Odger also wrote supporting the basic principles of the Millite position. As discussed above the O'Brienite radicals sought to influence Mill's organisation and did contribute to the shift to a more radical approach, including a demand that the state should purchase estates in the market and let them to co-operative societies or to individual small holders, even if Mill remained unpersuaded on nationalisation. Odger, Cremer and Weston actually joined the platform at the LTRA's public meeting in May 1871 (Moberg, 1954).

In 1869, Boon published a pamphlet on *Home Colonisation*. Boon's basic argument was that the working class did not need to emigrate as there was enough uncultivated land in England to provide work and food for everybody. The pamphlet, published under the name of the National Rational League, stated that it included 'a plan showing how all the unemployed might have profitable work and thus prevent WANT, PAUPERISM, and CRIME.' Boon calculated that 20 million acres of wasteland could create 310,000 farms and employ 1,920,000 men. He argued that £120 million initial investment would soon generate £92.4 million worth of wheat 'exclusive of cattle, poultry, fruit and vegetables and other farm produce such as butter and eggs'. He argued that the investment

would give employment to builders, agricultural implement makers, furniture makers and in fact to all who are employed in any way making the necessaries and conveniences of life ... This money would eventually find its way into the hands of surveyors and contractors, who would be able to employ a large number of navvies, carpenters, bricklayers, iron workers and other mechanics, for making supplementary railways as feeders to our large termini and thus open up all the districts throughout the country , bringing about a closer union between the citizen and peasant; also, in making waterworks that would supply our towns with pure water – cutting irrigating canals throughout the length of the land, so that when we have hot and dry summers the crops should not suffer, and the supply fall short, making subways and sewers in all our towns, and erecting establishments to receive the excrements of our cities, to be converted into deoderised guano – making embankments to all our rivers, so as to utilize the mudbanks, which at the present time only create fever and pestilence – pulling down the worst parts of our towns and rebuilding them on a good sanitary system – building large schools, with playgrounds attached – and houses with all the latest domestic accommodation for our working classes , the producers of all our wealth – also in making cheap trains and railways to carry lime, clay, sand and rich alluvial soil of our river beds to the poor, bog, fen and moorlands, wherever situated. Men being employed on these useful works would be the means of increasing trade throughout the country, which would bring prosperity to all.

(Boon, 1869)

Boon had submitted his pamphlet to the *Beehive*, whose editor said he did not have room to print it. Boon also submitted his paper to the Social Science Association, who also refused to publish it (Whitehead, 1999). Boon's pamphlet is significant in that it pre-empted the writings of both Ebenezer Howard and of John Maynard Keynes. He argued that his National Rational League was based on the social system of Robert Owen and the political programme of Bronterre O'Brien, but in many ways his views were far more advanced than the writings of either of his mentors.

Boon's argument for resettlement of London's unemployed on vacant land was taken up by other radicals and philanthropists. George Howell, former secretary of the IWMA, the Reform League and the London Trades Council and later secretary of the London Municipal Reform League and Lib–Lab MP, published in1871 a pamphlet on *Wasteland and Surplus Labour*, based on a lecture given to the Greenwich Advanced Liberal Association. Howell followed Boon's approach by estimating the amount of wasteland and uncultivated land. His estimates were very specific – apparently derived from a paper by the radical Captain Maxse in the *Fortnightly Review* – 7,215,125 acres for England, 1,969,410 for Wales, 14,219,272 for Scotland and a slightly less specific figure for Ireland of 6,290,000 acres, giving a total of 29,694,807 acres. He suggested of this figure of nearly 30 million acres, 15 million could be cultivated, with the remaining 15 million left for 'picturesque scenery, deer forests, game preserves, rabbit warrens and similar purposes, and for places of recreation for the great mass of the people'. Howell then referred to the number of paupers at 1,554,169 (again disaggregated by country) and the number of prisoners at 90,000, with a combined cost to the state of £18 million pounds a year. He also referred to the number of emigrants at 1,250,000 over the previous ten years. Howell then calculated that on the basis of each acre providing work for two men, jobs could be provided for 1,500,000 men and produce worth £150 million. Prisoners would be made to work the hardest ground as punishment for their crimes. He argued that the annual produce would be double the value of the country's imported food and that Britain could actually be self-sufficient. He concluded that 'in years to come, the Land will give its fair quota towards the expenses of the State, give remunerative employment to those out of work, and at the same time yield the means to abundantly feed and clothe the people' (Howell, 1871; Leventhal, 1971).

Boon in 1873 produced a second pamphlet – *How to Nationalise the Commons and Wastelands*, followed by a more detailed outline of how to fund his proposed programme in *National paper money and its use* in 1885. In 1884, Henry Solly of the Working Men's Club and Institute Union, who was a Unitarian minister and Christian socialist, published a pamphlet on *Industrial Villages* on behalf of the Society for Promoting Industrial Villages. Solly published a further pamphlet in 1884 *Home Colonization*, with the subtitle *Rehousing of the industrial classes – village communities v town rookeries*. Solly's object was to promote industrial villages, rather than actually set up a company to develop new settlements, a task taken up later by Ebenezer Howard's Garden Cities Association (Solly, 1893). Solly was not looking for state aid, but suggested that working men 'organise themselves in clubs for saving funds'. While he set out a vision of the 'best conditions for healthy, cheerful and moral life', including well built and well ventilated cottages, leisure facilities, a public hall, schools, public libraries, art galleries and museums for local collections, coffee taverns but no public houses, with each cottage having a garden and a belt of land around every village, Solly seemed to assume that the new settlements would be funded by the promoter, who would also select the residents. 'Only those who are ready will go in with their brethren to the marriage-feast, and the door must be inexorably shut, for a time, on those who would only mar the order and destroy the peace of a new community' (Solly, 1884).

Karl Marx was somewhat ambivalent on the issue of land nationalisation. Marx recognised that 'the property in the soil is the original source of all wealth, and has become the great problem upon the solution of which depends the future of the working class' (Marx, 1872). Marx was opposed to the concept of peasant proprietorship which had been advocated by O'Connor. However, he also argued that

> To nationalise the land in order to let it out in small plots to individuals or working men's societies would, under a middle class government, only engender a reckless competition among themselves and this result in a progressive increase of 'rent' which, in its turn, would afford new facilities to the appropriators of feeding upon producers.
>
> (ibid.)

At the 1868 Brussels congress of the IWMA, the Belgian socialist, Cesar de Paepe, in his report on land property had proposed that:

> Small private property in land is doomed by the verdict of science, large land property by that of justice. There remains then but one alternative. The soil must become the property of rural associations or the property of the whole nation. The future will decide that question.
>
> (De Paepe, 1868, cited by Marx, 1872)

Marx argued that

> I say on the contrary; the social movement will lead to the decision that the land can be owned by the nation itself. To give up the soil to the hands of the associated labourers, would be to surrender society to one exclusive class of producers.
>
> (ibid.)

So, while Marx supported the nationalisation of land, which he recognised would 'work a complete change in the relations between capital and labour', he argued that nationalisation of land was but one component of the 'national centralisation of the means of production' and should not be pursued independently of the nationalisation of the other components – labour and capital.

The English branches of the IWMA however gave greater priority to the land issue than the General Council, which was dominated by Marx. The more moderate trade unionists such as Howell, Applegarth and Cremer left the IWMA after the dispute over Marx's support for the Paris commune and his publication of his polemic *The Civil War in France*, to which Marx attached the General Council's signatures without their permission (Evans 1909; Humphrey 1913; Moberg 1954; Collins and Abramsky 1965; Collins 1967; Leventhal 1971). However, some of the radical trade unionists including John Hales, the IWMA secretary, not only stayed in the IWMA but established a Federation of English branches. The Federation, established in 1871 only lasted until 1873 and only had two conferences – in Nottingham in July 1872 and in London in January 1873. The Nottingham conference published a statement, written by Thomas Smith of the Nottingham branch and the Scot, Gavin Clark, land reformer and later an advanced Liberal MP for the Highlands. The statement had only five points of which the third was

> the emancipation of land – the right of the people to the soil, and the abolition of privileged political land cases: and socially, the emancipation of labour – and the advocacy of measures that shall make capital the servant of labour, and not labour the servant of capital.
> (IWMA cited in Harrison, 1971, pp. 241–2)

With the winding up of the Reform League in 1869, the radical working class movement split. Howell established the Labour Representation League which worked with the Liberal Party and focused on trying to get working men nominated as official Liberals for parliamentary seats. He was supported by most of the leading trade unionists including radicals such as John Hales and Alfred Walton. The League did not however publish any political programme (Leventhal, 1971). A number of their leading members were to become Liberal MPs, including Howell, Broadhurst and the Scottish miners' leader, Alexander MacDonald. The northern-based National Reform Union had been established under middle class leadership in 1864 under the presidency of George Wilson, formerly chairman of the Anti-Corn Law League. It survived the abolition of the London based Reform League, and employed George Potter of the *Beehive* as a lecturer. After a conference in 1875, it published a set of new objects which now included land reform – but in effect promoting the LTRA's Millite position –

> a thorough Revision of the Land Laws, so as to provide such systems of tenure as will promote the best cultivation of the soil, and secure a fair valuation of the land for the purposes of national taxation in proportion to its increased value.
> (cited in Cole and Filson, 1951, pp. 595–6)

The London IWMA radicals tended to cluster round the O'Brienite group, led by Boon, John Weston and Charles Murray, who in the early 1870s established a series of relatively small and short lived organisations including the Mutual Land Emigration and Colonisation Society and the British Democratic Convention, led by Thomas Mooney which met in the Grafton Hall in Soho in the winter of 1873. The Land and Labour League also participated in the Birmingham Republican conference in May 1873, together with a number of London radical clubs, many of which had developed out of branches of the Reform League.

An attack on the aristocratic ownership of land was a central component of the republican position. Pamphlets and speeches were full of information on the land holdings of specific members of the royal family or aristocrats. The Democratic Convention's *Fifteen Cardinal Principles of Democracy*, included 'Nationalise the land – Sell or let it in small parcels to actual cultivators only; Property and income alone to bear all taxation, to be levied by an ascending scale to reach large accumulations of wealth; and Nationalise all Church, college and "charitable" property'. This was supported by an analysis on land holdings in England, Scotland, Wales and Ireland.'No man had ever the right to sell the earth; it is for all men, from generation to generation. Man may own what he has made, but it is impious to claim exclusive ownership of earth, ocean or air' (British Democratic Convention, 1873).

It is also important to acknowledge that the late 1870s and early 1880s also witnessed an increasing interest in land amongst advanced Liberals at a national level. The issue was taken up by the radical Birmingham Mayor, Joseph Chamberlain, but can also be seen in the debates of the established provincial Liberal leadership within the National Liberal Federation. The radicalism of Boon, Walton and Mooney was for example reflected in a speech by the Manchester advanced Liberal, Richard Pankhurst in 1878. Pankhurst together with his wife the leading suffragette Emmeline and daughter Sylvia, were later to join the Independent Labour Party.

> At the root of privilege and of the privileged classes in England lies one thing – the way in which land is held and used. . . Land is looked upon as an instrument to be employed by the privileged classes to maintain their power, to perpetuate their supremacy and to constitute them for ever the great governing class. What is the result? The whole of the kingdom is virtually in the hands of a handful of privileged families
>
> . . .
>
> Land must be made the subject to special taxation. When land rises in value by the increasing wealth of the community, that land ought to pay to the State the increase due to the wealth of the community . . .There is no robbery in England more shameless than that of people putting into their pockets the fruit of other people's industry, as is now often done in the case of landed property near large towns . . . It is a shameful fraud that the population and enterprise of London should not have their share of the wealth they create. Therefore in this great realm on this land question there must be a great political, great social, and great economical transformation effected in obedience to the principle that the land of the country, being the property of the nation, must be administered for the benefit and interest of the whole of the nation.
>
> (Pankhurst, 1878)

In the late 1870s and early 1880s there was increasing agitation about the overcrowded housing conditions in parts of London and the failure of the local vestries to ensure the improvement of existing homes and the provision of new homes, both to replace those slum dwellings demolished or cleared to make way for railway lines and new roads.

In 1878, the inveterate radical pamphleteer, Dan Chatterton published an attack on the Metropolitan Board of Works which was responsible for the street improvements in a pamphlet – *The Homes of the Poor and the Board of Works Swindle*. Chatterton attacked the Board for demolishing homes without replacing them and leaving families homeless. Chatterton then went on to argue for the programme of the Land and Labour League:

> We demand that the land, houses, money, fisheries, railways and mercantile marine of our country shall be nationalised under a poor and just State; a government of the people by the people for the people, the only justifiable rent being a merely nominal charge to be in support of the imperial taxation of our country, all other taxation to cease at once. The Metropolitan Board of Works shall at once proceed to clear the land-map out, and rearrange good wide streets, and to build thereon good six-roomed houses, with say, twelve feet square rooms, with every accommodation, back and front rooms same size, with gardens at the back, the ash-house, dust-bin, and water-closet to be at the bottom of the garden, the whole of the drainage to run under the wash-house, dust-bin, and water-closet, till it comes to the end of the street, where a house should be left down, and a subway made to carry such drainage out into the main road sewer, by this means avoiding all foul smells and poisoning of the blood – sickness, disease, and death.
>
>   ... The rooms in these houses to be let at a rental of one shilling per week for each room ... These houses would stand sixty years ... we should then have good homes, good food, good clothes, health, life, liberty, and happiness for all.
>
> (Chatterton, 1878)

The development of a distinctive working class agenda

This chapter, which has focused on London working class radicals in London in the mid-19th century, has demonstrated the active engagement of radicals in land reform campaigns, which also touched on the wider issues of housing and the planning of new settlements. It has demonstrated both a level of continuity across several generations, but a distinctly separate approach to that of the middle class Liberals and radicals. Working class radicals and early socialists engaged with the organisations established by middle class radicals, but continued to advocate their own interests. The debates over land reform in the 1870s and 1880s, with the working class radicals advocating land nationalisations as distinct from the more moderate reforms propounded by John Stuart Mill's Land Tenure Reform Association is the clearest example. The assertion of the importance of land nationalisation by the London radicals in countering Marx's emphasis on nationalisation of industry in the debates within the IWMA is also significant. Land nationalisation was also introduced into the programmes of the Democratic Federation, the Socialist League and the ILP by the working class radicals and not by the intellectuals. The depth of the analysis provided in some of the pamphlets they published and the foresight shown in much of the writing, noticeably by Martin James Boon and his O'Brienite colleagues, is both surprising and impressive. Boon and others focused not just on the vision of public ownership of land but on the mechanisms for achieving this objective, with a focus on both means and ends which was lacking from the arguments of more romantic utopian writers.

Primary sources

Boon, M (1850) *Home Colonization* (London: National Rational League)

Boon, M (1873) *How to Nationalise the Commons and Wastelands* (London: E Truelove)

Boon, M (1885) *National Paper-Money and Its Use* (London: Longman and Davies)

Bray, J F (1839) *Labours Wrongs and Labour's Remedy* (Leeds: D Green)

British Democratic Convention (1873) *Fifteen Cardinal Principles of Democracy* (London: Charles Watts)

Chatterton, D (1878) *The Homes of the Poor* (London: D Chatterton)

Cooper, T (1848) *Land for the Labourers* (London: E Wilson)

Dick, R (1856) *On the Evils, Impolicy and Anomaly of Individuals being Landlords and Nations Tenants* (London: John Chapman)

Dove, P (1851) *The Theory of Human Progression* (Boston, MA: Benjamin Mussey)

Dove, P (1854) *Elements of Political Science* (Edinburgh, UK: Johnstone and Hunter)

Evans, H (1913) *Radical Fights over Forty Years* (London: Daily News and Leader)

Federation of the English Branches of the IWMA (1872) Nottingham Conference Statement

Hall, C (1805) *The Effects of Civilization on the People in European States* (Reprint 1965, New York: Augustus M Kelley)

Howell, G (1871) *Wasteland and Surplus Labour* (London: T S D Floyd for Borough of Greenwich Advanced Liberal Association)

Jones, Ebenezer (1849) *The Land Monopoly* (London: Chas Fox)

Jones, Ernest (1856) *Evenings with the People: The Hereditary Landed Aristocracy* (London: The People's Paper)

Land and Labour League (1869) *Address to the Working Men and Women of Great Britain and Ireland* (reprinted in Marx and Engels Collected Works, (1985), Vol 21, p. 401, London: Lawrence and Wishart)

Linton, W (1850) *The People's Land* (London: J Watson)

Maccall, W (1865) *The Land and the People: An Argument for an English Land League* (London: Austin and Co)

Marx, K (1872) The Nationalisation of Land. Paper read to Manchester section of the IWMA published in *The International Herald*, No 11, 15 June

Mill, J S (1871) *Programme of the Land Tenure Reform Association* (London: Longmans, Green, Reader and Dyer)

O'Brien, B (1847) *National Reformer* 17 April 1847, quoted in Plummer, 1971.

O'Brien, B (1885) *The Rise, Progress and Phases of Human Slavery* (London: William Reeves)

O'Connor, F (1847) *A Practical Work on the Management of Small Farms* (Manchester, UK: Abel Heywood)

Pankhurst, R (1878) 'Dr Pankhurst on the Future of Liberalism', Speech at Leigh Liberal Club (Leigh, UK: The Journal)

Solly, H (1884) *Industrial Villages: A Remedy for Crowded Towns and Deserted Fields* (London: Sonnenschein)

Solly, H (1893) *These Eighty Years* (London: Simpkin and Marshall)

The First International (1868–70) Documents, Vol 3 (London: Lawrence and Wishart)

Walton, A (1865) *History of Landed Tenures* (London: Charles Clarke)

Walton, A (1868) *Our Future Progress* (London: Effingham Wilson)

Secondary sources

Armytage, W H G (1961) *Heavens Below: Utopian Experiments in England 1560–1960* (London: Routledge and Kegan Paul)

Beer, M (1920) *The Pioneers of Land Reform: Thomas Spence, William Ogilvie, Thomas Paine* (New York: Alfred A Knoff)

Biagini, E (1992) *Liberty, Retrenchment and Reform* (Cambridge: Cambridge University Press)

Bronstein, J (1999) *Land Reform and Working Class Experience in Britain and the United States 1800–1862* (Stanford, CA: Stanford University Press)

Carr, H J (1940) 'John Francis Bray' in *Economica*, Vol VII, No 28, pp. 397–414

Chase, M (1988) The People's Farm: English Radical Agrarianism 1775–1840 (Oxford: Oxford University Press)

Chase, M (1991) 'Out of Radicalism: The Mid-Victorian Freehold Land Movement' in *English Historical Review*, Vol 106, No 419, pp. 319–45.

Chase, M (2003) '"Wholesome Object Lesson": The Chartist Land Plan in Retrospect' in *English Historical Review*, Vol 116, No 465, pp. 59–85

Cole, G D H and Filson, A W (1965) *British Working Class Movements* (London: Macmillan)

Collins, H (1967) 'The English Branches of the First International' in Briggs, A and Saville, J (eds), *Essays in Labour History* (London: Macmillan)

Collins, H and Abramsky, C (1965) *Karl Marx and the British Labour Movement* (London: Macmillan)

Barry, E (1965) *Nationalisation in British Politics: The Historical Background* (London: Jonathan Cape)

Englander, D (1973) The Workman's National Housing Council (unpublished MA dissertation, University of Warwick, UK)

Englander, D (1983) *Landlord and Tenant in Urban Britain* (Oxford: Oxford University Press)

Entz, Gary and Whitehead, Andrew (2005) 'John Radford' in Gildhart, K and Howell, D (eds), *Dictionary of Labour Biography*, Vol 12, pp. 233–40 (London: Palgrave Macmillan)

Epstein, J (1982) *The Lion of Freedom. Feargus O'Connor and the Chartist Movement 1832–42* (London: Croom Helm)

Evans, H (1909) *Sir Randal Cremer: His Life and Work* (London: T Fisher Unwin)

Hadfield, M (1970) *The Chartist Land Company* (Newton Abbott, UK: David and Charles)

Hardy, Dennis (1979) *Alternative Communities in Nineteenth Century England* (London: Longman)

Harrison, R (1964) *Before the Socialists* (London: Routledge and Kegan Paul)

Harrison, R (ed.) (1971) *The English Defence of the Commune* (London: Merlin Press)

Howkins, A (2002) 'From Diggers to Dongas: the Land in English Radicalism' in *History Workshop Journal*, Vol 54, No 1 (Autumn), pp. 1–23

Humphrey, A W (1913) *Robert Applegarth* (Manchester, UK: National Labour Press)

Leventhal, F M (1971) *Respectable Radical: George Howell and Victorian Working Class Politics* (London: Weidenfeld and Nicolson)

Lindsay, J (1978) 'Ebenezer Jones, 1820–1860- An English Symbolist' in Cornforth, M (ed.), *Rebels and their Causes* (London: Lawrence and Wishart)

Maw, B (2005) Bronterre O'Brien, class and the advent of democratic anti-capitalism; the social and political ideas of Chartism's 'schoolmaster' (University of Wales unpublished PhD thesis)

Moberg, D R (1954) George Odger and the English Working Class Movement 1860–77 (University of London, unpublished PhD thesis)

Owen, J (2014) *Labour and the Caucus* (Liverpool, UK: Liverpool University Press)

Packe, M St J (1954) *John Stuart Mill* (London: Macmillan)

Peacock, A J (1961) Land Reform 1880–1919 (University of Southampton, UK, unpublished MA dissertation)

Plummer, A (1971) *Bronterre* (London: Allen and Unwin)

Postgate, R W (1923) *The Builders History* (London: Pelican Press)

Saville, J (1952) *Ernest Jones, Chartist* (London: Lawrence and Wishart)

Schoyen (1958) *The Chartist Challenge: A Portrait of George Julian Harney* (London: Heinemann)

Shipley, S (1971) *Club Life and Socialism in Mid-Victorian London* (Oxford: History Workshop, reprinted London: Journeyman Press 1983)

Smith, F A (1973) *Radical Artisan: William James Linton 1812–97* (Manchester, UK: Manchester University Press)

Tate, G (1950) *London Trades Council 1860–1950 A History* (London: Lawrence and Wishart)

Taylor, A (2005) '"A Melancholy odyssey among London public houses": radical club life and the unrespectable in mid nineteenth century London' in *Historical Research*, Vol 76, No 199 (February)

Taylor, A (1995) '"Commons stealers", "Land-Grabbers" and "Jerry-Builders": Space, Popular Radicalism and the Politics of Public Access in London 1848–1880' in *International Review of Social History*, 40, pp. 383–407

Turner, M (2012) 'Chartism, Bronterre O'Brien and the "Luminous Political Example of America"' in *History* (Oxford: Blackwell)

Whitehead, Andrew (1999) 'Martin James Boon' in Bellamy, J and Saville, J, (eds), *Dictionary of Labour Biography*, Vol 9 (London: Macmillan)

Wohl, A (1977) *The Eternal Slum: Housing and Social Policy in Victorian London* (London: Edward Arnold)

8   Social reform and social science

Intellectuals and the labour movement

While the primary focus of this work is on the attitudes to land, housing and planning within the working class radical and socialist movement, the role of liberal, radical and socialist intellectuals cannot be discounted. As discussed at the end of Chapter 6, mid-19th century socialism in England did not produce the cohort of middle class intellectuals and professional technocrats equivalent to the Saint-Simonians and Fourierists in France. While there may have been individual social reformers and engineers with radical or socialist inclinations they did not operate in England as an organised group. In the mid and late Victorian period, the organised leadership of socialism came from within the trade union movement and was largely artisan-led rather than professional or technocratic. There was little direct participation by labour leaders in government, though there were occasional invitations to labour representatives to appear before government commissions, normally through the formal representative structure of the Trades Union Congress established in 1868. There were no working class Members of Parliament until the election in 1874 of Thomas Burt and Alexander Macdonald as working class Liberals, known as Lib–Labs, to be joined by the former TUC general secretary, Henry Broadhurst, in 1880. Until that point, Labour leaders had to rely on sympathetic radicals and Liberals to promote legislative reform which was in their interest.

There were two groups of middle class social reformers in the second half of the 19th century who took a socialistic perspective on politics and social policy and who directly provided support to working class organisations – the Christian Socialists of the 1850s, and the positivists who were most active between 1860 and 1880. It is also helpful to refer to the role of the Social Science Association, which operated between 1857 and 1886, in which members of both groups participated. It is however necessary to first set the scene for these interventions by briefly reviewing the Benthamite origins of the social reform movement.

Utilitarianism and sanitarianism

The social reformers of the mid-19th century can be viewed as following Benthamite principles. The leading public health reformer, Edwin Chadwick had been Bentham's secretary, while his colleague Thomas Southwood Smith had, with Chadwick, helped Bentham in writing his *Constitutional Code*. It is therefore not surprising that the reforms promoted by Chadwick, Southwood Smith and their fellow reformers followed the utilitarian principle. The utilitarians can be viewed as laissez faire in economics but interventionist in social policy. Chadwick adopted the Benthamite principle that the right ordering of society aided individual happiness and that matters such as health required communal rather than individual action. Graham Wallas argued that Chadwick took the details of the 1834 Poor Law and that Joseph Parkes and Francis Place took much of the draft of the Municipal Corporations Act of 1835 from the *Constitutional Code* (Wallas, 1923).

Chadwick and his colleagues produced a set of reports and legislation which fundamentally changed not just the relationship between central and local government, but extended the role of government to regulate a wide range of organisational and individual behaviour. The legislation generated a new profession of civil servants whose role was to inspect, regulate and if necessary prosecute offenders (Fry, 1970; Lubenow, 1971). The 1834 Poor Law generated a mass opposition movement in the North of England (Edsall, 1971). Chadwick was the author of the 1834 *Poor Law Report*, and the 1842 *Report on the Sanitary Conditions of the Labouring Population*, which he published on his own initiative and led to the establishment of the Royal Commission on the Health of Towns and their reports in 1844 and 1845. He was also the main proponent of the Public Health Act of 1848 and sat on the General Board of Health and the Metropolitan Commission for Sewers (Wohl, 1983; Brundage, 1990).

The growth of central government control, exercised through a new series of public boards led to an anti-centralisation campaign under the leadership of Joshua Toulmin Smith who published a series of volumes defending local self-government, including *Government by Commissions Illegal and Pernicious* in 1849, *Local Self Government and Centralisation* in 1857, *The Parish Council* in 1859 and *Local Self-Government Unmystified*, also published in 1859. Toulmin Smith argued that 'local self government was the true socialism.' (Toulmin Smith 1857; Weinstein, 2008) As Hamlin (1998) has shown, Chadwick also met considerable opposition from medical critics, such as Thomas Wakley of *The Lancet* who was MP for Finsbury between 1835 and 1852, the medical journalist, James Kay-Shuttleworth, and the Scottish professor of medicine, William Pultney Alison, who argued that more attention needed to be given to causes of ill health such as poverty (Hamlin, 1998, pp. 74 ff). Alison was concerned that Chadwick focused on 'applying remedies to diseases which have obviously been the result of privations ... (and) known that they could be only temporarily useful simply because he had no remedy for the privations from which they originated' (Alison, cited by Hamlin, 1998, p. 79).

The Public Health legislation of this period also set the framework for later housing legislation, the history of which is narrated in Wohl's classic work *The Eternal Slum*, and does not require repetition here (Wohl, 1977).

The Christian socialist intervention

The Christian Socialist group were progressive Christian philanthropists, who in response to both the Chartist agitation in England and the 1848 revolution in Paris decided to provide active assistance to working class organisations. The leaders of the group were Frederick Maurice, John Ludlow, Edward Vansittart Neale and Thomas Hughes (Stubbs, 1900; Raven, 1920; Norman, 1987). The group had relatively limited support from working class activists, the main exception being the former Owenite, Lloyd Jones, who was to co-author with Ludlow a book on the *Progress of the Working Class* in 1867.

The group was influenced by the French associationist movement, especially the writings of the French Christian co-operator, Philippe Buchez. Ludlow had strong links with elements of the socialist movement in Paris and the former Saint-Simonian and Fourierist, Jules Lechavalier, was a close friend of Ludlow's. Lechavalier was now an associate of the French anarchist Proudhon and editor of his journal *La Voix du Peuple* and was also involved in anti-slavery campaigns and trying to establish a new community in French Guiana. He was exiled to London in 1849, and, known as J L St Andre, was an associate of the Owenite co-operator and secularist, George Jacob Holyoake. He worked with Lloyd Jones in establishing a co-operative tailoring house and then the London Co-operative and General Store at Charlotte Street in Fitzrovia (Ludlow, 1981, p. 157; Corcoran, 1983, p. 175). However, according to Holyoake's memoirs and McCabe's *Life of Holyoake*, he was actually a paid secret agent of Napoleon III (Holyoake, 1893, Vol 2, pp. 4–5; McCabe, 1908, Vol 1, pp. 191–2).

The Christian Socialists were advocates of associationism and co-operation. In May 1848, the group started a weekly journal – *Politics for the People*. The purpose of the journal was to study 'the questions which are most occupying our countrymen at the present moment'. The editors argued that politics and religion could not be separated – 'that Liberty, Fraternity, Unity, under some conditions or other, are intended for every people under heaven.'

In addition to articles on Chartism, the suffrage and the progress of the revolution in France, the journal had an interest in wider issues of social policy. Three of the early issues included lectures on sanitary reform, written by Professor W A Guy. The first article commented that 'to leave this subject out of popular politics would be to strike health from the list of blessings, and air, light and water from the catalogue of the necessaries of life' *(Politics for the People, 1848, pp. 7–10, 53–6,121–4).* Guy was a leading sanitarian, a member of the Health of Towns Association, and had in 1846 written a pamphlet entitled *On the Health of Towns, as influenced by Defective Cleansing and Drainage, and on the Application of the Refuse of Towns to Agricultural Purposes.*

In 1849, however, the group as a whole decided to take up the issue of sanitary reform. Responding to a series of articles published by Henry Mayhew in the *Morning Chronicle*, Ludlow together with Kingsley, the scientist Charles Mansfield and Charles Walsh, who had been a health inspector during the cholera epidemic, established a Health League. The object was to collect information on health conditions and promote the need for public health. The League wrote a letter to the Commissioner of Sewers on the conditions in Jacob's Island in Bermondsey exposed by Mayhew. Maurice was however opposed to any idea of a campaigning league and shut down the campaign (Ludlow, 1981, pp. 155–6). This however did not stop Kingsley later writing a number of essays on health issues. In 1850 he established the Society for Promoting Working Men's Associations, to help establish co-operatives, but abandoned any practical intervention in health or housing issues. In May 1851, Kingsley gave a lecture to the association on *The Application of associative principles and methods to agriculture*, which was published by the former Chartist, John James Bezer on behalf of the Office of the *Christian Socialist*. Kingsley argued against competition in the land market – 'I cannot but think that it would be a very bad thing to let land to go freely into the market to be struggled for by every speculator.'

Kingsley then criticised both O'Connor's Chartist land plan and the idea of land nationalisation as impractical, offering up instead the notion of an association of farmworkers renting collectively from a sympathetic landlord. He then contrasted what he saw as the failure of socialist experiments with the success of the Moravian settlements, which he also referred to as 'socialist' – socialist land colonisation failed through self-conceit, while the Moravian settlements succeeded because they were "undertaken in the fear of God, and with humility and caution . . .founded on the rock of everlasting justice." There is no evidence that Kingsley's organisation actually sponsored any home colonisation initiatives or plans for new settlements, though it did support a number of co-operatives including a builders' co-operative as well providing support to trade unions and establishing the Working Men's College in Islington (Harrison, 1954; Masterman, 1963).

Thomas Hughes was elected to parliament in 1865 and was a member of the Royal Commission on Trade Unions, together with the positivist Frederic Harrison. However, by 1854, the group had disbanded, without making any substantial contribution to social policy or health and housing reform, though Kingsley continued to pursue sanitary reform. In 1857, he gave a lecture on *Great Cities and their Influence for Good or Evil* and in 1869 a lecture on the need for clear air, called *The Two Breaths*. In the first essay, Kingsley called for improvements in education and working conditions, model homes and for athletic activity. He pointed to the improved homes in the suburbs but noted that the working class still lived in city centres in overcrowded conditions. In the second he argued for ventilation of homes and factories (Kingsley, 1880).

Thomas Hughes was, however, to maintain an interest in co-operative communities. The *Manual for Cooperatives* he wrote for the Co-operative Congress with Edward Vansittart Neale in 1881 included a section on 'The Practice of Co-operation in Social Life'. This included reference to the projects of Titus Salt, Owen and Fourier but focused mainly on the experience of Godin's Familistère at Guise in France. The manual also referred, in a footnote, to philanthropic housing schemes and the possibility of communal housing or 'associated homes' (Hughes and Neale, 1881). Hughes was however to put some of these ideas into practice. In 1870, he toured America with the idea of establishing a new settlement. He persuaded a group of Boston business men to form a Board to Aid Land Ownership in 1877, and in 1879 the Board raised funds to buy 50,000 acres in Tennessee to sell to colonists. A purchaser was required to pay a third of the cost up front and pay the rest within two years.

Hughes named the colony Rugby after his old school. The colony was not intended for the working class. Hughes sought 'young men of good education and small capital, the class of which, of all others, is most overcrowded today in England' (Hughes, 1881). Hughes had hoped that the English public schools would send their young men to the colony but this did not happen. Most of the colonists were families from Britain or America. The settlement, which grew to some 400 families, included a public store, a library, a hotel and a non-denominational church, in accordance with Hughes' concept of muscular Christianity. The object was to support both petty capitalism and moral and physical regeneration. Hughes and his family actually lived in the colony between 1884 and 1887, selling his plots in 1892 (Mack and Armytage, 1952, pp. 227–50; Norman, 1987, pp. 91–2).

As will be discussed later in Chapter 9, the Christian socialist revival in the early 1880s, led by Stuart Headlam and the Guild of Saint Matthew, was to make a significant contribution to the land nationalisation movement.

Positivism and social reform

The positivists were a group of progressive Oxford-based academics who were followers of the French philosopher Auguste Comte. Comte had originally been a disciple of Saint-Simon but had then developed his own concept of a social system – a science of society – based on what he referred to as 'positivist social science'. Comte's summary work, pulling together a much more extensive work based on lectures given between 1826 and 1829, *A General View of Positivism*, was translated into English in 1865. Comte produced an analysis of the different stages of the development of society and a comprehensive social theory which appeared to set out a basis for the development of a new society, a society in which the role of the proletariat would be predominant. The proletariat however needed the assistance of an intellectual elite to bring them to a recognition of their role, a perspective which was not that different from the view of Marx. Comte's later work, like that of his mentor Saint-Simon, developed into a religious cult, with the establishment of a 'religion of humanity' (Kent, 1978). Comte's primary object, as he put it himself, was 'to generalise our scientific conceptions, and to systematize the art of social life'. The theory was a regenerating doctrine. Once a systematic view of human life was undertaken, there would be a basis for modifying its imperfections. Comte did not expect support from the upper classes but instead looked to women and the working classes. However, it was necessary for philosophers to promote the new doctrine to the working classes. Comte's motto was 'Love, Order, Progress' with the ultimate objective being 'Humanity' (Comte, 1865, pp. 2–5).

Comte's concepts received support from a number of members of the British liberal intelligentsia, including John Stuart Mill, who published a study of Comte in 1865 and Harriet Martineau who translated Comte's positive philosophy in 1853 (Martineau, 1853; Mill, 1865). The leader of the British Comtists was Richard Congreve, a tutor at Wadham College, Oxford. The original Comtist circle was centred on a group of Congreve's students, including J H Bridges, E S Beesly and Frederic Harrison. Beesly and Bridges both had religious backgrounds and their conversion to Comtism was to some extent based on a rejection of the established church. Comtism offered an optimistic social theory free of religious trappings, based on moral concepts which had a religious tone to them (McGee, 1931).

Comtism, and the English positivism that grew from it, was a system of analysis rather than being a philosophy of action. In this sense it was different from Marxism. Nevertheless, the fact that the two theories both focused on the role of the proletariat as the basis for a new society did allow for some collaboration between positivists and Marxists, or at least between positivist leaders and Marx himself. Like the Christian Socialists, with whom the positivists shared a number of attributes, the positivist leaders focused on working with the organised working class. Beesly was to assist in the establishment of the International Working Men's Association and in fact chaired the founding meeting at St Martin's Hall in London in 1864, though he never became an active participant or member of the General Council. Harrison became an active supporter of the trade union movement, advisor to the Trades Union

Congress and a member, with Charles Kingsley, of the Royal Commission on Trade Unions of 1867–9. Of the other positivist leaders, J H Bridges was a medical doctor and essayist and became medical inspector for the Local Government Board; Richard Congreve published essays on the religious aspects of Comtism and founded the Church of Humanity, separating the organised English positivist movement from the French positivists, led after Comte's death in 1856 by Pierre Lafitte.

Of the positivist leaders, it is Beesly and Harrison who became most involved in politics. Royden Harrison, the author of the main study of the English positivists (Harrison, 1963) has tracked at considerable length the relationship between Beesly and Marx (Harrison, 1959). There is also an excellent biography of Frederic Harrison (Vogeler, 1984), and a more traditional biography of Bridges (Living, 1928). There are also two recent studies of the role of Harrison and other positivists in opposing Britain's imperial adventures (Claeys, 2010; Matikkala, 2011).

Given the belief of both Saint-Simon and Comte in establishing a new social system (though in Comte's case the propositions were somewhat abstract), it might have been expected that the English positivists might have developed interests in communitarian settlements, housing reform, land policy and planning. This was however not the case. J H Bridges, who as a medical inspector was part of the professional civil service which actually implemented the Chadwickian sanitarian policies, did read a paper to the British Medical Association on the need for sanitary teaching in primary education and wrote a *Catechism of Health for Use in Primary Schools*, copies of which he sent to Harrison and to William Forster, who was Minister of Education (Living, 1928, p. 94). However not a single article in his published collected essays touches on public health or related subjects (Bridges, 1907, 1915).

Of the positivist leadership, it was Harrison who was most active in Liberal party politics. Harrison however, unlike the Fabian Sidney Webb, whose role will be discussed later, was not involved in the internal politics of the party and was more of a journalistic commentator. As Vogeler points out, he could write about the dockers' strike of 1889, without visiting the East End, although he did give a talk at Toynbee Hall. He could write about Irish Home Rule without visiting Ireland. His retreat was an isolated cottage on the Surrey/Sussex border and for the last years of his life he lived in the Royal Crescent in Bath. He was a member of F B Firth's London Municipal Reform League and supported the campaign that led to the creation of the London County Council. He was interested in historic buildings, no doubt influenced by the fact that he lived in one, and once gave a talk to Morris's Society for the Protection of Ancient Buildings, in which he opposed alterations being made to Westminster Abbey. He appears to have been a supporter of the de-urbanisation of London, arguing in his Toynbee Hall lecture, that the ideal population for London was half a million people – at the time it was 3.8 million for London and 4.8 million for Greater London.

Harrison's brother, Charles, was elected to the first London County Council for Bethnal Green in 1889, and went on to become vice chairman of the LCC under Lord Rosebery's chairmanship. Charles was a leading advocate of leasehold enfranchisement and 'betterment tax', which will be discussed in the next chapter. No doubt Charles had a role in ensuring Frederic was elected as one of the first London County Council aldermen. Charles took a leading role within the LCC Progressive party, chairing the Improvements committee and the parliamentary committee. When Charles became vice-chairman in 1892, Frederic took over the chairmanship of the Improvements committee and in that role promoted the proposal for the new thoroughfare in Holborn, that later became Kingsway. Speaking at the Industrial Remuneration Conference in 1885, he argued that 'no abstract rights of property' should prevent 'laying out our cities as health and convenience suggest'. Frustrated at the lack of support from government and the limited financial independence of the LCC, Frederic Harrison resigned his aldermanship, and retreated to his country cottage to focus on writing (Vogeler, 1984, pp. 207–11).

As none of the positivists were elected to parliament (Morley having moved away from positivism before his election), it was Frederic Harrison who was the only leading positivist to achieve a political position of responsibility, though it should be recognised that Vernon Lushington probably had more effective power as a senior civil servant than Harrison in his role as an LCC alderman. Though arguably the least theoretical of the positivists and the only one who actually got directly involved in the politics of planning, Harrison's lack of success in his role as practical politician perhaps exposes the limited ability of the positivists to relate Comtian theory to actual political practice. This is perhaps not surprising given that neither Comte nor his English followers tried to convert Comtian concepts into any form of programme for political action. This should not be surprising once Comtism is viewed as a system of analysis rather than as a set of principles for political and social reform.

The positivist circle was nevertheless influential. It included Geoffrey Lushington, prison reformer and permanent secretary at the Home Office, who on his retirement in 1895 became a London Council alderman; his brother Vernon Lushington who became a judge and was a friend of William Morris; Henry Crompton who became parliamentary legal adviser on the Trade Union Bill and the journalist and later Liberal MP and Minister, John Morley. One of the younger members of the positivist circle was the Edinburgh based sociologist and biologist, Patrick Geddes. The influence of positivism on Geddes will be considered in Chapter 10.

The Social Science Association

The National Association for the Promotion of Social Science was established in 1857 'to unite together as far as possible the various efforts now being made for the moral and social improvement of the people'. It was initiated by Lord Brougham, Whig lawyer and Lord Chancellor in Grey's 1830 reform government. The initial meeting involved some forty-three people, including leading Liberal MPs and social reformers. Rather unusually for a meeting of this time, fifteen were women. This group included Barbara Leigh Smith Bodichon, Bessie Raynes Parkes and Anna Swanwick. Amongst the male group were a number of MPs – the Liberals Viscount Ebrington, Samuel Whitbread, George Hadfield and two Conservatives – Lord Alfred Churchill and Charles Adderley, together with the textile magnate Samuel Courtauld, the statistician, William Farr, John Simon the public health administrator and a clutch of scientists and less well known reformers. G R Hastings, who had been secretary of the Law Amendment Society, was appointed secretary to the new body (Goldman, 2002).

The main activity of the society was to have an annual conference. This event rotated between the major British cities and became an impressive event, with two thousand or so attendees at each conference, with up to 100 papers presented. To be invited to speak was a major honour – an opportunity for a reformer to put a reform proposal to a large and well informed audience. Not surprisingly, it was a platform that Owenites, Christian Socialists and Positivists were happy to use. The ageing Robert Owen was himself to speak at one of the early conferences. The French socialist, Louis Blanc, in exile in London, welcomed the launch of the Society, arguing that socialism and social science were actually the same thing – 'socialism is nothing more than a sincere and scientific inquiry into matters which Lord Brougham declares to be eminently deserving of attentive study' (cited in Goldman, 2002, p. 253). Blanc was perhaps overoptimistic. The Society was under the control of the liberal establishment – some participants no doubt having socialistic tendencies, but few of the invited speakers could be viewed as putting forward explicitly socialist propositions.

The work of the Society was divided into a number of divisions: Jurisprudence and the amendment of law; Education; Punishment and Reformation; Public Health and Social Economy. Perhaps not surprisingly any papers relating to housing or planning came within the remit of the Public Health division. Most papers presented in this division – fifteen or so papers at each conference, dealt directly with medical and epidemiological aspects, presented by health academics and professionals. There were however papers that considered housing improvement as part of sanitarian reform. At the first conference, a paper on *Houses for Working Men, their arrangement, drainage and ventilation*, was presented by Rev C H Hartshorne. In 1863, James Begg gave a paper on *Co-operation as a Means of providing Houses for Working Men*. In 1864, George Godwin of *The Builder* presented a paper on *What is the Influence on Health of the Overcrowding of Dwelling houses and workshops and by what means could such Overcrowding be prevented?* In the economy and trade division of the same conference, a paper on *Houses for the People and how to provide them* was presented by John Holmes. This was followed by a paper on *The Principle of Association applied to Dwellings of the Working Classes and of the Poorer Classes generally* by William Westgarth, and a paper on the Euston Benefit Building Society by the Owenite co-operator George Jacob Holyoake. Westgarth had separately published plans for street improvements in London and was later to emigrate to Australia.

At the 1865 conference in Sheffield, there was a series of papers on the Health of Towns. John Morgan, a doctor and secretary of the Manchester and Salford Sanitary Association, presented a paper on *The Danger of Deterioration of Race from the too rapid increase of Great Cities*. In the same session, George Godwin of *The Builder* gave a detailed presentation on Godin's Fourierist phalanstery in Guise in France, complete with site plan and an impressive lithograph. The 1869 conference in Bristol included a paper by Frederick Wedmore on *The Supervision of Dwellings for the Poor*, which referred to the work of John Ruskin and Octavia Hill, while in another session Octavia Hill herself gave a paper *On the Importance of aiding the Poor without Almsgiving*. This summarised her approach to housing management – 'I see no limit to the power of raising even the lowest classes if we will know and love them, deal with them as human beings, stimulate their hope and energy'. Hill referred to the residents of the homes she managed, purchased due to the liberality of Mr Ruskin, as 'my people'.

By the 1874 conference in Glasgow, the issue of displacement was on the agenda. Two papers, by James Morrison of the Glasgow Improvement Trust and Rev J Simpson, vicar of St Clement Danes in London, were presented on *In what way can healthy working men's dwellings be erected in lieu of those removed for carrying out*

Sanitary or Municipal improvements or for other purposes? The first respondent in the discussion which followed was none other than Edwin Chadwick who pointed to the fact that the Peabody Trust had demonstrated that homes for working people could be built on a commercial basis, and that as long as large rooms were heated properly, housing constructed on good sanitary principles would reduce the death rate.

At the 1877 conference in Aberdeen, William Hardwicke, London medical officer of health and coroner, gave a presentation on *Accommodation for the Labouring Classes and of Utilising Open Spaces in Towns.* Hardwicke referred again to Godin's Guise project but also reported on his visit to the model workman's town or 'cité ouvrière' at Mulhouse in Alsace, at that time under German occupation and known as Mulhausen. Hardwicke argued for the provision of open space in residential areas, suggesting that the Open Space Act of 1877 should be amended to include compulsory as well as enabling provisions. In his view open spaces were essential

> for effecting improved conditions of infant life, and for lessening the high mortality existing; for preventing a larger number of street accidents, and lastly, for the cultivation of healthy tastes, which the sight of shrubs and flower culture is well calculated to promote.

Chadwick, who was chairing the session responded by commenting on ''the gross neglect on the part of local authorities and people in charge of towns', in not providing open spaces. He gave his view that:

> there was not sufficient education, taste and refinement on the part of the usual run of local authorities . . . In some cities on the continent such as Hamburg a very superior intelligence prevailed, open spaces were beautiful and the towns made pleasant . . . Unfortunately in this country the municipal government was not under the more educated but the less educated of the middle class.

The president of the Public Health section in 1875 was Benjamin Ward Richardson. His address was later published as a pamphlet under the title *Hygeia: A City of Health.* Richardson was later to publish other books – *The Future of Sanitary Science* and *The Health of Nations,* which was a review of the works of Edwin Chadwick in six volumes.

In *Hygeia,* Richardson set out his vision for a new city. This is worth quoting at some length as it provides the most substantive detailed plan of any writing in this period.

> The population of the city may be placed at 100,000, living in 20,000 houses, built on 4,000 acres of land,– an average of 25 persons to an acre. This may be considered a large population for the space occupied, but, since the effect of density on vitality tells only determinately when it reaches a certain extreme degree, as in Liverpool and Glasgow, the estimate may be ventured.
>
> The safety of the population of the city is provided for against density by the character of the houses, which ensures an equal distribution of the population. Tall houses overshadowing the streets, and creating necessity for one entrance to several tenements, are nowhere permitted. In streets devoted to business,

where the tradespeople require a place of mart or shop, the houses are four stories high, and in some of the western streets where the houses are separate, three and four storied buildings are erected; but on the whole it is found bad to exceed this range, and as each story is limited to 15 feet, no house is higher than 60 feet.

The acreage of our model city allows room for three wide main streets or boulevards, which run from east to west, and which are the main thoroughfares. Beneath each of these is a railway along which the heavy traffic of the city is carried on. The streets from north to south which cross the main thoroughfares at right angles, and the minor streets which run parallel, are all wide, and, owing to the lowness of the houses, are thoroughly ventilated, and in the day are filled with sunlight. They are planted on each side of the pathways with trees, and in many places with shrubs and evergreens. All the interspaces between the backs of houses are gardens. The churches, hospitals, theatres, banks, lecture-rooms, and other public buildings, as well as some private buildings such as warehouses and stables, stand alone, forming parts of streets, and occupying the position of several houses. They are surrounded with garden space, and add not only to the beauty but to the healthiness of the city. The large houses of the wealthy are situated in a similar manner.

Our model city is of course well furnished with baths, swimming baths, Turkish baths, playgrounds, gymnasia, libraries, board schools, fine-art schools, lecture halls, and places of instructive amusement. In every board-school, drill forms part of the programme. I need not dwell on these subjects, but must pass to the sanitary officers and offices.

At a distance from the town are the sanitary works, the sewage pumping works, the water and gas works, the slaughter-houses and the public laboratories. The sewage, which is brought from the town partly by its own flow and partly by pumping apparatus, is conveyed away to well-drained sewage farms belonging to, but at a distance from, the city where it is utilised.

The water supply, derived from a river which flows to the south-west of the city, is unpolluted by sewage or other refuse, is carefully filtered, is tested twice daily, and if found unsatisfactory is supplied through a reserve tank, after it has been made to undergo further purification. It is carried through the city everywhere by iron pipes. Leaden pipes are forbidden. In the sanitary establishment are disinfecting rooms, a mortuary, and ambulances for the conveyance of persons suffering from contagious disease. These are at all times open to the use of the public, subject to the few and simple rules of the management.

The gas, like the water, is submitted to regular analysis by the staff of the sanitary officer, and any fault which may be detected, and which indicates a departure from the standard of purity framed by the Municipal Council, is immediately remedied, both gas and water being exclusively under the control of the local authority.

The inspectors of the sanitary officer have under them a body of scavengers. These, each day, in the early morning, pass through the various districts allotted to them, and remove all refuse in closed vans. Every portion of manure from stables, streets, and yards is in this way removed daily, and transported to the city farms for utilisation.

The details of the city exist. They have been worked out by those pioneers of sanitary science, so many of whom surround me to-day, and specially by him whose hopeful thought has suggested my design. I am, therefore, but as a draughtsman, who, knowing somewhat your desires and aspirations, have drawn a plan, which you in your wisdom can modify, improve, perfect. In this I know we are of one mind, that though the ideal we all of us hold be never reached during our lives, we shall continue to work successfully for its realisation. Utopia itself is but another word for time; and some day the masses, who now heed us not, or smile incredulously at our proceedings, will awake to our conceptions. Then our knowledge, like light rapidly conveyed from one torch to another, will bury us in its brightness.

The Industrial Remuneration Conference

This conference was initiated by a group of trustees led by Frederic Harrison following a gift of £1,000 from an anonymous Edinburgh philanthropist. The trustees included Sir Thomas Brassey, who had been president of the 1874 Cooperative Conference and Admiralty Minister in Gladstone's government, Professor Foxwell, the economist, the Earl of Dalhousie, who was Secretary of State for Scotland in Gladstone's government and the Lib–Lab MP Thomas Burt.

The purpose of the conference, which was chaired by Charles Dilke, was to discuss the distribution of the profits of industry between different classes. This included consideration of wage rates and the general wellbeing of the working classes, distribution of wealth, forms of taxation and the ownership of land. What was significantly different from the Social Science Association conferences was the list of those participating. This was dominated by representatives of political organisations trade unions and cooperative societies. The Social Democratic Federation (SDF) had three representatives – John Burns, James MacDonald (of the London Trades Council – not James Ramsey MacDonald) and J E Williams: Beesly represented the Positivist Society, William Saunders the English Land Restoration League, Hubert Bland and J G Stapleton the Fabian Society, Stewart Headlam the Guild of St Matthew, Gavin Clark the Highland Land Law Association, J Bruce Wallace the Irish Land Restoration Society, Charles Bradlaugh the Land Law Reform League and Patrick Geddes, the Edinburgh Social Union. Invited speakers included, in addition to Harrison: Lloyd Jones, Alfred Russell Wallace, Professor Alfred Marshall, John Morley and Arthur Balfour. The only trade union speaker was James Mawdsley of the Manchester cotton spinners, who was the current chairman of the Trades Union Congress.

The whole of the third day of the three-day conference was devoted to a debate on land nationalisation, an issue which had not been on the agenda for the Social Science conferences. The first speaker was Arthur Balfour, who in effect defended the status quo. Alfred Russell Wallace then propounded a system of peasant proprietorship, by which every adult could claim a portion of land for personal occupation at a fair rent and with security of tenure. Professor Newman speaking on behalf of the Land Nationalisation Society, put forward the case for the recovering of land by the state on behalf of the community and replacing landlords by occupying cultivators, who would not own the land but would own whatever had 'been added to the soil by human industry'.

The first speaker in the afternoon session was Lord Bramwell, a lawyer and representative of the Liberty and Property Defence League, who not surprisingly argued against any form of land nationalisation or redistribution. He was followed by Frederic Harrison who gave an extended and devastating critique of Henry George's arguments that land was a different form of property from all other property and that all individuals had a natural and God given right to land ownership. The third speaker was Shield Nicholson, Professor of Political Economy at Edinburgh University, who argued that the direct management of land by the state was neither advantageous nor necessary on financial or utilitarian grounds.

The two sets of papers generated a vigorous debate. Participants in the morning discussion include J E Williams of the SDF, who argued that land nationalisation on its own was insufficient and that factories and railways needed to be nationalised as well, a proposition that clearly was not welcome, as there was loud cheering when the chairman told Williams that his oratory had exceeded his allotted time. George Bernard Shaw of the Fabians spoke to argue that the subdivision of land proposed by Wallace would be inefficient. Henry Solly intervened to promote the resettlement of London workers in agricultural communities on the edge of the city. He argued that workers could not afford to be freeholders but should have security of tenure. He believed his proposal would reduce overcrowding in London and reduce the distress in agricultural districts. The growth of the new settlements needed to be limited to avoid recreating the problems of the urban areas.

The afternoon discussion was also lively. The first respondent was Gavin Clark speaking for the Highland land reformers, who narrated the story of how the landlords had cleared crofters to make way for sheep and were now clearing away sheep to make way for deer as deer hunting was more profitable than sheep farming or crofting. He was followed by John Burns representing the SDF, who criticised Harrison for arguing that land nationalisation was unnecessary as industry and capital could be moralised – 'You might as well try to moralise the lion who was about to devour the lamb; you might as well try to moralise the boa constrictor that had its coils around the body of the victim.' He responded to Harrison's contention that the socialists had no theory. Referring to Marx and Lassalle, he argued that 'the battle of the future lay between individuals on the one hand and socialists on the other'. He pointed to the success of existing socialistic experiments such as the Birmingham Corporation's ownership of the sewage works, gasworks and waterworks. He also pointed to the fact that in Belgium, the government owned the railways. He concluded his contribution by asserting that

A revolution was germinating in the bowels of society through the inequalities of condition which prevailed. To the middle class he would say: Will you guide the revolution or be driven by it, or try to suppress it by force? If you do the latter, upon you rests the responsibility of the strife that is coming – the responsibility of pushing back the hopes and aspirations of the workmen of the world.

A contribution that unlike that of his colleague, J E Williams, was met with applause (Industrial Remuneration Conference, 1885).

Radical and socialist intellectuals and the built environment

The main conclusion from this review of radical and socialist intellectuals in the mid-19th century is that little attention was given to planning. The focus of social reform debate, so far as it related to the built environment, was public health. This led to campaigns and legislation relating to sanitary reform, which then led to laws relating to the improvement or clearance of existing housing in poor condition. While there was an increasing recognition that overcrowding was a key source of the public health problem, there was little recognition that this reflected both an overall shortage of housing and the inability of the working class to afford to live in better conditions. There was little discussion of the need for a new house-building programme the planning of new settlements or the need for changes in the management and ownership of land. In fact, land reform was not on the agenda for the Christian Socialists, the positivists, or perhaps surprisingly for the Social Science Association.

This presents a contrast with the attention given to the subject by radical working class movements as shown in the previous chapter, and the significance of the issue to the new socialist movements of the 1880s discussed in the next chapter. It is also significant that the Christian Socialists, who were involved in their initial period in sanitary agitation, shifted their attention elsewhere, and that their only settlement project was Hughes' Tennessee initiative of 1881, not a project targeted at helping the working class or relieving the pressures on overcrowding in London – more a personal escapism, an attempt to recreate the muscular Christianity of Thomas Arnold's Rugby on the American frontier.

It could be argued that the failure of progressive intellectuals to take the issues of housing, land and the planning of new settlements sufficiently seriously was one of the reasons for the dissatisfaction of working class organisations with the existing government structures and more specifically with the Liberal party. It should not be forgotten that the main housing legislation of the 1880s and 189's was introduced by Conservative governments rather than by Liberal governments. Gladstone was more concerned with Ireland and temperance and moral regeneration than he was with government intervention on social policy. The radical domestic policy promoted by Chamberlain in the early 1880s disappeared from the Westminster agenda with Chamberlain's establishment of the Liberal Unionist party – the radicals he left behind such as Labouchere focusing on imperial rather than domestic issues. The Lib–Lab MPs showed little interest in housing, land and planning, with the notable exception of Henry Broadhurst's agitation on leasehold reform. It was in fact not until after the Boer War and the controversy over why so many working class men were unfit to fight, that attention was paid to these State of the Nation issues, with the beginning of agitation by New Liberals such as Charles Masterman arguing that if Britain was to defend its Empire, then the problems at the Heart of the Empire needed to be remedied. This debate will be considered in Chapter 10.

Primary sources

Bridges, J H (1907) *Essays and Addresses* (London: Chapman Hall)

Bridges, J H (1915) *Illustrations of Positivism. A Selection of Articles from the Positivist Review* (London: Watts)

Comte, A (1865) *A General View of Positivism*. Translated and edited by J H Bridges (London: William Reeves)

Holyoake, G J (1893) *Sixty Years of an Agitators Life* (London: Fisher Unwin)

Hughes, T and Neale, E V (1881) *A Manual for Co-operators* (Manchester, UK: Central Cooperative Board)

Hughes, T (1881) *Rugby Tennessee, being some Account of the Settlement Founded on the Cumberland Plateau by the Board of Aid to Land Ownership* (London)

Industrial Remuneration Conference (1885) *Report of Proceedings and Papers* (London: Cassell)

Kingsley, Charles (1851) *The Application of Associative Principles and Methods to Agriculture* (London: J J Bezer)

Kingsley, Charles (1880) *Sanitary and Social Lectures and Essays* (London: Macmillan)

Ludlow, J (1981) *The Autobiography of a Christian Socialist* (London: Frank Cass)

Lechavalier, J (1854) *Five Years in the Land of Refuge, A Letter on the Prospects of Co-operative Associations in England* (reprinted London 2013)

Martineau, H (1853) *The Positive Philosophy of Auguste Comte* (London: Chapman)

Mill, J S (1865) 'Auguste Comte and Positivism', reprinted from *Westminster Review* (London: Trubner)

National Association for the Promotion of Social Science Transactions 1857–1887 (London: John W Parker)

Politics for the People (1848) May to July 1848 (reprinted New York: A M Kelley, 1971)

Richardson, Benjamin Ward (1876) *Hygiea: A City of Health*

Toulmin Smith, J (1849) *Government by Commissions Illegal and Pernicious* (London: Edward Stafford)

Toulmin Smith, J (1851) *Local Self Government and Centralisation* (London: J Chapman)

Toulmin Smith, J (1857) *Local Self-Government Unmystified* (London: H Sweet)

Toulmin Smith, J (1859) *The Parish Its Powers and Obligations* (London: H Sweet)

Secondary sources

Backstrom, P N (1974) *Christian Socialism and Cooperation in Victorian England* (London: Croom Helm)

Brundage, A (1990) *England's Prussian Minister: Edwin Chadwick and the Politics of Government Growth 1832–54* (Philadelphia, PA: Penn State University)

Claeys, G (2010) *Imperial Sceptics. British Critics of Empire* (Cambridge: Cambridge University Press)

Corcoran, P (1983) *Before Marx: Socialism and Communism in France 1830–1848* (London: Macmillan)

Edsall, N C (1971) *The Anti-Poor Law Movement* (Manchester: Manchester University Press)

Everett, E M (1939) *The Party of Humanity* (Chapel Hill, NC: University of North Carolina Press)

Fry, G K (1970) *The Growth of Government* (London: Frank Cass)

Goldman, L (2002) *Science, Reform and Politics in Victorian Britain: The Social Science Association 1857–1886* (Cambridge: Cambridge University Press)

Hamlin, C (1998) *Public Health and Social Justice in the Age of Chadwick* (Cambridge: Cambridge University Press)

Harrison, J F C (1954) *History of the Working Men's College* (London: Routledge and Kegan Paul)

Harrison, R (1959) 'E S Beesly and Karl Marx' in *International Review of Social History*, Vol 4, No 1 (April), pp. 22–58 and Vol 4, No 2 (August), pp. 208–38

Harrison, R (1963) *Before the Socialists: Studies in Labour and Politics* (London: Routledge and Kegan Paul)

Kent, C (1978) *Brains and Numbers: Elitism, Comtism and Democracy in Mid-Victorian England* (Toronto: University of Toronto Press)

Living, S (1928) *A Nineteenth Century Teacher: John Henry Bridges* (London: Kegan Paul)

Lubenow, W C (1971) *The Politics of Government Growth: Early Victorian Attitudes towards State Intervention* (London: David and Charles)

Mack, E and Armytage, W (1952) *Thomas Hughes* (London: Ernest Benn)

McCabe, J (1908) *Life and Letters of George Jacob of Holyoake* (London: Watts)

McGee, J E (1931) *A Crusade for Humanity: The History of Organised Positivism in England* (London: Watts)

Masterman, N C (1963) *John Malcolm Ludlow* (Cambridge: Cambridge University Press)

Matikkala, M (2011) *Empire and Imperial Ambition* (London: I B Tauris)

Norman, E (1987) *The Victorian Christian Socialists* (Cambridge: Cambridge University Press)

Raven, C R (1920) *Christian Socialism 1848–1854* (London: Macmillan)

Roach, J (1978) *Social Reform in England 1780–1880* (London: Batsford)

Stubbs, C W (1900) *Charles Kingsley and The Christian Social Movement* (London: Blackie and son)

Vogeler, M (1984) *Frederic Harrison: Vocations of a Positivist* (Oxford: Clarendon Press)

Wallas, G (1923) *Jeremy Bentham*, lecture reprinted in *Political Science Quarterly*, March

Weinstein, B (2008) 'Local Self Government is True Socialism' in *English Historical Review*, Vol 133, pp. 1193–1228

Wohl, A (1977) *The Eternal Slum* (London: Edward Arnold)

Wohl, A (1983) *Endangered Lives: Public Health in Victorian Britain* (London: Dent)

Wright, T R (1986) *The Religion of Humanity: The Impact of Comtean Positivism on Victorian Britain* (Cambridge: Cambridge University Press)

9   The socialist revival, land and housing reform

The revival of land reform agitation

The late 1870s also saw a revival of agitation for land reform. In 1878 an anonymous pamphlet appeared on *Our Land*, published as *No 1 of Papers for the People By One of Them*, though I have not been able to trace any subsequent pamphlets in the series. The pamphlet does however bear some similarities with other writings of the O'Brienite, Alfred A Walton. The pamphlet reviews a range of options for land reform and while sharing the view of John Stuart Mill and the Land Tenure Reform Association, criticised its proposed plan to tax the increment in land value as impractical, as 'a more practical man would have seen at once the impossibility of distinguishing the source of increment and that the attempt to do so would lead to endless contention and litigation, costing, with the valuation, probably more than it was worth'. The author argued that 'the only practicable method is to make the land national property and the simplest way of doing this is to give landlords in exchange an annuity of equivalent value' (anonymous, 1878).

Henry George's *Progress and Poverty* was published in 1879. In 1880, a group of George's followers in England established the Land Reform Union. Henry Champion, editor of the *Christian Socialist* was treasurer; the secretary was R P B Frost. The Union's objective was stated simply as 'The Restitution of the Land to the People'. It published a number of short pamphlets, including *Land Common Property* by the Birmingham former Chartist John Sketchley, and *The Right to the Use of the Earth* by J L Joynes, an Eton schoolmaster who had accompanied George on his tour of Ireland, who were both to be founding members of the Democratic Federation, established under the leadership of Henry Hyndman the following year. Joynes' short pamphlet reprinted an extract from Herbert Spencer's *Social Statics*. Sketchley gave an erudite history of arguments for land nationalisation with quotations from Judge Blackstone, Archdeacon Paley, Julius Caesar and William Cobbett, followed by an analysis of the unequal distribution of land ownership in England and Scotland concluding with the argument that there were enough resources for everybody:

> Why then should England be dependent on the foreigner? Let us then restore the land to the people. Let the ground rents be paid into the National Exchequer. Let fixity of tenure by lease be secured to every cultivator. Let all indirect taxes cease. On this question let there be no compromise. Let principle not expediency be our guide. Let the happiness of the whole people, not a part, be our aim. And we shall not have to wait many years before the cry of the land for the people will resound from one end of the country to the other.
>
> (Joynes, 1880)

The republican Charles Bradlaugh, who had previously published pamphlets on land reform, issued a programme for a Land Reform Convention. This included a compensation scheme for compulsory purchase of uncultivated land. He convened a conference in January 1880 at St James' Hall in London. This attracted contributions from Joseph Arch and Thomas Burt, both now MPs, as well as a representative of the London Trades Council, J Grout, who announced that the Trades Council supported land nationalisation. The meeting established a Land Law Reform League. Based in Mile End, with R Forder of the National Secular Society as secretary, the French republican and former IWMA council member, Le Lubez, as treasurer and Peter Taylor MP, Edward Aveling, Annie Besant, Joseph Arch, Alexander MacDonald, Stewart Headlam and Ashton Dilke all as vice presidents, Bradlaugh himself taking the presidency. An attempt to convert the organisation to supporting land national-isation failed. The organisation seems to have achieved little, though it did publish a leaflet opposing payment of state pensions to members of the royal family and other aristocrats. Bradlaugh nevertheless retained considerable influence amongst London's radical clubs.

The rediscovery of the East End

The mid and late Victorian period also saw a growth of middle class interest in hous-ing conditions, with a focus on London's East End. The editor of *The Builder*, George Godwin, had published in 1854 *Long Shadows: a Glance at the Homes of the Thousands*. The Charity Commissioner, Thomas Hare, had published in 1862, a polemic *Usque ad Coelum: Thoughts on the Dwellings of the People, Charitable Estates, Improvement and Local Government in the Metropolis*. In 1873, the Charity Organisation Society published its report on *Dwellings of the Poor*, based on the work of a committee of MPs, representatives of dwelling companies, Medical Officers of Health and other clerics and professionals including Godwin and the COS secretary C B P Bosanquet. Octavia Hill published her essays on *Homes of the London poor* in 1875. In 1883, the journalist G R Sims published an illustrated book of *How the Poor Live* and in the same year, the Congregationalist, Andrew Mearns, published *The Bitter Cry of Outcast London: An Enquiry into the Condition of the Abject Poor*. William Booth's *In Darkest England and the way out* was published later – in 1890.

The London Trades Council also began to give attention to housing. In 1882, the Trades Council gave evidence before the Select Committee of the House of Commons on Artisans and Labourers Dwelling Improvements. Their representative, T Eckford Powell, argued that the state should build working class suburban housing, that rent payment should be postponed in times of depression, and that the artisan tenant should eventually become the owner of the house. Homes for the poorest should be subsidised from the rates. This position was also supported by the trade unionist and former London Trades Council secretary, George Howell in an article on *The Dwellings of the Poor in the Nineteenth Century* (cited in Stedman-Jones, 1971, p. 226). In 1884 the Trades Council had a meeting with the Wholesale Co-operative Society at which a presentation was given by Benjamin Jones on a scheme for housing of the working classes.

George Shipton, the Trades Council secretary, presented its evidence to the Royal Commission on Housing of the Working Classes in 1884. Shipton's main argument was that the provisions of the 1875 Act were not being enforced by most vestries and that the provisions should be compulsory and not just permissive. He also argued that municipal authorities who demolished unfit houses should be required to 'first provide suitable and sufficient home accommodation for those about to be displaced before they are turned adrift'. He stated that 'it is totally impossible that private enterprise, philanthropy, and charity can ever keep pace with the present demands, and those involved in the rapid increase of population. . . What the individual cannot do the State municipality must seek to accomplish'. He also proposed that for lowest income households, who could not pay a rent sufficient to cover the building cost, the municipality should let the tenancies at a loss. Shipton also pointed out that when working people are displaced from central London to the suburbs, they may have to spend two hours getting to work and back. They could not afford the train fares and the train companies could not afford to subsidise their fares. (*Commissioners on the Housing of the Working Classes* 1884–5 – evidence, pp. 475–81)

One of the most vigorous campaigners against inaction by the vestries was Samuel Brighty, a member of the Clerkenwell vestry, who had political experience from his previous role as a paid agent of the Reform League. Brighty was highly critical of his vestry colleagues and the vestry clerk and was also called as a witness at the Royal Commission on the Housing of the Working Classes in 1894. The Commission paid special attention to the problems of Clerkenwell, summoning the vestry clerk, W Robson, who later published a pamphlet defending his record. Sir Charles Dilke, the Commission chairman, attacked the vestry in parliament. At the Commission hearings, Brighty together with another vestryman, Thomas Jennings, gave a number of examples of schemes, including road improvement schemes and a new development by the Peabody Trust, which had led to displacement of existing residents. Brighty's main argument was that schemes should be undertaken incrementally to avoid displacement. He also argued that the cost should be spread rather than carried solely by the local vestry and suggested that a new central authority should be established.

The Commission appears to have accepted many of the arguments put to them. They agreed that there should be a reform of the London government system, and that the government should be empowered to require a municipal authority who was failing to do so to carry out improvements. They also proposed a more favourable arrangement for the Public Works Loan Board to provide local authorities with loans to fund the provision of new dwellings. They also supported the argument that sudden clearances should be avoided and that 'it should be made compulsory for displacement and rebuilding to be as nearly as possible simultaneous'. They proposed taxing vacant land to put pressure on landowners to bring sites forward for development. Perhaps most controversially, they supported the principle of betterment – that rates should be levied in a higher measure upon the property which derives a distinct and direct advantage from an improvement, quoting American legislation as a precedent. The Commission also responded to Shipton's comments about train fares and suggested that the Workmen's Trains legislation should be strengthened to compel all train companies to provide cheap workmen's trains earlier in the morning.

It is also relevant to refer to the campaign of Henry Broadhurst on leasehold reform. Broadhurst was a stonemason and secretary of the Trades Union Congress from 1875, who became a Liberal MP in 1880, and was later to become a junior Minster in the Home Office in Gladstone's 1885 government. He was a member of the Royal Commission and after the defeat of Gladstone's administration in 1886, he returned to his previous post at the TUC. Broadhurst wrote a memorandum on leasehold reform which was published as an annex to the Commission report. His main objective was to make it easier for the working classes to be able to own their own homes, by cutting the legal costs of acquisition. His proposal was that the municipal authority should pay the legal costs and then attach a charge of 2 per cent to the property, with the charge repaid on resale. The municipal body would therefore retain a register of ownership and charges. The proposal was supported by six other members of the sixteen-member commission, including Jesse Collings, Samuel Morley and Cardinal Manning. Broadhurst expanded on these proposals in a book on *Leasehold Enfranchisement* written with Robert Reid and published in 1885.

The work of the Royal Commission eventually led to the 1890 Housing of the Working Classes Act. In 1885, Conservative politicians including Lord Salisbury and C T Ritchie, the President of the Local Government Board collaborated with the Lord Mayor of London to convene a conference of housing philanthropists. This led to the establishment of the Mansion House Council on the Dwellings of the Poor. With the Lord Mayor as president and a grouping of Bishops, other religious leaders, including the Chief Rabbi and some members of the House of Lords as vice-presidents, the work of the Council was undertaken by its secretary, W Craies, its medical officers, Dr Louis Parkes and Dr A H Hogarth and its architect, Keith Young. There was also an executive committee including LCC members, N L Cohen and Hon Rupert Guinness, Rev Samuel Barnett of Toynbee Hall and a number of representatives of the local sanitary committees. The chair of its sanitary committee was James Hole, the Leeds housing reformer, who had returned to London. The Council's objects were:

1   To study all questions relating to Housing and sanitation, especially in London and its suburbs, to watch parliamentary action, and to influence public opinion in connection with the same, and generally act as a bureau of investigation in regard to such matters.
2   To encourage and press for efficient sanitary administration on the part of Central and Local Authorities, and to undertake inspection where expedient for testing the efficiency of such administration.
3   To form, and assist the work of, Sanitary Aid committees in London and its suburbs, and to affiliate to the Council, when desired, any other societies or committees working on similar lines within that area.

The Council issued instructions to local committees, stressing that 'it is imperatively necessary that no distribution of charity shall be made in the name of local committees, as that is not the object of the Mansion House Council on the Dwellings of the Poor' (Mansion House Council on Dwellings of the Poor. Reports – 1890–1906).

The Council's main focus was on sanitary measures and control of existing dwellings rather than new building. The Council also argued that the LCC should have powers to intervene if the local vestry (after 1900 the local council) refused to do so.

Socialists, Fabians, the radical clubs and land nationalisation

Many of the O'Brienites and other veterans of the IWMA and the Land and Labour League were to take their views on land nationalisation into the new socialist organisations founded in the early 1880s. The most significant of these new organ-isations was the Democratic Federation founded by Henry Hyndman in 1881, which was to become the Social Democratic Federation in 1884. The Democratic Federation was a combination of a wide range of radical traditions – the radical conservatism of Hyndman and his fellow Tory MP, Butler Johnston; positivists such as E S Beesly and Henry Crompton; Joseph Cowen, the Newcastle advanced Liberal MP; the veteran Owenite and Christian socialist, Lloyd Jones; the German and Austrian exile republicans such as Adam Weiler, Andreas Scheu and Herman Jung; the London O'Brienites, members of London radical and republican clubs such as Edwin Dunn, John Williams and J Lord; ultra radicals and land campaigners such as the journalist Morrison Davidson, Gavin Clark and Helen Taylor, who was Mill's step-daughter; radicals from the Magna Charter association; the Irish nationalist Justin McCarthy; the ethicist Herbert Burrows; the secularist Annie Besant and the disillusioned Liberal, William Morris. Dunn and Lord both had key roles in setting up the original meetings with Hyndman and in writing the Democratic Federation manifesto. Given the role of the O'Brienites and land reformers in establishing the Democratic Federation, it is not surprising that the land issue was prominent in the organisation's programme, despite the fact that Hyndman, following Marx, had little interest in the issue, nor did William Morris.

It should be noted that the East End radicals maintained their own organisational base. In 1882, Ambrose Barker, Joseph Lane, Frank Kitz and Tom Lemon of the Stratford Radical and Dialectical Club established the Labour Emancipation League, based at Mile End, which included nationalisation of land, mines and transport in its programme, before joining the renamed Social Democratic Federation in 1884, which then adopted key elements of its programme.

The founding document of the Democratic Federation was Hyndman's *England for All*, copies of which the author handed out to the attendees of the first meeting. The first chapter was entitled 'The Land'. Most of the chapter is historical. It does however conclude with a programme:

> Reform of the law of settlement and entail, putting an end to the existing system altogether.

> Compulsory registration of title, so as to make transfer of land as easy as it is in America.

> Extension of the powers of local bodies to acquire land for all purposes and lease it in small portions.

> Compensated expropriation of property-owners in large cities.

This programme is accompanied by a footnote:

> 'Nationalisation' of the land is, of course, the only logical outcome of any thorough suggestion for reform; but this, unless accompanied by nationalisation of railways and of capital, would be of little use to the mass of the workers of the country. Meanwhile, however, the only safe course is to work in the direction of steadily restricting the rights of private property in land.

The section continues:

> The nation has always both the power and the right to take any land at a fair valuation. By immediate limitation of the right of inheritance, and an application of the power of purchase, the State or the local authority would speedily come into possession of land, which could be used for the common interest, and some comfort and security obtained for those who at present have neither.

> (Hyndman, 1881)

In its early years the Democratic Federation was active on the issue of rents in London. The O'Brienite Manhood Suffrage League had in 1880 run a campaign in favour of municipal housing, though abandoned when the agitation to improve properties led to evictions and rent increases. In 1881, the Democratic Federation announced that 'it had taken up the question of Fair Rents in London and intended to carry out a vigorous agitation for Rental and Sanitary Reform' (Labour Standard 24 November 1881, cited in Englander, 1973, p. 103). Hyndman claimed in a letter to Helen Taylor that the appointment of the Royal Commission on Housing of the Working Classes was a recognition of the socialist presence (cited in Englander, 1973, p. 104). The rent agitation was rather lacking in success, with the anarchist leaning SDF member Frank Kitz later commenting that the agitation had had 'about as much effect upon the masses as trying to tickle an elephant with straw' (*Voice of Labour* 18 Jan 1907, cited in Englander, 1973, p. 105).

In 1884, the Democratic Federation published a *Summary of the Principles of Socialism*, written jointly by Hyndman and Morris and signed by all the members of the executive committee. This included a policy on land:

> We claim then the land for the people, that the soil of our country with whatever is useful or beautiful in or upon it, should no longer be held by a small minority for their aggrandisement and greed, but that it should be owned by all for all collectively, to be occupied, cultivated, enjoyed, mined or built over as the majority of people shall see fit to ordain. That the economical forms are not yet fully ready for the completest development of agricultural management is no reason why a handful of persons should draw vast revenues from a monopoly fraudulently seized from their countrymen; still less why the land in towns and the minerals below the land in country should be held for the benefit of the few.

> (Hyndman and Morris, 1884)

Later in 1884, Morris took a group opposed to Hyndman out of the newly renamed Social Democratic Federation into a new organisation which was named the Socialist League and which immediately established the *Commonweal* newspaper. The manifesto of the new organisation was however more critical of land nationalisation:

> Nationalisation of the land alone, which many earnest and sincere persons are now preaching, would be useless so long as labour was subject to the fleecing of surplus value inevitable under the Capitalist system ... no number of merely

administrative changes, until the workers are in possession of all political power, would make any real approach to Socialism.

(Socialist League, 1885a)

The second edition of the manifesto published in July 1885 added a note by Morris and Ernest Belfort Bax:

Now that the feudal system with the consequent public duties of the landowner is abolished, land is but one of the forms of capital. The land that a factory stands upon is part of the constant capital of the manufacturer, just as much as the building is, or the machinery within it. A landowner's rent for his land is exactly analogous to a money-lender's interest on his money; it is one of the many forms of squeezing surplus value from labour.

(Socialist League, 1885b)

It is now appropriate to return to review the progress of the land nationalisation movement. In 1881, Alfred Russell Wallace, the naturalist, published a book on *Land Nationalisation: Its Necessity and Aims*, and then initiated the Land Nationalisation Society, which was 'established to equitably restore to the Nation the Land of the Nation, so that all may equally benefit by the revenue from the Land and have equal facilities to use and enjoy it.' Wallace had in his youth attended meetings of the Owenite Hall of Science and in his memoir referred to Owen as 'my first great teacher in the philosophy of human nature and my first guide through the labyrinth of social science' (Wallace, 1908; Clements, 1983). As mentioned above, he had been an active member of Mill's Land Tenure Reform Association. The land agitation in Ireland reactivated his interest in the land issue, and in November 1880 he had written an article for the *Contemporary Review* on *How to Nationalise the Land* (Peacock, 1961, p. 31).

Wallace criticised the Liberal Cobden Club's proposals for Free Trade in Land, as advocated in George Brodrick's *English Land and English Landlords*. He argued that the labourer 'had a right to refuse to be treated as a mere portion of the farming stock, to be housed well or ill as the landlord chooses'. Wallace argued that free trade would add to the evils of landlordism and the engrossing of land rather than stop it (Peacock, 1961, p. 33).

Wallace was himself president of the Society, with vice presidents – Desmond Fitzgerald, E D Girdlestone, Professor Newman and Helen Taylor. Members of the executive committee included E T Craig (former leader of the Ralahine Owenite settlement), Charles Murray and the publisher W Reeves. Gavin Clark, William Saunders and David Urquart also joined the organisation. The first report of the society included some fifty-seven names including Stewart Headlam (of the Guild of St Matthew), Ben Lucraft (now a member of the London School Board), R P B Frost, Robert Dick and H S Salt. The Society ran a lecture programme and published a series of pamphlets.

The social democrats, as well as supporting Wallace's organisation, also attempted to capture the Land Reform Union. In 1884, just after Henry George had started his tour of Britain (apparently at the invitation of Helen Taylor), Champion and Frost tried to persuade the LRU leadership to endorse the Social Democrats' position on land nationalisation. George himself made it clear that he was opposed to both land nationalisation and socialism. The challenge was resisted and the LRU was re-established as the English Land Restoration League, with an explicit Georgeite single tax programme (Peacock, 1961, p. 51).

The English Land Restoration League then ran its own lecture programme and published a series of leaflets, including extracts from Henry George's work and pamphlets by Helen Taylor, Sidney Webb and a number of Liberal MPs. Though London based, both the ELRL and the LNS seemed to focus their attention on the provinces. The ELRL propaganda was targeted mainly at agricultural labourers. The Christian Socialist, Frederick Verinder, was its secretary, and Stewart Headlam its treasurer. Its general committee included Helen Taylor, Tom Mann and W C Steadman of the London County Council. The LNS sent yellow vans around the country to distribute their propaganda, while the ELRL used red vans.

It is however significant that working class radicals and trade unionists do not appear to have been active in either organisation, with the exception of Charles Murray who wrote a poem *Free Land for a Free Society* for the Land Nationalisation Society.

It should be recognised that the LNS approach was based on Wallace's support for nationalisation rather than just taxation of land value and was more fundamentalist than the position of the ELRL. In an appendix to the third edition of *Land Nationalisation*, Wallace argued that the principle of nationalisation was also applicable to house property. Wallace envisaged that freeing up access to agricultural land would lead to an outflow of population from the congested areas of large towns to the countryside where they could build homes – artisans who had moved to the cities to get work would be able to return to their home towns. While this would ease some of the pressure in urban areas, he argued that it would still be necessary for the State or the municipality to become the sole ground-landlord in urban areas, while every householder should be able to obtain possession of his house or premises on the easiest terms.

> Every municipality should have the power to take any land required for the use of its inhabitants, either for health and recreation, for the sites of public buildings, or for the erection of dwelling houses, paying only the official valuation price.
>
> (Wallace, 1882)

The middle class based Fabian Society, founded in 1884, was somewhat ambivalent on the issue of land nationalisation. Their founding statement, the *Fabian Basis*, included

> to work for the extinction of private property in land, and of the consequent individual appropriation, in the form of rent, of the price paid for permission to use the earth, as well as for the advantages of superior soils and sites.

Tract 7, *Capital and Land*, written by Sidney Olivier, and published in 1888 consisted of an appeal to land nationalisers to support the nationalisation of industrial capital. It also proposed that the English Land Restoration League – single tax followers of Henry George – should support taxation of all income and not just income from land. The 1890 tract on *Practical Land Nationalisation* written by Sidney Webb while reasserting the principle of collective ownership sought a compromise between the land nationalisers and the land taxers by proposing what they referred to as a practical programme. This had four points: public rights in land were to be preserved; taxation of land values was supported; private rights of individual landowners should be limited and public authorities (such as the new London County Council) should take over all leading public services.

In 1885, Joseph Chamberlain published his *Radical Programme*. While the programme discussed the land reform proposals of George and Wallace, it was inconclusive arguing only that municipalities should control land transactions while a progressive income tax of up to 10 per cent should be introduced on the highest incomes. The programme instead focused on housing as the key challenge. While Lord Salisbury had argued that the state should cover the cost of improving housing, Chamberlain argued that the costs should fall on the owners. He commented that 'the working classes are at last realising the true extent of their sufferings, and it is high time for Parliamentary Reformers to show themselves aware of the fact.' The programme proposed that local authorities should be able to purchase land at market value as fixed by an arbitrator 'with no allowance for prospective value or compulsory sale', what today would be referred to as existing use value. It should also be made an offence, punishable by heavy penalties, to hold property unfit for human habitation. The housing chapter of the programme concluded:

> The state has too long made itself the champion of the rights of the individual; it must now assert the rights of the many – of all. It is apparent that in open competition the fittest obtain more than they deserve, and the less fit come too near perishing.
>
> (Chamberlain et al. 1885)

The London Liberal and Radical Union also engaged in the housing debate. On 8th February 1889, its council adopted a set of policies on the housing of the working classes, which were then adopted at a meeting in St James Hall on 14th February. This included:

1 Opposition to eviction without rehousing;
2 The London County Council should be given powers to prevent overcrowding and to prohibit the use of insanitary dwellings;
3 The LCC should be given powers to acquire land and 'erect and hold dwellings for the industrial classes, and manage and let the same direct to tenants of those classes. That in erecting such dwellings, special regard should be had to the health and convenience of the probable tenants'.
4 In fixing rents of tenants, the LCC 'should take into consideration the character and condition of the district'.
5 The funding of the housing programme to come from a tax on developed and undeveloped land.
6 Compensation for any tenants evicted for improvements made under the authority of parliament.

Some of these provisions had been included in a Bill promoted the previous year by the Liberal MP, R T Reid, apparently supported by a number of the London working men's clubs, while all the provisions were to be promoted in a new Bill by another Liberal MP, Professor James Stuart, leading member of the Metropolitan Reform League, who was later elected as an LCC alderman and was leader of the LCC progressives between 1890 and 1892.

A detailed justification of the proposals was published by the Liberal Publication department in an 1889 pamphlet by J Theodore Dodd on *The Housing of the Working Classes*, which also summarised the report of the Royal Commission. The pamphlet concluded with a peroration:

> Let me conclude by saying that the Liberal party must now begin an AGITATION which shall grow and never cease till every working man in London can have, at a fair rent Three Rooms and a Scullery.
>
> One room for self and wife, one for the sons and daughters, for comfort health and decency; that 'thy sons may grow up as the young plants and thy daughters as the polished corners of the Temple',

followed by the rather more practical point

> But to obtain such Homes the men of London must send to parliament forty or fifty Liberal and Radical members all pledged to obtain them.
>
> (Dodd, 1889)

The London progressives were also involved in a conference on Housing of the People in April 1890 at the National Liberal Club. It was chaired by James Stuart MP, with Theodore Dodd as secretary. The conference included representatives of the London Liberal and Radical Union, the Metropolitan Radical Federation and the Mansion House Council on the Dwellings of the poor. Attendees included Emma Cons, recently elected as an LCC alderman, Sidney Webb and Stewart Headlam. It set up five sub committees, including a committee on London housing, led by Benjamin Costelloe, LCC member for Stepney, and a financial sub committee led by Sidney Webb. The financial and compensation committee, which included R T Reid MP, R K Causton MP, Theodore Dodd and the Fabian and Metropolitan Radical Federation adviser, Graham Wallas, produced its own report, which in effect endorsed the London progressives' position as set out in the Reid and Stewart bills and Dodd's previous pamphlet. The report opposed funding from an increase in the rates or from indirect taxation, arguing that there was no alternative to a tax on property and that councils should be able to raise a levy on all property owners through the landlord's property tax component of schedule A to income tax. The report also proposed a tax on property on death of the owner.

Not all the London radical clubs joined the Democratic Federation. In 1886, the combined club federations of Chelsea, Hackney and Finsbury established the Metropolitan Radical Federation (MRF), which became the representative body of the working class left of the Liberal party and rivalled the official London Liberal and Radical Union which was formed in 1887 (Davis, 1989). From its origin, the MRF supported Irish nationalism and land reform and republicanism. In 1887, it organised a protest against Queen Victoria's Jubilee celebrations. It also campaigned on the issues of unemployment and free speech. In 1894, the MRF established a lecture bureau 'to provide lecturers and speakers at club meetings and public demonstrations'. Its executive met on a monthly basis.

The MRF collaborated with the Social Democratic Federation and other socialist organisations. It was actually the MRF, not the SDF, which called the Trafalgar Square demonstrations in 1887, including the event which became known as 'bloody Sunday'. The MRF also actively participated in elections, with individual clubs initiating radical candidacies, sometimes ousting the 'official' Liberal Party representatives. Radical candidates stood in council and school board elections. The MRF supported the proposals in Sydney Webb's *London Programme*, which became the basis of the progressives' election manifesto in the 1892 London County Council elections. James Timms, the MRF secretary was elected as LCC member for Battersea, while Aeneas Smith of the MRF and the Eleusis Club, was elected for Chelsea. Both joined the progressive group together with nine Labour members.

During the 1890s some of the radical clubs, notably those in the East End, affiliated to the ILP, and later to the Labour Representation Committee and the Labour Party. The Eleusis club in Chelsea however put up James Jeffrey, the MRF chair, as an independent radical in the 1900 general election. The MRF and individual clubs opposed the Boer war, at a time the Fabian Society was divided on the issue. Many of London's socialists were active participants in individual clubs and in the MRF, including Herbert Burrows, Graham Wallas and John Scurr, the latter becoming a Labour MP in Tower Hamlets, having been the MRF's lecture secretary. The MRF had no leader, with the chairmanship rotating between representatives of the different radical clubs, which may explain why it receives so little coverage in most of the histories of the period. It however played a significant role in London politics. According to one observer, it could put 50,000 people onto the streets in a few hours.

In December 1897, the MRF published the *Radical Programme* as its political manifesto, under the names of H A Rundlett, MRF secretary and Bessie Biddlecombe, MRF assistant secretary.

> The Liberal Party was defeated in 1895 because the confidence of the People in the Liberal leaders had been shaken. Even the almost unprecedented combination of monopolies and vested interests would have been powerless to return Lord Salisbury to power, if the mass of workers had believed the Liberal leaders to be earnestly desirous of carrying out the Radical reforms to which they were pledged.
>
> The Radical Programme.
>
> (A)   FOR THE FIRST RADICAL BUDGET –
>
> > 1 Payment of Members and of Election Expenses
> > 2 Abolition of the Breakfast Table Duties
> > 3 Old Age Pensions
> > 4 Taxation of Land Values
>
> (B)   AS SOON AS MAY BE –
>
> > 5 Home Rule All Round
> > 6 Universal Suffrage
> > 7 Registration Reform
> > 8 Second Ballot
>
> (C)   IF THE LORDS REJECT OR MUTILATE THESE –
>
> > 9 Abolition of the House of Lords

We submit these proposals to the consideration of Radicals with confidence and hope, believing that upon them may be grounded an appeal to which the electorate will respond with enthusiasm. We do not set forth our Programme as the last word on Social and Political Reform. It is rather the first step; but it is a step worth the making. There is no proposal in this pamphlet which cannot easily be realised. If the Liberal 'leaders' are in earnest, and mean to abide by their pledges, they will be realised. If the present leaders are not prepared to take the lead, other men will lead the Radical Party to an assured triumph for Justice and Freedom over Privilege and Monopoly.

(Metropolitan Radical Federation, 1897)

The programme argued that the taxation of land values was the best way for the government to raise revenues to fund old age pensions, the 'freeing of the breakfast table' and the payment of salaries of members of parliament, which would remove the dependence of working class members in trade union sponsorship. To take the step of taxing land would be

a step towards crippling the power of the land monopolist, while at the same time giving the people cheaper food, lightening the terrors of old age, and democratising the House of Commons, might form a worthy ambition for a Radical chancellor of the Exchequer.

The London progressives and the London County Council

The debates over housing and land tax became a central feature of the debates over the reform of the London governance structure which led up to the establishment of the London County Council in 1889 and the replacement of vestries by borough councils through the London Government Act of 1899. The 1880s had seen a radicalisation of the London Liberal Party, with the clubs pushing for more radical policies as well as working class representation in parliament, on the London School Board, and on the London County Council. As shown by John Davis (Davis, 1989), both the discussions at the Housing of the Working Class Commission and in parliament over the 1884 London Government Bill had used the criticism of vestry performance on slum clearance and housing provision to support the case for the establishment of a new London wide governance body.

The increased radicalisation on the Liberal Party nationally as demonstrated by the adoption of the Newcastle programme by the October 1891 conference of the National Liberal Federation is often portrayed by historians, for example in McBriar's *Fabian Socialism and English Politics* (McBriar, 1962) as a victory by the London progressives over the established provincial Liberal leadership. This tends to focus on the role of Sydney Webb in the London Liberal and Radical Union and the similarities of the Newcastle programme to Webb's London programme published earlier in the year.

The Newcastle programme was similar to Webb's position in not going as far as supporting land nationalisation, but endorsed the position of the ELRL which was supported by the London progressives, including the repeal of the laws of primogeniture and entail, freedom of sale and transfer, the just taxation of land values and ground rents, compensation to town and country tenants for both disturbance and improvement and the enfranchisement of leaseholds. The programme also called for full municipal powers for the LCC and all other municipalities, including the control of its own gas and water supplies, markets and police; the taxation of ground values and other financial reforms.

Many of these proposals can be traced back to Chamberlain's radical programme. Webb and his fellow Fabians may have contributed facts to support the arguments, but the adoption of the Newcastle programme and the programme of the London progressives reflected a wider movement for change among middle class and working class radicals not just in London but also in core Liberal centres such as Birmingham, Manchester, Sheffield and Newcastle which had their own histories of municipal radicalism. The Fabian historiography tends to focus on the changes in party policy rather than on the fact that the Liberal government of 1892 to 1895 failed to implement much of the programme. In a pamphlet in 1893, *How it Strikes a Radical*, the LCC radical, William Saunders, who was also MP for Walworth between 1892 and 1895, referred to the waste of the first year by Gladstone's ministry in not seeking to carry forward the Newcastle programme, arguing that the Cabinet still represented the class interests of the landlords and excluded Labour and were driving the political train in the opposite direction to the one on which they had been elected. Saunders argued that the focus on home rule for Ireland had led to the sacrifice of social progress in England, Wales and Scotland.

With the establishment of the Independent Labour Party (ILP) in 1893, some working class radicals transferred their affiliations. Some of the London radical clubs joined the ILP, but the ILP was relatively weak in London, despite Keir Hardie's election as MP for West Ham (which was actually just outside the LCC area) in 1892. John Burns elected in Battersea in 1892, represented the Battersea Labour League and was supported by the Liberal Party. Howell, elected for Bethnal Green North East in 1885, 1886 and 1892 sat as a Liberal. Cremer was elected for Haggerston in 1885, 1886 and 1892 as a Liberal. W C Steadman, former secretary of the TUC, elected for Stepney in 1898, was a Liberal. After Keir Hardie's defeat in 1895, Labour did not in fact have an MP sitting for a seat in the London area until 1903 when Will Crooks was elected as Labour MP with Liberal support. The trade unionist, Will Thorne, a member of the SDF, was elected for West Ham South in 1906. In 1910, George Lansbury was elected as MP for Poplar, again with Liberal support. There were no other Labour MPs in the London area until after the First World War.

Both LCC progressives and some London working class Liberal MPs, Burns and Steadman having dual roles, nevertheless were actively engaged debates on land taxation and housing, and in the early years of the 20th century, in what was referred to as town planning.

The London progressives were actively engaged in a campaign to introduce a land tax. In 1887, the United Committee for the taxation of ground values was established, with Lord Hobhouse as president and Frederik Verinder of the ELRL as secretary. The radical MP and later LCC councillor, William Saunders, was an active member and in 1886 had proposed a motion in parliament for the introduction of a land value tax, referring back to the recommendation of the Royal Commission (Saunders, 1891). As soon as the LCC was in session, even before its powers came into effect, Saunders put forward a proposal to set up an investigation into the adoption of ground values taxation in London and this was agreed with a committee on land valuation established under the chairmanship of J F Torr with Saunders as a member (Saunders, 1892). The committee then put forward a proposed mechanism for taxing land value and recommended that the LCC prepare a parliamentary bill. However, this proposal was not supported by the full LCC and the matter was referred to the Council's Local Government and Taxation committee. That committee accepted that part of the rates should fall on owners rather than occupiers, but did not accept that the basis of rating should be capital values (Saunders 1891).

The LCC was however to accept the principle of betterment. In October 1896, the LCC Housing Committee agreed to promote a number of amendments to the 1890 Act. The previous year, the LCC had promoted an Act relating to the development of the southern approach to Tower Bridge. This Act had included a betterment clause which required contributions to the cost of the redevelopment from landowners who benefited from it. This legislation appears to have been passed by parliament, without recognising the precedent it created. In 1896, the progressive-controlled Housing Committee used the precedent to argue that the LCC, a vestry or district board should have the power to insert a betterment clause into any redevelopment scheme (London County Council, 1900).

The main debate within the LCC was however on whether the LCC should itself undertake a programme of building new working class homes. In 1893, the council built a common lodging house in Drury Lane. It was however not until 1898, following the lobbying of the Workman's Housing Council discussed below, that the LCC's Housing of the Working Classes committee won the support of the Council as a whole to adopt the provisions of the 1890 Act relating to acquiring land for building homes. The moderates tried to block the proposal. In August 1899, the London Trades Council organised a protest meeting in support of the progressives' proposals. One of the challenges faced was the cost of buying land within the LCC area – but the LCC in 1900 won an amendment to the Act to allow them to acquire land in the suburbs and beyond. The first estates were developed in central London between 1892 and 1914. Suburban estates were at Totterdown fields in Tooting, Old Oak in Hammersmith, Norbury in Croydon and White Hart Lane in Tottenham. The architect Robert Williams, who was active in the Workman's Housing Council and a member of the LCC housing committee, persuaded the LCC to focus on building larger homes. When the Moderates won control of the LCC in 1907, they stopped the suburban development programme. The Moderates then tried to sell of part of its Tottenham and Norbury estates, which generated a protest meeting which included representatives of the London Trades Council, the ILP, the SDF, the Workmen's National Housing Council and a number of trade unions (Wohl, 1977).

The 1892, 1895 and 1898 elections generated considerable debate on housing, though in three elections the main controversy was on the record of the public works department, which the Moderates wanted to abolish.

For the 1892 election, the LCC Progressive, William Saunders, published a book which set out the progressive record on the first three years of the LCC. This gave the record of voting and contributions to every substantive debate and decision.

John Burns published two articles on the LCC in the *Nineteenth Century* in March and April, the first under the somewhat provocative title *Towards a Commune*, the second, replying to an attack by R E Prothero, headed *Towards Commonsense*, was titled *Let London Live!* Burns defended the use of the term *commune* – 'a free city in a free country – a community possessing all the powers of a free people for its civic, social and artistic development, uncontrolled by any power other than that to which it voluntarily consents'. He pointed out that 'the revolution in decentralised government and civic control' which had in Paris been achieved by the commune, had been 'secured by the vote of London's craftsmen' (Burns, 1892b, p. 774).

For the 1895 election, the London Liberal and Radical Union manifesto included:

> That the Council should vigorously enforce the Housing Acts against the owners of slum property (while discouraging large and costly schemes on the basis of Cross's Act).
>
> That the County Council shall use its powers to provide proper dwellings, at rents sufficient to secure them from loss, in those parts of the metropolis and suburbs where proper housing for the working population has been swept away or does not exist.
>
> (London Liberal and Radical Union, 1895)

The progressive controlled *Daily Chronicle* published a book length pamphlet defending their record, with illustrations by Walter Crane and Edward Burne-Jones – *New London: Her Parliament and its Work*. In the section on housing, the Moderates were criticised for relying on 'the cheap and hollow expedient of entrusting the industrial dwelling companies with the unrestricted right of planting their barracks on the areas from which the slum-owner has been swept' (*Daily Chronicle*, 1895, p. 44). The progressives' alternative was to provide new cottages in the suburban areas on the basis they could travel back into central London to work on the cheap workmen's trains.

> Of course homes will have to be found for those who must live near to their work; but there is no reason why the citizens of new London, the young ones, at any rate, into whose blood the conservatism of locality has not passed, should not hear the nightingales singing in Epping forest in the summer when the days work is over, or take their children to pick primroses in Bostall Wood in spring-time.
>
> (*Daily Chronicle*, 1895)

Sidney Webb wrote a pamphlet for the London Reform Union on *The Work of the London County Council*. This included a defence of the work of the LCC's Building Act committee which carried a new Act through parliament and the work of the LCC's Public Health and Housing Committee (Webb, 1895, pp. 6–7). Webb had the previous year presented a paper on the *Economic Heresies of the London County Council* to the British Association for the Advancement of Social Science, which had defended the Council's practices of requiring fair wage clauses in contracts and undertaking direct works (Webb, 1894).

For the 1898 elections, the progressives' London Reform Union published leaflets defending their record. In *Progressive Leaflet No 13 – The Housing of the People*, it set out *The Claim of the Workers*:

> The housing problem must be faced. Better dwelling accommodation for the labouring population must be provided. Overcrowding and insanitary areas will

have to be dealt with. Wealth has increased in our midst by leaps and bounds, and the unearned increment has been piled up mainly by the industry of the people; and yet vast numbers of the wage-earners are unable to procure decent accommodation.

The workers of London have largely contributed to the luxury and comfort of mansion and villa, and for the most part they may be said to be all but homeless. Driven into the miserable lodgings of outlying districts, or into the wretched tenements of central areas, they are exposed to the evils and overcrowdings of insanitary surroundings, Death and disease are rampant in their midst. The rate of mortality in these overcrowded areas registers the price paid by the wage-earners for a little breathing space in this great city; and it is a melancholy fact, that the high death-rate in the slums bears a distinct relationship to the rise in ground values.

But the time has now arrived when decent homes at a fair rent must be placed within the reach of the workers. As citizens, they claim to be freed from the tyranny of land monopolists, ground-rent speculators, jerry-builders and slum owners.

The pamphlet also argued that

This want of proper dwellings and consequent overcrowding saps the health and energies of the workers and breeds indifference and despair ... until decent homes are placed within the reach of the labouring population, the work of all the social agencies for the improved condition of the people will to a large extent be counteracted.

(London Reform Union, 1898)

The progressives argued that they needed greater powers to 'deal more rapidly with the clearance of slum property and the erection of healthy dwellings'.

In a separate leaflet – No 14 – *Nine Years Good Work for the People*, the progressives set out a list of 30 achievements. This list included

7   **Demolished whole areas of slums** at Bethnal Green, Deptford, and elsewhere;
8   Erected **Healthy Homes at the lowest possible rents**, Cottage dwellings wherever practicable, and, where Blocks were inevitable, the most comfortable and healthy Flats that can be designed.
9   Opened a **Model Common Lodging House,** in Drury Lane, for homeless men
10 Greatly improved the **Sanitary Administration** all over London, and put down many nuisances and noxious trades.
16 Obtained a New Building Act to put down jerry-building and slum-making
26 promoted in every possible way the direct Taxation of Ground Values
27 established the principle of **Betterment** by introducing into several private Acts provisions levying contributions on Owners whose property is improved.

(London Reform Union, 1898)

Progressive Leaflet No 30 argued the case for taxing *The Unearned Increment,* using the figures in Webb's Fabian pamphlet.

After the election, in 1899, the London Reform Union, a Progressive led organisation which campaigned for the replacement of the vestries, published a pamphlet on *The Housing Problem in London* by C M Knowles. The pamphlet argued that

> the Housing Problem is undoubtedly the most difficult of all the questions with which the London County Council has had to grapple. The magnitude of the population needing re-housing, the tightness of the grip of vested interests, the ever-increasing value of the land, the poverty of the people, the relationship between public and private enterprise – all these factors make the problem seem well-nigh insoluble.
>
> (Knowles, 1899, p. 6)

The purpose of the pamphlet was not just to set out the achievements of the LCC, but also to encourage the new Borough Councils being established under the1899 London Government Act to help the LCC. Knowles pointed that only one vestry, Shoreditch, had carried out a new housing scheme, with a second scheme being undertaken by the Rotherhithe vestry. Knowles argued that the Boroughs had responsibility for clearing away unhealthy areas, and that the council should prepare plans for the erection of working class dwellings, with the council fixing the maximum rent. He concluded that

> It must be recognised that the Housing of the People Question has now reached a critical stage and can no longer be ignored with safety. It has assumed proportions which defy the puny efforts of the local authorities; it demands the anxious and immediate attention of Parliament and calls for statesmanship of the highest order. The occasion calls for legislation of the heroic type; and the nation waits the advent of the statesman who will lead the people out of the bondage of the slum.
>
> (Knowles, 1899, p. 21)

Socialists and home colonisation

The mid 1880s saw a revival of socialist interest in home colonisation.

Herbert Mills, a Unitarian minister in Liverpool and member of the Liverpool Poor Law Guardians published in 1886 *Poverty and the State*, subtitled *Work for the Unemployed*.

In his book, Mills provided a history of the poor laws before reviewing previous attempts at new settlements to respond to unemployment, distinguishing between initiatives he saw as failures and those he viewed as successes. In the first category, he included the phalanxes of Fourier and the national workshops of Louis Blanc. In the second category was the Oneida settlement in the United States, and ET Craig's Ralahine commune in Ireland. Mills's main proposition was that poor law guardians should stop paying dole to the unemployed and instead use the resources to establish co-operative settlements – to buy the land, stock it with cattle and seed and machines 'to enable the inmates to earn their own food, and clothing and shelter. As far as possible competition shall be abolished within the walls of this estate'. The workers would not be paid, but would have housing, clothing and food provided for them.

However once the workers had worked for the co-operative for six hours a day, they would be free to undertake additional work on a commercial basis. The objective was 'to cultivate able and tender men and brave and independent women; and not to accumulate wealth' (Mills, 1886, pp. 183–5).

Mills moved to Kendal in Cumberland in 1887. In 1888 he gave evidence to the House of Lords Select Committee on the Poor Laws, calling on the government to set up a series of land colonies, on which urban workers would learn to live by practicing their skills and trading with one another. Mills established the Home Colonisation Society, which in 1892 acquired a small farm at Starnthwaite, near Kendal. By 1893, some twenty-two settlers were working on the estate. These included Dan Irving of the SDF, later a Labour MP, and the Bristol socialist and feminist Enid Stacy, both of whom were expelled from the colony after challenging Mills on his autocratic style of management. Mills apparently stopped the supply of food to the colony before evicting the dissidents, with the assistance of the police. Irving wrote in the *Clarion* that 'We claim that we have been misled and unfairly treated; having been drawn into this place in the belief that it was a commune, whereas it is an outdoor workhouse conducted on more arbitrary lines than any known to bumbledom' (cited Marsh, 1982, p. 125). In 1900, Mills abandoned the project and handed over the farm to the Christian Union for Social Service (Armytage, 1961; Hardy, 1979; Marsh, 1982). This controversy did not stop A R Wallace, the land nationaliser, from writing a two-part article in the *Socialist Review* in 1908 promoting Mills' book and endorsing his ideas (Wallace, 1908).

Mills' initiative was not the only settlement aimed at housing the unemployed. In London, General William Booth of the Salvation Army, to follow up his 1890 *In Darkest England and the Way Out* polemic, established a colony for the poor of London at Hadleigh in Suffolk in 1891, which had also provided for some of Poplar's unemployed. The project was supported by both Charles Booth and Beatrice Webb (Brown, 1968).

Despite the difficulties experienced by the Starnthwaite project, other socialists were attracted to the idea of home colonies, especially in the context of increasing unemployment in London. In 1895, a conference on Co-operative Labour on the Land was held at Holborn Town Hall, the report of which was edited by the ILPer and economist J A Hobson and published by Swan Sonnenschein (Hobson, 1895). George Lansbury, SDF member and member of the Poplar Guardians, had promoted in his 1893 manifesto the 'formation of Labour colonies for the treatment of the habitual casual and the loafer'. In 1895, however, he denied that he was in favour of 'pauper colonies or in any way perpetuating the workhouse system'. He argued for self-supporting colonies in his evidence to the Select Committee on Unemployment. In his speech to the 1897 central poor law conference, Lansbury stated 'I do not wish for penal settlements, for you will never drive out wickedness by wickedness, you cannot do good work with the devil's tools' (Shepherd, 2002 citing Harris 1972). In 1903, Lansbury was approached by the American philanthropist and land tax reformer, Joseph Fels, who proposed to finance a farm colony for the unemployed of Poplar. Fels, who had already established a Vacant Land Cultivation Society, had originally approached the President of the Local Government Board, Walter Long, with a proposal, but hearing of Lansbury's work in the East End asked Keir Hardie to introduce him to Lansbury. Fels bought a 100-acre farm at Laindon, near Basildon in Essex, which he leased to the Poplar guardians at a peppercorn rent. The farm provided employment in fruit growing and market gardening for 200 men.

This project was followed by a larger colony at Hollesley Bay on the Suffolk coast sponsored by Fels for the London Central Unemployment Board. Fels bought an agricultural training college for would be colonial emigrants, on a 1300-acre estate. Some twenty-two cottages were built, designed by Raymond Unwin. Lansbury was a member of the Central Unemployment Board, where he chaired the Working Colonies Committee and also served with Beatrice Webb on the Royal Commission on the Poor Laws, being a signatory to the Minority Report.

The Hollesley Bay project had three objectives:

1 The provision of special work for periods of exceptional distress.
2 The provision of more continuous work for men who are not only in exceptional need of work, but who have either already lived upon the land, or show a marked aptitude for country life;
3 The establishment of suitable men and families in agricultural or other rural industry in various forms.

(Lansbury,1908, pp. 223–4)

However, in October 1906, the Local Government Board, under the presidency of none other than John Burns declared the Hollesley Bay project ultra vires, and whereas Lansbury had envisaged permanent smallholdings, the Board ruled that the provision of cottages and development of smallholdings were not contemplated by the Unemployed Workmen Act and limited the stay of residents to sixteen weeks. Lansbury protested that this restriction contradicted both the objective of Joseph Fels in funding the scheme and the intentions of the Poplar guardians of permanently resetting the unemployed in a new community. In an article in the ILP's *Socialist Review* in May 1908, Lansbury argued that

The colony is a considerable distance from London – about eighty miles – and is situated eight miles from the nearest railway station. In these circumstances the only justification for its purchase and for the expenditure on fares from London were, firstly, its adaptability for every kind of horticulture and agriculture, and, secondly, the splendid accommodation in the college building, not only for living arrangements, but for educational purposes generally. There would have been no question of buying such an estate merely to serve the purpose of temporary relief.

(Lansbury,1908, p. 225)

Lansbury concluded by criticising Burns for his view that a colony should be 'a sort of semi-penal place of detention where only the most abject failures of society would be sent' and appealing to

the younger men of the Liberal Party to stand side by side with the Socialists in demanding that the Right to Work shall be acknowledged without any reference to the old poor law, but under terms and conditions that will not only preserve to the unemployed their self-respect but lead them on to independence.

(Lansbury, 1908, pp. 232–3)

In a submission to a new Royal Commission in 1909, Lansbury commented that under the new regime 'Hollesley Bay is a glorified workhouse. I think it is a shocking waste of time and money to be sending men all that way merely for sixteen weeks and then letting them come back to London' (Lansbury, 1928; Postgate, 1951; Shepherd, 2002).

In 1938 the London County Council sold the Hollesley Bay colony, which was then converted into a borstal and prison, Jeffrey Archer being one of the more celebrated inmates.

Fred Knee, Robert Williams and the Workman's National Housing Council

The main socialist pressure group on housing in the first decade of the 20th century was the Workman's Housing Council (WHC), formed in 1898 'as a delegate body representing 150 labour organisations, including Trade Unions, Trades Councils, Co-operative Societies, having for its object the provision by public authority of good houses for all its people.'

While Wohl made reference to the work of the WHC in the final chapter of his classic study of housing and social policy in Victorian London (Wohl, 1977) it is through the research of David Englander, undertaken for his (regrettably as yet unpublished) MA dissertation, that we have a detailed study of the origins and role of the organisation (Englander, 1973). The following section relies largely on Englander's dissertation.

A London Workman's Committee on Housing was established in June 1898 by three members of the London Society of Compositors who were employed at the Twentieth Century Press and were also members of the Social Democratic Federation – Fred Knee, Charles Coleman and H W Hobart. While Hobart was well known within the SDF, it was Fred Knee who led the initiative and who became secretary of the Workman's Housing Council formed in September 1898. Knee had been a member of the Frome Liberal and Radical club in Dorset, had embraced socialism on reading the Danish American Laurence Gronlund's *Co-operative Commonwealth* and moved to London in 1891. Knee wrote a diary which was subsequently edited and published by Englander (Englander, 1977), so we have a detailed record of his political activities – Knee joined the Fabian Society, the Chelsea branch of the SDF, the Eleusis radical club, the Chelsea Liberal Council and the Regent Street Polytechnic Parliament, where he established a Social Democratic Party.

Chelsea radicals had a record of activity on housing issues, with the Eleusis club establishing an anti-eviction society, which also campaigned for Millbank and Clerkenwell prison sites to be redeveloped for housing – the first site was redeveloped by the LCC as the Millbank estate; the second was to become a school. Knee was also involved in the Working Men's Home Union formed by the Mile End radical James Hayman, which also established a Fair Rents Union.

The WHC's statement of 'What it Does' states that:

> It promotes annually legislation having for its object the provision of healthy houses. Especially for the poorer section of the working classes;

> It seeks to move local authorities to a sense of their responsibility in the matter of slums and insufficiency of house accommodation, and urges them to use their

present powers for the building of houses while asking for greater powers in that behalf.

It provides lecturers, arranges meetings. Supplies information, publishes leaflets and pamphlets, and issues an official Housing Journal.

(Williams and Knee, 1905, annex)

The WHC's president was W C Steadman, the secretary of the barge builders' union who had just been elected as Lib-Lab MP for Stepney. Steadman was to become president of the Trades Union Congress, secretary of its parliamentary committee and in 1900 the first chairman of the Labour Representation Committee, though he was to stay with the Liberal Party rather than join the Labour Party on its establishment in 1906. The WHC executive committee included Harry Brill of the porters' union, the carpenter alderman George Dew who was also involved in the workmen's trains lobby and who was on the LCC as councillor or alderman between 1895 and 1916 and was on the housing committee between 1901 and 1907, Florence Grove of the Fabian society and Robert Williams, architect and ILP member. Williams had been a member of the executive committee of the Land Nationalisation Society and had argued in an article in *Land and Labour* that 'housing reform then remained closely identified with some form of land taxation'. Williams was also a member of the executive committee of the London Reform Union. He had stood unsuccessfully for the LCC in Woolwich in 1895. He wrote a series of articles on housing in the progressives' journal *London*, which were published by the London Reform Union in 1894 as *More Light and Air for Londoners*.

Williams campaigned for the LCC to adopt more stringent housing standards. He took his campaign to the national conference of the Sanitary Institute and to the Church Congress. He was frustrated by the response he received. In an 1895 pamphlet on *The People and the Nation's Wealth*, he commented:

Never was hypocrisy so abominable as this . . . these people actually tell you, by their discourses, that the labourer to whom they owe their very bread is not worth a home, because the providing of such home cannot be made the means of screwing out a further percentage.

(Williams, 1895, p. 5 cited in Englander, 1973, p. 56)

In an 1897 pamphlet entitled *Face of the Poor or the Crowding of London's Labourers. The Rent they Pay and the Evils they endure*, based on a study of housing conditions in North Lambeth, which had been reported in the *Clarion*, *Labour Leader* and *Justice*, Williams argued that 'First and foremost is the need of breeding a healthy spirit of discontent with their surroundings and conditions among the crowded' and that

considerations of profit over public welfare was at the heart of the matter . . . it seems but idle mockery to talk about pure air and lungs but try to think of acting on a plan and you are met with the hard and impenetrable wall – WILL IT PAY?

Williams noted that T H Huxley had argued that 800 cubic feet was a minimum standard for health and that Benjamin Richardson in *Hygeia* had argued for a maximum density of twenty-five persons a hectare, while the 1894 Building Act had set 150 cubic feet as a minimum room size:

> The palliatives of legislation go but little way after all and cannot go far toward engrafting on the lives of London's working poor the benefits of sanitation, because the very best that is done and reaches the poor is but a compromise ... always weighted against the original intention ... through which the speculator can easily trundle his mud cart.
>
> (Williams, 1897, p. 18 cited in Englander, 1973, pp. 59–60)

Williams argued that overcrowding, which meant that people did not have enough good quality air to breathe, was the result of housing being too expensive. The LCC was limited in what it could achieve so long as it had to pay interest at 3 per cent. Williams presented a detailed analysis of population density in different parts of London. His conclusion was that Londoners be dispersed into the countryside, and that rural residents should be encouraged to stay in the country by being allocated allotments to work, so that they did not have to move to London to get employment (Williams, 1897, p. 20).

Englander recounts the struggle the housing reformers had to separate the housing issue from the issue of land reform. In December 1897, the Land Nationalisation Society held a conference to discuss policy for the forthcoming LCC elections and published a manifesto prioritising both housing reform and rating reform. In January 1898, a London Land Reform committee was established which distributed some 300,000 leaflets. It also campaigned against rent increases on the LCC Boundary Street estate in Bethnal Green and in conjunction with the radical Fred Soutter, against rent increases in Bermondsey. The formation of the WHC was a conscious strategy to set up a separate housing campaign and to seek to avoid the increasingly adversarial rivalry between Wallace's Land Nationalisation Society and the Georgites of the English Land Restoration League. In practice the LNS was to be supportive of the WNC, while the Georgites refused to allow housing to be considered independently of their single tax policy. The WHC therefore initially focused their campaign on calling on the LCC to implement part III of the 1890 Housing of the Working Classes Act – the provisions relating to the provision of working class houses independent of the requirements for the clearance of slums in unhealthy areas. The WHC argued that the LCC should acquire land outside its boundary in order to reduce overcrowding in the central area.

The WHC put its proposals to the LCC Housing Committee who recommended to the full Council that they should defer implementation of part III of the 1890 Act. A second delegation, preceded by lobbying of all LCC members with support of the bricklayers' union, however, persuaded the LCC housing committee to change its mind and agree to implement the provisions. The WHC argued for a programme of 2000 homes. The full LCC carried the proposals in November 1898 with a large majority. It was however only a partial victory as the LCC was not convinced of the argument that they should seek powers to build outside the LCC boundary, though they later conceded to the WHC lobbying and this provision was included in the 1900 Housing of the Working Classes Act.

With its success in London, the WHC decided to extend its campaign nationally, becoming the Workman's National Housing Council (WNHC). Knee presented a paper on *The Financial Side of the Housing Question* to the ILP annual municipal conference in Leicester in 1901. He pointed out that the key housing issue was not slum clearance but the provision of new homes for working people at realistic rents. The sinking fund by which councils could finance new housing required councils to repay compound interest and was too expensive. The loan repayment period should be extended from forty years to sixty years. Knee advocated municipal banking, with the local authority being able to use their assets as security for the loan. He also argued that rents should be no more than a sixth of a household's income.

> It is not the housing of the poor but the housing of the people by the people themselves that we must work for – not the herding into slums for the benefit of private enterprise, not the crowding into barracks in order to provide interest to municipal bondholders but by a feasible, honest system and plan.
>
> (Knee, 1901 cited in Englander, 1973, pp. 89–90)

Following this conference, the WNHC sought to reach agreement with the land reform bodies. John Scurr of the Poplar Labour League and also a member of the executives of both the Metropolitan Radical Federation and the English Land Restoration League (and later Labour MP for Stepney Mile End) proposed that the WNHC draw up a statement on ' the bearing of the land question upon housing'. However at the special meeting with the LNS and ERLR, while Joseph Hyder the LNS secretary supported the WNHC, Frederic Verinder of the ELRL ridiculed doing anything until the taxation of land values had been secured and had an argument with Robert Williams (Englander, 1973, p. 91). The WNHC executive agreed that

> recognising the connection between the land question and the housing question, this meeting urges upon workman's organisations, in addition to compelling the LCC to carry out its housing policy and the local authorities to enforce the rating of empty houses and vacant sites, to press upon their representatives in parliament, the importance of at once taxing land values and of giving municipal authorities the power to acquire land compulsorily at a valuation on a more equitable basis than at present prevails.
>
> (WNHC minutes 4th January 1899 cited in
> Englander, 1973, p. 92)

Knee nevertheless had to continue his argument with the single taxers. In October 1899, he wrote to the *Municipal Journal* –

> We regard taxation as helping to settle the housing question by fixing the value of land for public acquisition, while your correspondent imagines that the taxation of ground values will, of itself solve the housing question and every other troublous question.
>
> (*Municipal Journal* 6th October 1899 cited in
> Englander, 1973, p. 92)

Englander comments that the ELRL's hostility was an obstacle to the WNHC winning support in the radical clubs. Knee wrote again to the *Municipal Journal* in September 1899:

You sir do not tell us why the housing problem is not to be solved by part III of the Act but find the way at the end of your editorial to that usual slough of despond, the taxation of ground values – a thing as far off as ever, mainly through its advocates tactless and avowed opposition to London improvements ... Unless a firmer attitude is taken the present road leads to a possible violent revolution or more probably and worse, abject degeneration of London's industrial population.

(*Municipal Journal* 1st September 1899, cited in Englander, 1973, p. 101)

The ELRL continued to lobby the Metropolitan Radical Federation to oppose the NWHC position and argued that the LCC should consider the potential impact of taxing land values before acquiring land for housing schemes. Of the London radical clubs, only the Eleusis, the Camberwell Radical and Mildmay in Hackney (of which Copeland was a member), the Bethnal Green Radical, the Marylebone Liberal and Radical and the Bow and Bromley Progressive supported the WNHC (Englander, 1973, p. 108).

In 1900, the National Housing Reform Council was established by the housing reformer William Thompson of Richmond. The NHRC at one time proposed to amalgamate with the WNHC, but this was rejected by the latter as the NHRC favoured private enterprise while the WNHC focused on municipal provision. The NHRC turned its attention to town planning, the garden city movement and co-operatives. Knee was scathing: 'In London escape to garden city was quite meaningless for the mass of the working population ... Running off to Letchworth would not improve conditions in Shoreditch or Hoxton' (cited in Englander, 1973, p. 112).

Knee considered that the Garden City Association and its secretary Thomas Adams were hostile to the WNHC's promotion of council housing and instead were partisans of paternalistic housing schemes, which ignored the interests of and participation by workers (Buder, 1990, p. 102 citing letter 9 September 1902 from Knee to Adams).

The WNHC continued to draft bills to amend what they considered to be inadequate housing legislation. They drafted a Bill for Steadman to present in parliament. This won support from the London Reform Union, the London Liberal and Radical Union and the Trades Union Congress. In response, the government made some amendments to its own Housing Bill including introducing the power for the LCC to undertake suburban housing schemes. Steadman lost his seat in the 1900 'Khaki' election and his role as WHNC parliamentary advocate was taken on by the Liberal MP for Camberwell North, T J Macnamara, who was to become parliamentary secretary to the Local Government Board in 1907.

In August 1901, the WNHC collaborated with William Thompson of the National Housing Reform Council to hold a Housing and Transit conference. Supporting suburban development, the WNHC had recognised that the provision of cheap public transport was essential if working people living in the suburbs were to get to their workplaces in central London. The demands included:

1   the provision of money from savings bank deposits and other sources for housing loans at low rates of interest
2   the relaxation of building regulations imposed by the Local Government Board

3   extension of loan repayments
4   more effective dealing with slum areas by means of increased powers of representation and registration of slum ownership; and
5   the granting of larger powers to acquire land on the basis of its assessable value for the purposes of developing municipal housing estates.

(cited in Englander, 1973, p. 172)

These proposals were put forward in a Bill by Macnamara in January 1902. The government responded by appointing a select committee on the repayment of loans, which proposed extending the loan repayment period from sixty years to eighty years – the WNHC had wanted a 100-year period. However, the WNHC annual conference decided that it should have a Labour MP to be its parliamentary advocate rather than the Liberal, Macnamara. Macnamara had won third place in the ballot for a private members' bill but decided to pursue legislation on land values rather than housing. The labour movement was by then recognising the importance of the housing issue, with the TUC holding a special conference on housing at Holborn Town Hall in March 1903. In April 1904, the TUC general council declared 'that for the future it has confidence in any MP or candidate who is not a direct Labour representative'. Knee wrote to Kier Hardie asking him to take up housing reform, but Hardie said he was too busy working on other issues. So the WNHC hoped that Steadman, despite officially being a Liberal MP, would return to parliament to represent their interest. Knee attempted to get adopted by the ILP as parliamentary candidate for Clapham. Although he had local support, he appears to have been blocked by the national ILP leadership, not surprising that as a prominent SDF member, he had been critical of Hardie and other ILP leaders.

In 1905, Williams and Knee wrote a book – *The Labourer and his Cottage*, which was published for the WNHC. The authors in a preface stated that the book was produced

in the hope that it may help stem the tide of revolt against what is called – the tyranny of bye-laws – by which is meant the extremely small amount of control the public can exercise over the health of a district by and through its local authority.

The purpose was to protect the bye-laws which sought to ensure minimum housing standards.

The book argued for an amendment to the Housing Acts to allow for government to provide interest free loans to councils to provide homes. They now proposed that costs to the exchequer be covered by a graduated tax on big incomes, assisted by a land tax.

Williams and Knee pointed out the irony of relating space standards to household income –

if we were to argue that because a man with only 18s should have less air space ... than the £2 a week man, then logically a man who is unemployed should be requested to take himself off the planet altogether... It is useless also to leave the matter of housing the agricultural worker to private enterprise, which can only act when there is a return promised on capital invested. Unless with brutal callousness you drop bye-laws and let the landowner benevolently lead the way for the unscrupulous jerry-builder, who will always provide something cheap, especially if there is a bigger margin of profit to be gained thereby.

Despite their hostility to the view that garden cities were a panacea, Knee and Williams did recognise that town planning had a role

> For many years we have advocated the planning beforehand of villages and towns as is done in some German towns and admirably carried out by the Soudanese Government in the planning of the new Khartoum. Bye-laws might contain a clause empowering local authorities to prepare a tentative plan showing new roads, open spaces, and for the scheduling of belts of land surrounding the village or town.
>
> (Williams and Knee, 1905, p. 67)

We will return in a later chapter to considering the role of the WNHC in the debates that led to the 1909 Housing and Planning Act. It is however necessary to first consider the contribution made by other labour movement organisations to the housing reform campaign.

Fabian tracts and the Independent Labour Party

In 1900, the Fabian Society published Steadman's pamphlet on *Overcrowding in London*. This was based on his speech in parliament on a Bill to amend the 1890 Housing of the Working Classes Act, which was enacted as the Housing of the Working Classes Act 1900. Steadman claimed that in ten years, the LCC had spent £2 million and housed 42,000 people, but was restricted in what it could do by the Local Government Board and the Home Office. He argued that because the LCC could only borrow at the market interest rate, the rents were so high 'that the places rebuilt do not come within the purview of the poor unskilled worker or general labourer, and therefore, we are accommodating people today who could find not better but other accommodation elsewhere, and the poor people are entirely neglected.' Steadman argued for lower interest loans, which were repayable over 100 years rather than the 60-year term. He argued that land should be treated as an asset and not as a charge on the building repayable through rent. He also objected to the requirement of part III of the 1890 Act that compulsory purchase had to be on the basis of 10 per cent above market value. He also proposed that vacant land should be taxed. He referred to the previous argument put forward by Joseph Chamberlain, now Colonial secretary, that private owners should demolish unfit buildings and rebuild at their own expense without compensation. Steadman claimed that his proposals had support of a trades union movement of 1,250,000 working men and referred to a recent mass meeting in Hyde Park attended by 100,000 trade unionists.

This pamphlet, while advocating the policies promoted by the Workman's National Housing Council discussed above, was actually published in conjunction with the National Housing Reform Council, later renamed as the National Housing and Town Planning Council. This organisation had been established 'to advocate and work on non-party lines for practical housing reform', and as discussed above sought to be broader based than the WNHC. Its secretary was Henry Aldridge and its membership included housing reformers such as Edward Bowmaker, William Thompson (of Richmond), George Haw, George Dew of the LCC, and the Lib–Lab MPs Sam Woods, Thomas Burt and John Wilson as well as trade unionists, G N Barnes and Richard Bell, both later MPs. It supported councils having the power to acquire land and build homes, the extension of co-operative enterprise in housing supply and the taxation of land values.

Later, in December 1900, the Fabian Society published another pamphlet on *Houses for the People*, which summarised the provisions of the 1890 and 1900 Housing Acts, which also gave examples of how local authorities had used the powers, with the LCC as the main example. It should be acknowledged that the Fabian society, mainly led by intellectuals although a number of trade unionists, ILP and SDF working class radicals and socialists were also members, had an interest in housing, land and planning issues, partly because of the leading role of the main pamphlet drafter, Sidney Webb, who was from 1892 a member of the LCC. Webb had a special interest in land taxation and in 1891 wrote a Fabian tract on *The Unearned Increment*, as the first in a series of short pamphlets on what was referred to as the 'Fabian Municipal Programme'. Webb argued that the annual rental value of land within the LCC area was £40 million, with a capital value of £600 million. He calculated that the value had increased from a value of £335 million in 1870, giving an increase in value of £245 million in twenty-one years. He calculated that if the value of new buildings was discounted, the unearned increment in annual rental was £7 million, giving an unearned increment in capital value of £110 million. Webb suggested that a tax of 10 per cent on land value, payable on transfer on death of the owner, would yield £3 million a year – 'more than enough to pay all the expenses of the London School Board and county council put together without the need of any rates at all for these authorities.'

The Fabians also published in 1900 a series of papers on the *House Famine and How to Relieve it*, which included a paper on urban overcrowding by Edward Bowmaker, a paper on London by Mrs Phillimore of the Women's Cooperative Guild, a paper on the powers of local authorities by councillor William Thompson of Richmond and a seven-page bibliography contributed by Sidney Webb.

The Workmen's National Housing Council continued to put pressure on both parliament and the LCC. While TUC conferences supported the WNHC arguments for the extension of municipal housing and for rent courts, they were not convinced of the argument that direct state taxation should fund housing, the TUC thinking that cheaper loans and cheaper workers' trains were sufficient. However, in 1908, Fred Knee claimed that he had persuaded Arthur Henderson, chair of the Labour Party, to support direct government grants for council housing (*Housing Journal* July 1908 cited in Wohl, 1977, p. 328). When in 1909, Dew attempted to get the LCC to adopt the rent courts proposal, he was defeated by 45 votes to 33, as the LCC was by then under control of the Moderates. It should also be noted that the WNHC would not collaborate with the National Housing and Town Planning Council as the latter body, headed by Alderman William Thompson (now Mayor of Richmond) thought that councils should leave house building to private builders rather than build themselves (*Housing Reformer* July 1901 quoted by Wohl, 1977, p. 330).

Some reference should also be made to the Independent Labour Party which was founded in 1893. The ILP was largely of northern origin, with its founding conference held in Bradford. Although there were ILP branches in London, it was less influential in London politics than the SDF or the Lib–Labs, despite the fact that its leader Kier Hardie was MP for West Ham from 1892 to 1895. The Fabian attempt to influence the ILP, in which Webb was involved, was largely unsuccessful, and the ILP, as an explicitly working class organisation, rejected the London based intellectuals. It is interesting that the ILP's first programme focused on agricultural issues including the establishment of a state agricultural land department and fixity of tenure for farmers. The second set of policies focused on working conditions including the campaign for an eight hour working day and state pensions. The programme also called for the nationalisation of the railways, free education and the 'taxation to extinction of all unearned incomes'. The programme does not include any points on housing or the planning of new settlements. In the agricultural section, there is a statement that 'Land values, urban and rural, to be treated as public property'. However, in Tom Mann's commentary, there is a reference to

> The bitter cry for decent house room in London, provincial towns, and rural districts, is as urgent now as ever; Tens of thousands of homes are wanted in London alone; the building of these would necessitate a considerable extension of the Works Committee of the LCC and would absorb many of the unemployed.
>
> (Mann, 1893, pp. 13–14)

Another ILP perspective is shown in Leonard Hall's 1899 *Clarion* pamphlet *Land, Labour and Liberty*. In contrast with Mann's earlier pamphlet, Hall saw land as the key issue.

> Not only is the land monopoly in itself the greatest and most vicious of all monopolies; it is the parent, the source, the pillar of all other monopolies ... Freehold property in land gives the land-interest a death grip on everything and everybody – up to heaven and down to hell.
>
> (Hall, 1899, pp. 3–4)

> The LAND (including ,of course, the minerals under it, and the roads, railways, canals, and harbours on and around it) being the source of all production and all livelihood, should be public property, not private property; should be the collective trust of the whole community, not the monopoly perquisite of individuals and cliques; and should be administered and allotted by the community on lines and terms that would secure the equal rights of each and produce the greatest benefits for the whole.
>
> (ibid., p. 8)

> to abolish Land Monopoly by thoroughgoing methods of LAND SOCIALISA-TION is the next thing to do of those things that are really worth doing. Any proposal short of out-and-out Socialisation not only fails to meet the case, but risks aggravating and prolonging the evil.
>
> (ibid., p. 12)

Hall also argued with the orthodox Marxists who argued that the focus of socialists should be on socialising the means of production and not land: "monopoly of capital would be impossible if there were no monopoly of land. Capital is the offspring of labour on land. Freed labour on freed land can always produce fresh capital at will and without limit' (ibid., p. 14).

The Lib–Lab MPs

The Lib–Lab MPs have been largely ignored by labour historians, with the notable exception of John Shepherd (Shepherd, 1991). Reference has already been made to the role of the Lib–Lab MP W C Steadman as president and parliamentary advocate of the Workman's National Housing Council. Given the relative inactivity of Keir Hardie and his ILP parliamentary colleagues on housing and planning issues, it is interesting to note the extent to which other Lib–Lab MPs were active on housing issues.

Henry Vivian, who was elected as the Lib–Lab MP for Birkenhead in 1906, had started his career as a carpenter and became secretary of the Pimlico branch of the Amalgamated Society of Carpenters and Joiners at the age of twenty-two, was secretary of the Labour Association for Promoting Co-operative Production amongst the Workforce, founded at the Co-operative Congress in 1884 by Edward Owen Greening and Edward Vansittart Neale. Vivian became the promoter of Labour Co-Partnership (Vivian, 1898), and initiated a programme of housing co-partnership schemes, initiating the Ealing Tenants co-partnership scheme at Brentham as well as projects at Penge and Epsom. Vivian was the main sponsor of the Brentham Garden Suburb as well as the founder of the Co-operative Building Society, which later became the General Builders Co-operative Society and by 1897 had sixteen London branches (Birchall, 1988; Reid, 2000).

The Lib–Lab MP for Sheffield Brightside, Fred Maddison, was also an active member of the Labour Association. As previously mentioned, the Lib–Lab MP, Henry Broadhurst, was also active on housing issues. Broadhurst and Maddison were active participants in the debate over the Housing of the Working Classes Amendment Bill in 1900, together with W C Steadman who was advocating the policies of the WNHC. As discussed above, this amendment enabled London boroughs to use part III of the 1890 Act and the LCC to purchase land outside their boundaries.

In the debate, Maddison stressed that 'the housing question was neither more nor less than the land question'. Steadman stated that 'I am in favour of purchasing all the land which the municipality can purchase, and holding it instead of allowing the increased value to go into the pockets of the landowner'. He argued that

> A local authority may acquire land compulsorily at a price based on the annual value assessed for taxation ... The landowner to-day can keep his land vacant as long as he likes. Fifty years back it may have been only worth a song, but land is increasing in value year after year, and the landowner knows that. What does it matter to him if the working classes cannot be housed? A man called on me on Saturday afternoon in my own constituency. He had been bundled out of his house with his wife and family, and had not a place to lay his head. He had to go round to some friends seeking accommodation until such time as he could find one or two rooms. The landowner is indifferent to all that. He says, 'The land belongs to me '– though I should like to know who gave it to him in the

first place – and like Shylock he insists upon having his pound of flesh before he parts with it. If land is not assessed I say it should be assessed, and if vacant land were compelled to pay rates landlords would not be so ready to hold it, and would be prepared to sell it at a reasonable price, let the local authority, who assess our buildings and houses at present, assess the land also, and let them have the power to purchase that land on its assessment value.

Maddison supported his colleague:

The House will have to face this problem some of these days. We shall have to assert the sound economic and sacred principle that land does not exist for private convenience and profit, and that wherever that private convenience or profit runs athwart the very necessities of the people in the matter of housing, the landlords will have to sell their land at a fair price. The purpose of the clause is to preserve the very life of the people. Everybody knows that the landowners are exacting what is really a blood tax on the community. More than that, sometimes the corporations are not prepared to pay the blood tax, and something still worse happens. Therefore, when my hon. friend seeks to secure a more equitable basis for the purchase of land than now exists, he wishes to establish a principle which has had the support of some of the greatest economists of the day, and which cannot at all be called revolutionary.

While the amendment to extend the LCC's powers to purchase land was incorporated in the Bill, the Steadman amendment on the basis of land valuation was defeated by 161 votes to 78 (Parliamentary Debates, 1900, Vol 84, cc 923–1021).

In the third reading debate, Steadman continued to argue the case for extending the borrowing powers of local councils, linking the issue of housing provision to the cause of temperance advocated by a large group of Liberal MPs:

How can anybody expect the workman of to-day to be a bright and good citizen, living as he does in the slums, where the very atmosphere which he breathes is evil, and when you take into consideration his miserable surroundings? A workman may be crushed, heart-sore, sick and sorry, and walking the streets seeking employment, but a good Samaritan comes along and takes him by the hand and gives him a lift and alters his entire surroundings. What we have to do, if the Government want to turn out bright citizens, is to level up the employees more nearly to themselves, instead of keeping them down as they do to-day. Put them into decent dwellings, so as to improve their social conditions, because while they remain in the slums they will remain as they are. Alter the surroundings of the working man and you alter his disposition. The workmen are accused of spending their time in public houses. Visit the slums to-day, and it will be found there are more public-houses there than in any other part. Is it any wonder that a man who lives and sleeps with his wife and family in one room, where everything has to be done, if he has a penny in his pocket should be tempted to spend a few hours in the glare and glitter of a public-house, rather than go to the miserable hovel he calls home?

(HC 12 July 1900 Vol 85 cc1394–423)

The Act was carried without incorporating Steadman's LCC sponsored clause to xtend the loan repayment period from seventy to 100 years.

The continuity of the radical tradition

This examination of socialist attitudes to land and housing reform in the late-19th century demonstrates considerable continuity with the radicalism of the mid Victorian period considered in Chapter 7. What is perhaps significant is the evidence that this tradition was largely unaffected by the Liberal reforming, Christian socialist and positivists traditions considered in Chapter 8. This is partly due to the survival of radical working class politics, especially in London, through what is often regarded as the quiet period in English socialism – the period between the disintegration of the Chartist movement and the socialist revival of the early 1880s. Although some of the later Christian socialist intellectuals such as Stuart Headlam and Morrison Davidson were proponents of land reform, land nationalisation was also introduced into the programmes of the Democratic Federation, the Socialist League and the ILP by the working class radicals and not by the intellectuals. What is also significant about the period is the engagement of radicals and socialists with the institutions of government – demonstrated most clearly through the engagement of John Burns. W C Steadman and William Saunders and colleagues in the London County Council but also evidenced by the willingness of trade union leaders such as Henry Broadhurst to be active participants in Liberal governments, with Broadhurst's position as a junior Minister enabling him to pursue his leasehold reform campaign within government. There is also considerable evidence that working class trade unionists working through the Liberal party as Lib–Lab MPs did have a significant impact on housing legislation, specifically in the case of the 1900 Housing of the Working Classes Act. Though they failed to achieve all their objectives, further progress was to be made in the 1909 legislation which will be in the penultimate chapter. In this context the European debates over whether socialists and trade union leaders should collaborate with and participate in government looked somewhat irrelevant.

Primary sources

Anonymous (1878) *Papers for the People: Our Land* (London: Reeve and Co.)

Boyle, A (1888) *The Right of the State to Control All Monopolies of Necessary Articles* (London: Land Nationalisation Society)

Broadhurst, Henry and Reid, R T (1885) *Leasehold Enfranchisement* (London: Sonnenschein)

Burns, J (1892a) 'The London County Council: Towards a Commune' *The Nineteenth Century*. March 1892, pp. 496–514

Burns, J (1892b) 'Let London Live!' *The Nineteenth Century*, April, pp. 673–85

Chamberlain, J with others (1885) *The Radical Programme* (London: Chapman and Hall)

Charity Organisation Society (1873) *Dwellings of the Poor. Report of the special committee on Metropolitan Dwellings* (London: Longmans, Green)

Commissioners on the Housing of the Working Classes. 1884–5: First Report (Irish University Press 1970)

Daily Chronicle (1895) *New London: Her Parliament and Its Work* (London: *Daily Chronicle*)

Dodd J T (1889) *The Housing of the Working Classes* (London: The Liberal Publication Department)

English Land Restoration League (1897) *Land Values: The Country's Bank* (London: English Land Restoration League)

Fabian Society (1888) Capital and Land. Tract 7 by Sidney Olivier (London: Fabian Society)

Fabian Society (1890) Practicable Land Nationalisation. Tract 10 by Sidney Webb (London: Fabian Society)

Fabian Society (1891) The Unearned Increment. Tract 30 by Sidney Webb (London: Fabian Society)

Fabian Society (1900a) Houses for the People. Tract 76 by Arthur Hicknott (London: Fabian Society)

Fabian Society (1900b) The House Famine and How to Relieve It. Tract 101 (London: Fabian Society)

Fawcett, H (1883) *State Socialism and the Nationalisation of the Land* (London: Macmillan)

George, H (1879) *Progress and Poverty* (New York: Lovells Library)

Godwin, G (1854) *Long Shadows: A Glance at the Homes of Thousands* (London: The Builder)

Hall, L (1899) *Land, Labour and Liberty*, *Clarion* pamphlet No 30 (London: Clarion Newspaper)

Hare, T (1862) *Usque ad Coelum* (London: Sampson Low)

Haw, G (1900) *No Room to Live* (London: Wells, Gardner, Darton)

Haw, G (1902) *Britain's Homes* (London: Wells, Garner, Darton)

Hill, O (1875) *Homes of the London Poor* (London; Macmillan)

Hobson, J A edited (1895) *Co-operative Labour on the Land* (London: Swan Sonnenschein)

Hole, J (1866) *Homes of the Working Classes* (London: Longmans)

Howard, E (1892) *Tomorrow: A Peaceful Path to Real Reform* (London: Sonnenschen)

Howell, G (1871) *Waste Land and Surplus Labour* (London: T S D Floyd at the Reformers Library, Greenwich)

Hyndman, H (1881) *England for All* (London: Democratic Federation)

Hyndman, H and Morris, W (1884) *A Summary of the Principles of Socialism written for the Democratic Federation* (London: Democratic Federation)

Joynes, J L *The Right to the Use of the Earth* (London: Land Reform Union)

Knee, F (1901) *The Financial Side of the Housing Question* (London: Independent Labour Party)

Knowles, C M (1899) *The Housing Problem in London* (London: London Reform Union)

Lansbury, G (1908) 'Hollesley Bay' in *Socialist Review*, Vol. 1, No. 1, May 1908, pp. 220–33

Lansbury, G (1928) *My Life* (London: Constable)

Ley, H (1888) *Land Nationalisation. Who Shows the Way?* (London: W Reeves for Land Nationalisation Society)

Linton, W J (1850) *The People's Land* (London: J Watson)

London County Council (1900) *The Housing Question in London 1855–1900* (London: LCC)

London Liberal and Radical Union (1895) *Statement of Progressive Policy for the London County Council*

London Reform Union (1898) *The Housing of the People* (London: London Reform Union)

London Reform Union (1898) *Nine Years' Good Work for the People* (London: London Reform Union)

London Reform Union (1898) *The 'Unearned Increment'* (London: London Reform Union)

London Reform Union (1898) *Why London Must Maintain the Works Department* (London: London Reform Union)

London Reform Union (1899) *The Housing Problem in London* (London: London Reform Union)

Mann, T (1893) *The Programme of the ILP and the Unemployed* (London: Clarion Pamphlet, No 6)

Mansion House Council on Dwellings of the Poor (1891–1907) *Reports 1890-1906* (London)

Marshall, A (1885) *Where to House the London Poor?* (Cambridge)

Mearns, A (1883) *The Bitter Cry of Outcast London* (London: London Congregational Union)

Metropolitan Radical Federation (1897) *The Radical Programme*

Mills, H (1886) *Poverty and the State* (London: Kegan Paul, Trench)

Parliamentary Debates (1900) Vols 84-5 (London: House of Commons)

Phillimore, Mrs (1897) *Housing of the People* (Kirkby Londsdale: Women's Co-operative Guild)

Report of a Committee of Working Men (1896) *Improved Homes for Working Men in London* (London: George Hutchinson)

Report of the Financial and Compensation committee of the conference of delegates on questions concerning the Housing of the People (1895) (London: Veale, Chifferel)

Report of Conference on Housing of the People (1890) (London: Theodore Dodd)

Saunders, W (1891) *The Land Struggle in London and the contest in the London County Council on the taxation of land values* (London: National Press Agency)

Saunders, W (1892) *History of the London County Council* (London: National Press Agency)

Shaw Lefevre, G (1881) *Freedom of Land* (National Liberal Federation)

Sketchley, J (nd) *Land Common Property* (London: Land Reform Union)

Socialist League (1885a) *Manifesto*. First edition

Socialist League (1885b) *Manifesto*. Second edition

Solly, H (1884) *Industrial Villages: A Remedy for Crowded Towns and Deserted Fields* (London: Sonnenschein)

Steadman, W C (1900) *Overcrowding in London and its Remedy*. Tract 76 (London: Fabian Society)

Taylor, H (1888) *Nationalisation of the Land* (London: Land Nationalisation Society)

Vivian, H (1898) *Partnership of Capital and Labour as a Solution of the Conflict between them* (London: Labour Association)

Wallace, A R (1882) *Land Nationalisation: Its Necessity and its Aims* (London: W Reeves)

Wallace, A R (1885) *How to Experiment in Land Nationalisation* (London: Land Nationalisation Society)

Wallace, A R (1908) 'The Remedy for Unemployment' in *Socialist Review*, Vol 1, No 4, pp. 310–20; Vol 1, No 5, pp. 390–400 (London: Independent Labour Party)

Wallace, A R (1908) *My Life: A Record of Events and Opinions* (London: Chapman Hall)

Webb, Sidney (1894) *The Economic Heresies of the London County Council* (London: London Reform Union)

Webb, Sidney (1895) *The Work of the London County Council* (London: Office of London Journal)

Williams, R (1895) *More Light and Air for Londoners* (London: London Reform Union)

Williams, R (1895) *The People and the Nation's Wealth* (London: Office of 'London')

Williams, R (1897) *The Face of the Poor* (London: W Reeves)

Williams, R and Knee, F (1905) *The Labourer and his Cottage* (London: The Twentieth Century Press)

Secondary sources

Armytage, W H G (1961) *Heavens Below: Utopian Experiments in England 1560–1960* (London: Routledge and Kegan Paul)

Birchall, J (1988) *Building Communities the Co-operative Way* (London: Routledge Kegan Paul)

Brown, J (1968) 'Charles Booth and Labour Colonies 1889–1905' in *The Economic History Review*, Vol 21, No 2 (August), pp. 349–60

Buder, S (1990) *Visionaries and Planners: The Garden City Movement and the Modern Community* (New York: Oxford University Press)

Clements, H (1983) *Alfred Russell Wallace* (London: Hutchinson)

Davis, J (1988) *Reforming London: The London Government Problem 1855–1900* (Oxford: Oxford University Press)

Davis, J (1989) 'Radical Clubs and London Politics 1870–1900' in Feldman, D and Stedman Jones, G, (eds), *Metropolis London* (London: Routledge)

Douglas, R (1976) *Land, People and Politics* (London: Allison and Busby)

Barry, E Eldon(1965) *Nationalisation in British Politics: The Historical Background* (London: Jonathan Cape)

Englander, D (1973) *The Workman's National Housing Council* (unpublished MA Dissertation, University of Warwick, UK)

Englander, D (1977) *The Diary of Fred Knee* (Coventry, UK: Society for the Study of Labour History)

Englander, D (1983) *Landlord and Tenant in Urban Britain 1838–1918* (Oxford: Clarendon Press)

Gaudie, E (1974) *Cruel Habitations* (London: Allen and Unwin)

Hardy, D (1979) *Alternative Communities in Nineteenth Century England* (London: Longman)

Harris, J (1972) *Unemployment and Politics: A Study in English Social Policy 1886–1914* (Oxford: Oxford University Press)

Jones, P D'A (1991) *Henry George and British Socialism* (New York: Garland)

Marsh, J (1982) *Back to the Land* (London: Quartet Books)

McBriar, A M (1962) *Fabian Socialism and English Politics* (Cambridge: Cambridge University Press)

Peacock, A J (1961) Land Reform 1880–1919 (University of Southampton, UK, unpublished MA dissertation)

Postgate, R (1951) *The Life of George Lansbury* (London: Longmans, Green)

Readman, P (2008) *Land and Nation in England* (Woodbridge, UK: Boydell Press)

Reid, A (2000) *Brentham. A History of the pioneer garden suburb* (London: Brentham Heritage Society)

Shepherd, J (1991) 'Labour in Parliament: The Lib-Labs as the first working-class MPs' in Biagini, E (ed.), *Currents of Radicalism* (Cambridge: Cambridge University Press)

Shepherd, J (2002) *George Lansbury* (Oxford: Oxford University Press)

Stedman-Jones, G (1971) *Outcast London* (Oxford: Oxford University Press)

Thompson, P (1967) *Socialists, Liberals and Labour: The Struggle for London 1885–1914* (London: Routledge and Kegan Paul)

Wilkins, M S (1959) 'The Non-Socialist Origins of England's First Important Socialist Organisation' in *International Review of Social History*, Vol 4, pp. 199–207

Wohl, A (1977) *The Eternal Slum: Housing and Social Policy in Victorian London* (London: Edward Arnold)

10 Visions and politics of the garden city pioneers

Ideology and context

The purpose of this chapter is to examine the ideological background to the development of radical and socialist perspectives on planning in the period before the First World War. This will centre on an examination of the ideological influences on three of the central figures in the development of British planning and design in the pre-World War I period, first considering radical and anarchist influences on Ebenezer Howard, the influence of positivism on Patrick Geddes, and then the early involvement of Raymond Unwin with Edward Carpenter, the Socialist League, the Independent Labour Party and the Fabian Society.

The chapter will also briefly consider the contributions of John Ruskin, William Morris and the Arts and Crafts Movement, the environmentalist work of A R Wallace and the economic writings of Alfred Marshall, A C Pigou and Seebohm Rowntree. It will also examine the role of less well-known writers on new settlements and garden cities, including Herbert Mills, John Richardson, William Thomson (not to be confused with the Owenite of the same name), A R Sennett and Budget Meakin. It will also consider the pre-war debates within New Liberalism on The Heart of Empire and Darkest London.

This chapter seeks to examine the political and ideological context in which the pioneers developed their ideas as well as to demonstrate the extent to which the writings of the pioneers drew on a wide range of sources and traditions. Howard and his colleagues were synthesisers rather originators.

Radical and socialist influences on Ebenezer Howard

Ebenezer Howard is widely regarded by any as the founder of modern British town planning. He was not a professional town planner. At the time he published *To-morrow – A Peaceful Path to Real Reform* in 1898, the profession of town planner did not exist in England. Howard stood in a long tradition of reformers who sought to set out a framework for the development of a new society. As has been demonstrated in previous chapters, Howard was by no means the first English writer to put his ideas on to paper, though it could be, and has been, argued that he was the first writer on planning, at least in England, to successfully bring his plans into effect. The utopian experiments undertaken by philanthropists, Owenites and the followers of Cabet and Fourier had generally been on a smaller scale, and as we have seen more successful when carried out in the New World. Beevers (1988), Aalen (1992) and Hall, Hardy and Ward (2003) have all sought to examine the origins of

Howard's ideas. The following section seeks to re-examine the sources used by Hardy and the networks in which he participated, and focuses on his interaction with radical and socialist ideas and movements.

London in the 1880s and early 1890s witnessed a vigorous debate over a wide range of alternative solutions to the crisis of overcrowded slums in the major cities of England, with the focus being mainly on the East End of London. The followers of Henry George were advocating the taxation of land, while the naturalist and environmentalist, Alfred Russell Wallace, was arguing for the outright nationalisation of land, a position that as we have seen had been long argued by the O'Brienites, who had also put forward proposals for new settlements beyond London as 'home colonies' to provide homes and employments for slum dwellers. As early as 1893, Howard had collaborated with Russell's Land Nationalisation Society (Beevers, 1988) on a proposal to establish a Co-operative Land Society. At that time Howard supported the municipal ownership of enterprises.

Howard seems to have first picked up the idea of a planned city from reading Benjamin Richardson's *Hygeia*, which was published in 1876, while he was in Chicago. The term 'garden city' may have derived from Chicago itself, which at that time was often known as 'the garden city'. In fact, in 1893, Andreas Simon was to publish a book describing its parks, boulevards and cemeteries under the title *Chicago.The Garden City*.

Howard was not the first advocate of dispersing the overcrowded population of London. The economist Alfred Marshall in 1884 published a polemic in the Contemporary Review entitled *The Housing of the London Poor: Where to house them,* which proposed the formation of a 'colony in some place well beyond the range of London smoke' (Marshall, 1885).

In the year Howard published *Tomorrow*, the Russian anarchist and geographer Petr Kropotkin, in exile in England, published *Fields, Factories and Workshops*. Kropotkin's ideas had previously been published as a series of articles in *The Nineteenth Century*, and would therefore have been available to Howard at the time he was writing, though interestingly Howard only cited Kropotkin in the second edition of his own work published in 1902. Howard had become a member in 1880 of the Zetetical Society (Beevers, 1988), many of whose members were followers of Herbert Spencer, who had advocated land nationalisation in his *Social Statics*, and it was at the meetings of this group that Howard met the leading Fabians, Bernard Shaw and Sidney Webb, both of whom supported the taxation of land but not land nationalisation. Howard's lecture to the Zetetical Society was however on the subject of 'spiritual influences towards social progress' rather than garden cities. According to Beevers (1988), Howard was also involved in two unspecified 'very small social experiments' with Thomas Davidson, founder of the Fellowship of the New Life.

Through his role as a writer of Hansard, the official parliamentary report, Howard would also have been aware of the debates within parliament and on the Royal Commissions. Though Howard does not appear to have been involved in the Royal Commission on Housing of the Working Classes of 1883–5, he was the official reporter of the Royal Commission on Labour of 1892–4 (Beevers, 1988). Howard was also an official reporter for the London County Council, which as discussed above, was actively debating the merits of taxing development land as well as redeveloping slum areas. It was however the utopian novel of the American socialist, Edward Bellamy, *Looking Backward*, which was published in 1888, that appears to have had most impact on Howard. He was so enthusiastic that he paid the publisher William Reeves to publish an English edition, and went so far as to compile the index. In 1910, Howard recalled that Bellamy had convinced him 'that our present industrial order stands absolutely condemned and is tottering to its fall and that a new and brighter, because a juster, order must ere long take its place' (quoted in Beevers, 1988). Howard decided to test out Bellamy's ideas and first drafted a paper entitled *The City of Health and How to Build It*, which he sent to the elderly Benjamin Richardson. He then started promoting his ideas to various nonconformist meetings under the title *Commonsense Socialism*.

Howard's interest in Bellamy brought him into contact with the small circle of Bellamy's English supporters. In 1890, a group of admirers of *Looking Backward* established a Nationalisation of Labour Society. The Society had as president John Orme, a dealer in photographic supplies and as secretary, Walter Godbold, a printer. It published a journal *Nationalization News* to promote Bellamy's ideas. The group promoted the establishment of a co-operative colony in England, following the examples of the colony of Kaweah in California and that of Topolobampo in Mexico, the former established on the principles set out in the Danish American Gronlund's *Co-operative Commonwealth*, the latter in an attempt to fulfil Bellamy's dream. The group identified a site at Hockley in Essex for its first English colony, though it failed to raise the funds to establish it (Marshall, 1962, pp. 96–113).

Howard was in contact with the Bellamite group as his initial outline of his garden city proposals was published as early as February 1893 in *Nationalization News*. In fact, Howard was listed as one of the original twenty supporters of the Nationalisation of Labour Society. As analysed by Marshall, Howard had already modified some of Bellamy's propositions. He rejected Bellamy's assumption of integral co-operation in favour individual leaseholds. His 1893 paper included the main features of *Tomorrow*:

> The mingling of agricultural and industrial employment, the creation of municipal facilities, the planning of communal services, the existence of a master plan of development, and the hope that the financial success of the project would lead ultimately to the extinction of landlord's rents and the municipalizing of capitalist undertakings.
>
> (Marshall, 1962, p. 213)

One of the leading members of the NLS was the Congregationalist Minister John Bruce Wallace. Wallace was a follower of Henry George and after his association with the Bellamites, set up the Brotherhood Trust, which in partnership with the Tolstoyan, J C Kenworthy, ran the *Brotherhood* magazine and established two Brotherhood churches and co-operative stores on Tolstoyan principles in Southgate, North London and in Croydon (Bevir, 2011, pp. 260–1). Bruce Wallace was to be one of the founding members of Howard's Garden City Association in June 1899 (Macfadyen, 1970, p. 25).

The Bellamy group published a magazine – *Nationalisation News* – and had planned to set up a Home Integral Cooperative Colony, but the group soon collapsed having failed to win the support of working class movements. Sidney Webb, who was later to be critical of Howard's initiatives, commented that a cooperative commonwealth would not be created overnight but through 'such pettifogging work as slowly and with infinite difficulty building up a Municipal Works Department under the London County Council' (Marshall, 1962, p. 106). *Nationalisation News* was incorporated in Bruce Wallace's *Brotherhood*.

Howard, in a chapter in *Tomorrow* which was entitled rather grandly 'A Unique Combination of Proposals' stated that he was combining three distinct projects, which he believed had not been combined before:

> (1) the proposals for an organised migratory movement of Wakefield and of Professor Marshall; (2) the system of land tenure first proposed by Thos. Spence and afterwards (though with an important modification) by Mr Herbert Spencer; and (3) the model city (of somewhat different design, however) of Jas. S Buckingham.
>
> (Howard, 1898, p. 103)

In a footnote Howard however pointed out that these works reaffirmed rather than influenced his thinking:

> I may perhaps state as showing how in the search for truth men's minds run in the same channels, and as, possibly, some additional argument for the soundness of the proposals thus combined, that, till I had got far on with my project, I had not seen either the proposals of Professor Marshall or of Wakefield (beyond a very short reference to the latter in J S Mill's Elements of Political Economy') nor had I seen the work of Buckingham, which, published nearly fifty years ago, seems to have attracted but little attention.
>
> (ibid., pp. 103–4)

Howard was well-read and used a wide range of sources. It is perhaps significant that in the introductory chapter of *Tomorrow*, focusing on the need to reduce overcrowding in the cities, Howard quotes not only Lord Rosebery, Liberal leader, previously chair of the London County Council and former prime minister, but also quotes two leading socialist trade unionists, Tom Mann, Ben Tillett (ibid., pp. 3, 4). His first main chapter opens with a quote from John Ruskin's *Unto this Last* (ibid., p. 12). The second chapter opens with quotes from the republican Victor Hugo's *Les Miserables* and from Dr Benjamin Richardson's *Hygeia;* the third chapter with an extract from Marshall's *Housing of the London Poor*. The fourth chapter uses material from Marshall and the London School Board but also includes a footnote referring to John Richardson's *How it Can be Done*. The TCPA commemorative edition of *Tomorrow* incorrectly assumes this was a reference to Benjamin Richardson (Hall et al., 2003, p. 67). In fact, John Richardson was a Lincoln based mechanical engineer who was a member of the Social Democratic Federation, the English Marxist party led by Henry Hyndman. Richardson's book subtitled *Constructive Socialism*, a term which Howard himself had used, was published by Howard's publisher Swan Sonnenschein in 1894.The book had been written as a riposte to Blatchford's *Merrie England*, in which Blatchford had stated that he had not sought to answer the question as to how socialism could be accomplished. As a 'man of business', and as he puts it himself 'an intensely practical person', Richardson considered he was in a position to answer the question. His 'Plan of Campaign' was intended to complement Blatchford's 'Call to Arms.'

Richardson's book is an early and reasonably comprehensive statement of how to implement a socialist programme, complete with draft legislation. The book covered schools, technical schools and universities, state industries and how to fund them, public hospitals and orphanages, socialistic settlements, co-operation, the abolition of private property, emigration, poor law reform, prohibition of the drink traffic, the eight hour working day , municipal factories, allotments and small holdings, reform of the land laws, abolition of the standing army, currency reform (bi-metalism), provident societies and sick clubs, old age pensions as well as democratic reforms such as payment of members and abolition of the House of Lords. Richardson was later to write two further pamphlets for the SDF – *The Education Problem and Its Solution* in 1906 and *Work and Wealth for All* in 1908. Howard in his footnote comments that Richardson 'will, I am sure, welcome my proposals as bringing his suggestions within the realm of practical politics' (Howard, 1898, p. 42).

Howard made considerable use of J S Mill's *Principles of Political Economy*. He also refers not surprisingly to Henry George's *Progress and Poverty* (ibid., p. 125) and in fact comments in a footnote that he has derived much inspiration from George's work, though he disagrees with George's attack on private landlords. Howard also referred both to a lecture given by Henry Hyndman in 1893 and to the Social Democratic Federation's *Principles of Socialism Made Plain*, published pseudonymously under the name of 'Frank Fairman' in 1888. Howard however gave most attention to Blatchford's *Merrie England*, because he disagreed with Blatchford's statement that he 'would make all the lands, mines, factories, works, shops, ships and railways the property of the people'. Howard argues that socialists, whom he refers to as 'our friends', 'miss the essential point'.

> Their professed ideal is to make society the owner of land and of all instruments of production; but they have been so anxious to carry both points of their programme that they have been a little too slow to consider the special importance of the land question, and have missed the true path of reforms.
>
> (ibid., p. 125)

Howard's point, which he thought the socialists were missing, is that land had a different character than other wealth, a point with which George agreed:

> There is however one form of material wealth which is most permanent and abiding ... The earth for all practical purposes may be regarded as abiding for ever ... as every form of wealth must rest on this earth as its foundation, and must be built up out of the constituents found at or near its surface, it follows (because foundations are ever of primary importance) that the reformer should first consider how best the earth may be used in the service of man.
>
> (ibid., pp. 124–5)

Howard's response to the positions of both Blatchford and George was that while a reform of the land system is necessary, rather than nationalising land or appropriating rent values created by others, a more equitable system should be established which protects the individual against expropriation by others of the rent values which he creates or maintains (ibid., pp. 126–7). The method proposed in the book was the collective ownership of land and collectivisation of rent values through a trust.

In the 1902 edition published as *Garden Cities of Tomorrow*, Howard also acknowledged the work of William Light in Adelaide, in fact including a new diagram based on that of Light. As well as a footnote referring to Kropotkin's recently published *Fields, Factories and Workshops*, the new edition added some further references – to J W Petavel's *The Coming Revolution* and to Neale's *Economics of Co-operation*.

Captain James W Petavel of the Indian Polytechnical Association in Calcutta published a paper in 1909 on *The Town Planning of the Future* in the *Westminster Review*, which focused on the need for decentralisation of population and industry, the provision of cheap transport and the taxation of development land, proposing a 'lineal city' with 700 lineal settlements of six miles each, with each 'limb' providing for 12,000 dwellings and 60,000 residents. Petavel also wrote a number of books on Indian economics, self-government and how co-operation was preferable to the class struggle. In his 1911 work on the *The Coming Triumph of Christian Civilisation*, Petavel, now living in Stanford-le-Hope, Essex, included an updated version of his earlier essay as an appendix on *Town Planning and Railway Transport*.

Edward Vansittart Neale was a leading Christian socialist who had in 1877 given a series of lectures on the Economics of Co-operation, though the lectures were not actually published until 1885. It is interesting that, despite Howard's sympathy with co-operative approaches, Neale's short volume is the only reference Howard gives to the vast literature on co-operation available at the time he was writing.

There is one further footnote in *Tomorrow* which deserves a mention, as it epitomises the breadth of Howard's sources as well as demonstrating that Howard was far from unique in publishing proposals for new settlements. Howard's footnote to his famous diagram 7 – The Group of Slumless Smokeless Cities (1898, p. 130) comments that 'This drawing is, in many respects, very much like one to which (after making it) my attention was drawn in a work entitled *Palingenesia; or the Earth's New Birth*'. *Palingenesia* was published in 1894 by Gideon Jasper Ouseley, an Irish priest who claimed he had discovered the original gospel, called the *Gospel of the Holy Twelve*, from which the four gospels in the New Testament were derived. The Gospel was written in Aramaic, but apparently found by Ouseley in a Buddhist monastery in Tibet, having been hidden there centuries earlier by a member of the Essene society. After being suspended from the Catholic Apostolic Church for anti-Christian views, Ouseley founded the Order of At-One-ment and the United Templars Society (Hall et al., 2003, p. 159). Amongst his numerous works are volumes with the following titles: *The Science of the Aura, Colour Meditations, A Guide to Telepathy and Psychometry, Power of the Rays and the Science of Colour Healing* and *Changing and Projecting Thought*. Ouseley, who wrote under the pseudonym Theosopho, also produced a study of Persian poetry, a book on *How to Keep a Cat in Health, Why Eat Corpses* and *England Regenerated through justice to Ireland or a programme of reform proposals to a reformed parliament, with appendices on food and drink reform, burial and cremation*. The notion of planning new settlements based on religious and mystical imagery was part of a long standing tradition, traceable at least back to planning of New Haven based on a text from Ezekiel, discussed in Chapter 2.

It can be concluded that Howard's extensive study in developing his project had led him to derive ideas from a range of influences, many of which were radical and socialistic. He appears to have to a certain extent shared the anti-urbanism of Ruskin, though his approach to the need to disperse the overcrowded population of London was more practical than aesthetic and owed more to the hygienist and economic writings of Benjamin Richardson and Alfred Marshall. There is little evidence of the anarchistic self-help approach of Kropotkin, who is referred to more for his anthropological and geographical perspective than for his politics. Howard was in no way opposed to the state, though to a certain extent he shared Kropotkin's views on self-help and avoiding reliance on the state. In his references to John Richardson and to the work of the London County Council progressives, and specifically to John Burns, he was clearly a supporter of constructive socialism. However, Howard, while sharing the reforming objectives of the socialists, rejected the arguments for nationalisation and also rejected the Georgite argument for the taxation of land values. He believed that land and property owners could be won over to his project and that attacking landlords and other wealth owners was not a constructive way of realising his project. His promotion of his garden cities project was dependent on winning the support of the liberal and reforming establishment and his initial Garden Cities Association in 1899 was to be comprised mainly of Liberal MPs and municipal Liberal activists, including LCC progressives.

It is worth making one additional comment. Howard's influences were essentially English. Apart from Kropotkin, who lived in England and Henry George, a regular visitor to England, the only non-English source was the American writer Albert Shaw and the reference was to Shaw's study of Municipal Government in Europe. There is no evidence of Howard being familiar with European writing on town planning, municipal governance and economics. This is perhaps surprising given the extent of contact between British municipal reformers and architects with their colleagues on the continent. This is in contrast with the writings of other contemporary British writers on planning such as Inigo Triggs, Budget Meakin, Thomas Horsfall and A R Sennett, who will be considered later in this chapter and in the subsequent chapter.

The Fabian response to *Tomorrow*

The Fabian Society was hostile to Howard's approach. Fabians generally rejected the communitarianism of Owen and Fourier. H G Wells in his first paper to the Fabian Society on *Administrative Areas* in 1903 asserted that 'With these socialisms I have nothing in common.' As Stanley Buder points out (Buder, 1990, p. 77), the Fabian leadership had left the Fellowship of the New Life partly because they considered its focus on spirituality and communitarianism lacking in practicality. In the 1896 *Report on Fabian Policy*, George Bernard Shaw was dismissive of communitarian experiments:

> The Fabian Society desires to offer all projectors and founders of Utopian communities in South America, Africa and other remote localities, to apologise for its impatience with such adventures. To such projectors and all patrons for schemes for starting similar settlements and workshops at home, the Society announces emphatically that it does not believe in the establishment of socialism by private enterprise.

> (Fabian Society, 1896)

Edward Pease, the Fabian secretary, reviewing *Tomorrow* in *Fabian News* in December 1898, treating Howard and Wells as fellow Utopians, commented that 'proposals for building new (cities) are about as useful as arrangements for protection against visits from Mr Wells' Martians.' In his view the challenge was to learn to make the best of existing cities. Pease had early written in the *Clarion* that 'home colonisation and all cognate experiments are distinctly foreign to the Fabian method' (cited in Buder, 1990, p. 78). Sidney Webb considered colonization schemes were an attempt to introduce socialism horizontally (ie spatially) while socialism could only be created horizontally – by challenging the structure of capitalism. George Bernard Shaw on receiving his review copy from Howard, apparently 'glanced at the maps and put the book down with the thought – The Same Old Vision', clearly not studying the economic sections setting out how value was to be trustified, with which he might have agreed (ibid.).

Wells was actually an honorary vice-president of Howard's Garden Cities Association and apparently invited Howard to join the Fabian Society. In March 1905, Wells wrote an article in the *Daily Mail* entitled 'Utopianisms I – The Garden cities' (an article the following month was entitled 'Utopianisms II – State Babies'). In the first article, Wells commented that although Howard's scheme had many disadvantages, as a result of it

> people thought about housing who had never thought about anything in their lives before. . . It brought home to them that the way houses and roads and places are distributed on the earth's surface is within the province of intention and design.
>
> (Wells, 1905, quoted in Taunton, 2009, p. 63)

Wells had his own views on the growth of cities. His first novel, *When the Sleeper Awakes*, envisaged a London without urban sprawl. In his 1902 study *Anticipations*, Wells recognised that the growth of the city depended on transport facilities, with the population being concentrated within a 4-mile radius of the city centre (Wells, 1902). However, Wells saw the solution as distributing the population across the countryside, as put by Taunton (2009), a form of universal suburbanisation, rather than concentrating them in new towns. In his autobiography, Wells explains that in writing *Anticipations* he was seeking to examine the extent to which the change of scale of cities, with the redistribution of population through the evolution of transport was changing the social order (Wells, 1934). While Wells was critical of Howard, he focused in his books on envisioning the future, rather than as Howard did, planning for it. The Fabian Society did however publish a set of papers – Tract 101 in 1900 on *The House Famine and How to Relieve it*. In this tract, Councillor Lawson Dodd of Tunbridge Wells advocated decentralisation supported by cheap locomotion –

> It may be said that the further from the centre of our great towns and cities the housing of the people is carried out, the more hope there is for its ultimate success. For economic as well as for sanitary reasons, the further housing of the people in London is most undesirable and may become most disastrous . . . Decentralisation must be the aim of every housing reformer, and the more completely this can be attained the more success will attend his efforts. It must be for London no half-hearted decentralisation, for the housing of the people within the area of London will either mean, if done with any consideration for the people's health, a great burden on the rates, or else the overcrowding of those houses on area,

and a very probable increase in the prevalence of those diseases which are airborne While the problem is impossible for the great centres of population, it is comparatively simple for the provincial and rural authorities, They can purchase land on favourable terms, and the cheaper land thus obtained will allow for each house a proper site-area.

(Fabian Society, 1900, pp. 37, 40)

Howard was nevertheless invited to present his ideas to a Fabian Society meeting in January 1901. Shaw's main concern was the ownership of property transferred from the trust to the residents. Shaw then attended the Bournville conference later that year, in his capacity as a St Pancras vestryman rather than on behalf of the Fabian Society. Shaw did not believe that the capitalist investors would act in the interests of the residents, irrespective of the arrangements set out in the trust deed, and in fact wrote a long letter to this effect to the chair of the Garden City Association, the former Liberal MP, Ralph Neville (Beevers, 1988). Shaw still regarded Howard's project as a community which appealed to enlightened industrialists, but appeared to accept that the scheme was perhaps less utopian and more practical than some of its predecessors but not a socialist project (Buder, 1990, p. 82), Spurned by the socialists, Howard was to depend for his promotion and sponsorship on Liberals such as Neville and philanthropists such as James Leakey of the Letchworth Spirella corset factory.

Patrick Geddes and positivism

Geddes was in many ways the archetypical polymath, moving between different disciplines. Biologist and town planner, he was also a sociologist and in fact one of the founders of sociology in Britain. While Geddes had great respect for the work of John Ruskin and in 1884 wrote a study of Ruskin's economics, it was perhaps the positivism of Comte that had the greatest influence on his thinking. A study of the writings of the natural scientist, T H Huxley first drew him from Edinburgh to London in 1875, and then to the work of one of Huxley's intellectual opponents, the social scientist Herbert Spencer. This in turn led him to the writings of one of Spencer's challengers, the positivist Frederic Harrison, and he was then drawn to Richard Congreve's positivist church in Chapel Street, London (Meller, 1990, pp. 27–9). Study in Paris in 1878–9 introduced him to the social theories of the sociologist Frederic Le Play, a follower of Comte, and his focus on the three components of study – place, work and family, and then to the work of the geographer Élisée Reclus, with his focus on study of the region and his comprehensive *Geographie Universelle: La Terre et Les Hommes*. Geddes could not have been unaware of Reclus's political activity both in the Paris commune of 1871 and latterly as a leading proponent of anarchism. Geddes was later to be attracted to the work of the Russian geographer, proponent of natural evolution and anarchist, Petr Kropotkin.

The influence of Comte and Le Play can be seen in the methodology used by Geddes in developing his famous Valley Section which followed a Comtist system of categorisation. Geddes, in his search to understand the relationship between different disciplines, joined the British Association for the Advancement of Science and Art and was an active participant in its congresses. The group involved other positivists such as the sociologist and economist, J K Ingram. Geddes' earliest papers argued in

Comtist mode that all components of human society could be classified just as biological species could be classified.

Geddes work in the mid-1880s brought him a wider range of political contacts. In 1884, he helped establish the Edinburgh Social Union and as their representative attended the Industrial Remuneration Conference at which he presented a report, which is included in the published conference transactions. In his speech, Geddes was highly critical of legislators and socialist advocates such as Henry Hyndman, and instead argued that action should be taken in relation to what he referred to as the 'real wages' of the working class rather than the 'nominal wages' discussed in earlier contributions.

> What were we to do in these years of waiting (for reforms) for the people who had to live among present facts and not on future hopes? . . . Life is modified by its surroundings. . . that was very different from the current notion that life is mainly modified by Acts of Parliament. What were the actual surroundings of life for the working classes? Dirty little narrow streets, jerry-houses overcrowded and ill-ventilated, jerry furniture, parks generally so far away to be of little use; little playground for the children but the gutter; little repose for the women but to gossip about the street doors; no refuge for the weary men but to loaf at the street doors, if they did not muddle at the public house . . . They wanted better houses, and more inside them and more outside them.

Geddes then went on to describe what the Edinburgh Social Union was doing:

> It was bringing cheap and good art and beauty and culture into everyday life, so making pleasanter both work and play and providing cheap pictures, casts, flowers etc. It was also helping education, not only by lecturing and the like, but by preparing gymnasia etc; and it helped recreation, for their crusade against drink took the form of providing something better. The main material causes which hindered the well-being of the poor were bad housing – unwholesome and comfortless; lack of education; lack of simple yet real pleasure; and how were these to be remedied but by working at housing, at art, at education, at recreation?

It is interesting that Geddes's contribution was followed by James Macdonald of the SDF who in contrast to Geddes argued for state intervention rather than philanthropy. He called for the government to invest six million pounds to build houses for the poor, for their rights as citizens to be recognised, arguing that no man should live on another one's labour and 'that the system of private ownership be put an end to'. The conference report noted that while Geddes's contribution was greeted with applause, the more radical propositions of Mr McDonald were not (Industrial Remuneration Conference, 1885, pp. 240–3).

The Edinburgh Social Union involved itself in philanthropic housing projects following Octavia Hill's Marylebone example and Geddes appears to have met Miss Hill. By 1897, the Union was responsible for twenty-three properties housing some 450 families (Urquhart, 2003). Geddes however decided to take more direct action and bought up a tenement in the St James Court area of the Edinburgh Old Town, which he then let to students to establish the first University student hall in an attempt to replicate the activities of the university settlement movement in London. Geddes also undertook a number of initiatives to beautify the Old Town. He established an Environment Trust which first recruited artists to carve statues and provide drinking fountains before moving on to cultivating waste ground, making small gardens and planting trees to set up water fountains. This was the beginning of a civic initiative that was to lead to the establishment of the Outlook Tower as a centre for sociological investigation and display in 1892 and the Edinburgh Civic Survey of 1911.

Geddes, no doubt following on from his attendance at the Industrial Remuneration Conference, took an interest in the conditions of labourers. He contributed a lecture 'On the Conditions of Progress of the Capitalist and the Labourer' to a series of lectures delivered in the summer of 1886 in various Scottish cities on various aspects of the labour problem. Other lecturers in the series were John Burnett of the engineers' union, Benjamin Jones of the Co-operative, Alfred Russell Wallace, William Morris and H S Foxwell, economics professor at University College London. The lectures were published in Edinburgh by the Co-operative Printing Company as *The Claims of Labour*. Geddes's participation in the series gives an indication of the political profile he had already achieved. Geddes was critical of socialist writing on economics, which he referred to as

> only the old orthodox economics turned inside out – the old metaphysics, the hypothetical science, the one sided politics are there as much as ever. The propertied classes, however, are this time the wicked. The capitalist is merely a 'vampire', battening upon the wealth he does not help to create, He toils not, neither does he spin; even labour of superintendence – nay, too, those scarcest human qualities, power of foresight and organisation – now counting for little or nothing. The labourers are the blameless and long suffering elect.
>
> (Geddes, 1896, pp. 79–80)

Geddes's response was that the real life is more complex – that there are good and bad capitalists and good and bad labourers. After consideration of the challenges of increasing population, the lecture focused on the organic change brought about by the interaction of social processes and urban form. The key to the progress of labourers was 'life and surroundings, of "organism and environment", of evolution and degeneration' (ibid., p. 104).

> The working classes, like any other, will be in well-being in proportion as they become healthy organisms, leading fuller lives in richer surroundings both of art and nature. Reproduction has outrun individuation; the mere growth of our cities has outrun their real development. Our progress is as yet only 'quantity, not quality' . . . Remedial treatment then demands a raising of the whole character and aims of our civilization . . . It is no small matter to speak of reorganising cities, of reforming industries, of transforming the ideal of progress from an individual Race for Wealth into a social Crusade of Culture – not the Increase of Wealth, but the Ascent of Man.
>
> (ibid., pp. 104–5)

State interaction which intervened in this relationship could only be harmful. Each city within its region was an autonomous unit responsible for its own development. This perspective was maintained in his later paper on *Civics as Applied Sociology*.

Like many positivists, Geddes was not involved in organised party politics. Opposed to what he saw as the centralised bureaucratic approach of the London Fabians, his sympathies were more with the approach of the Fellowship of the New Life. Havelock Ellis was a friend and Geddes often acted as host to progressives speaking in Edinburgh including the positivist Beesly, Walter Crane and William Morris, though apparently the last was frustrated by Geddes's 'elusive style of discourse' (Meller, 1990).

Throughout his life, Geddes was an active member of the Sociological Association, and many of his papers between 1908 and 1931 were published in the *Sociological Review*. His sociological pursuits led him to collaborate with his fellow sociologist Victor Branford during and immediately after World War I, to publish a series of studies on *The Making of the Future*. Geddes contributed to three volumes: *Ideas at War* (co-authored with Gilbert Slater); *The Coming Polity* (with Branford) and *Our Social Inheritance* (also with Branford). The series as a whole, according to the introduction, was 'an endeavour towards a popular presentation of Civism as a doctrine combining the regional and humanist approaches', and was expounded further in Geddes's own *Cities in Evolution* as well as in Branford's separate work *Interpretations and Forecasts*.

The Coming Polity presented a manifesto for postwar reconstruction based on positivist concepts. It proposed a regionalism based on a form of anti-state localism and shared this approach with Kropotkin's *Mutual Aid* (Studholme, 2007). The book included a study of the Thames Valley. *Our Social Inheritance* was similarly eclectic with a large section devoted to a walking tour of Westminster. Geddes was to a large extent a *flaneur*, a strolling observer in the style later to be adopted by Walter Benjamin.

It is important to note the role of Geddes's partner in the civic reconstruction project, Victor Branford. Branford was one of the founders of sociology in Britain, establishing the London Sociological Society in 1903 and founding the *Sociological Review* in 1908. Like Geddes, he was a follower of Comte, though he was also influenced by Ruskin, having been involved in Ruskin's Guild of St George. Branford had been a student in Edinburgh and had become involved in Geddes's social projects. It was in fact Branford who set up the Geddesian Town and Gown Association, and Geddes's planning projects worked out of Branford's London office. A man of considerable business experience, with interests in South America, he negotiated the funding for a chair in sociology at the London School of Economics to create a London academic base for Geddes, only to find the post going to Leonard Hobhouse as Geddes presented an incoherent lecture. In the Sociological Papers published by the Society between 1905 and 1907, Branford engaged in debates with continental sociologists such as Durkheim and Tonnies, social Darwinists such as Francis Galton, Halford Mackinder and Benjamin Kidd and Fabians such as Bernard Shaw. Beatrice Webb, Graham Wallas and H G Wells, the latter having attacked the utopianism of Ebenezer Howard, now assaulted the 'scientific' pretensions of positivist sociology.

The *Sociological Review*, under the editorship of Hobhouse, continued this pluralist approach, but Hobhouse resigned in 1912 finding co-operation with Geddes and Branford problematic, with editorial control reverting to Branford. The *Review* had an interest in town planning, newly emerging as a discipline and included studies from Raymond Unwin, Patrick Abercrombie and Lewis Mumford. Branford, in his

Interpretations and Forecasts, promoted what he called the Third Alternative – an alternative to capitalism and socialism – uniting public and private enterprise to bring about civic reconstruction through education for citizenship. In later years his work focused on achieving a unity of science and sanctity, though he also contributed in 1926 to a symposium with Geddes, Abercrombie and others on a positivist response to the coal crisis and the general strike (Scott and Husbands, 2007; Scott and Bromley, 2013). Geddes meanwhile had transferred his interests to first Palestine and then India and drawing up plans for world governance (Meller, 1990).

The role of Branford's second wife, Sybella Gurney, was also significant. She was active in the housing co-partnership movement, editing the journal of the Labour Co-Partnership Association. She was involved in both the garden city movement through her involvement in Hampstead Garden suburb and the Ruskinian Arts and Crafts Movement. In 1910, she wrote a paper on *Civic Reconstruction and the Garden City movement* for the *Sociological Review*. Gurney promoted co-operative housing initiatives in the Midlands and Cheshire, in Brighton and had a specific interest in rural housing, founding a rural co-partnership housing association which built 200 homes. Gurney also wrote a history of the co-operative movement, a study of co-operative housing and an introduction to regional surveys for the cities committee of the Sociological Association, of which she was secretary (Scott and Husbands, 2007).

Geddes has rightly been portrayed as somewhat eccentric and unsettling (Kitchen, 1975). It is difficult to argue that he had a significant impact on planning practice. His main contribution was the mantra of 'survey, analysis, plan', but that notion was largely derived from Le Play. His organicist approach to urban development was to influence the thinking and practice of Abercrombie and Mumford. His anti-state and anti-collectivist perspective was however to receive little sympathy from the Labour Party and Labour governments, both interwar and post 1945, struggling to overcome economic crisis, war and austerity. It is interesting to contrast the lack of relevance of his ideas to the later period with the impact of William Beveridge, who made such an active contribution to postwar reconstruction after both wars. Geddes was after all primarily a writer and thinker, and to put it bluntly, not a very coherent or focused one, while Beveridge was both thinker and actor. Geddes was in practice not just disengaged from political life and party politics but hostile to the whole concept and practice of governance. It is perhaps ironic that as a thinker who argued that universities should engage in their communities, the actual practical outcome of Geddes's initiatives and creativity was so limited. At the same time ultra-localist and world travelling guru, Geddes missed the fundamental point that planning requires institutions and the power of government.

The ethical socialism of Raymond Unwin

Unwin was much more deeply engaged in the politics of the labour movement than either Howard or Geddes. He was a socialist both in theory and in practice. At the age of nineteen he attended the first meeting of Alfred Russell Wallace's Land Nationalisation Society. While still a student at Magdalen College Oxford, he met Samuel Barnett of Toynbee Hall and Edward Carpenter. Moving to Manchester in 1885 as an engineering draughtsman, Unwin joined Morris's Socialist League, becoming secretary of the Manchester branch. He also attended meetings of the Social Democratic Federation and the Ancoats Brotherhood founded by Charles Rowley, with which Thomas Horsfall, the proponent of German town planning, was associated. In 1905 Horsfall was to publish in Manchester *The Improvement of Dwellings and the Surroundings of People: The Example of Germany.*

In his contribution to a volume of tributes to Carpenter published after his death, Unwin reminisced on the happy weekends he spent with Carpenter in Millthorpe in 1883 and 1884. He referred to the fact that in Oxford he had grown up among Liberal ideas in religion and politics, his 'sense of escape from an intolerable sheath of unreality and superstition' on reading Carpenter's epic poem *Towards Democracy*, and the fact that his life and work had been profoundly influenced by Carpenter's writings. He had gained 'a new understanding, relation and unity to be realized between the spirit of man and his body, the animal man no longer a beast to be ridden, but an equal friend to be loved, cherished and inspired' (Unwin, 1931 cited in Beith, 1931, pp. 234–5).

Unwin became a regular contributor to the Socialist League's journal *Commonweal*, and contributed twenty articles between 1886 and 1890. His articles reflected the influences of Ruskin, Morris and the ethicist James Hinton. As suggested by Miller (1992), Unwin moved from a revolutionary position espoused in his first article *The Axe is Laid unto the Root* to proposals for social reform such as co-operative societies and associated houses in *Social Experiments*, to a critique of political institutions in *Broken Cisterns*, to the advocacy of a Third Course in an article on *Socialist Tactics* in 1887. In response to an article by Percival Chubb of the Fellowship of the New Life advocating socialism as a moral and religious gospel, Unwin argued for 'education towards enlightenment' as a way of resolving conflict between revolutionary and parliamentary routes to socialism.

A note written by Unwin in January 1886, at the age of twenty-two, entitled *The Dawn of a Happier Day* gives an idea of his early thinking:

> The wants and comforts which are conducive to a happy life are comparatively few. A house to live in, furniture, clothes, food, some books and a few works of art about comprise the list. Is it possible that with all the increase in our powers of production, through the use of machinery, steam and other agents, we cannot easily supply every member of the community with these without burdening him with more than a healthy amount of labour?
>
> It is only when we have learned to cooperate for our common needs that there will be the chance for all of sharing the enobling influence of honourably earned leisure, of study, art and science. Only then will the beauties of nature be open to every one, and will it be possible for every child to spend more of its summers digging in the sands by the seaside, for every man so inclined to roam over the hills and valleys of our country and learn to revere nature.
>
> Under such a system of co-operative work we shall soon learn to judge the values of things in something approaching a real and true manner. There will be no temptation to make cheap and nasty goods, because there will be no profit to be got by so doing. . . this system of work which Socialists wish to see established will be able to put happiness within the reach of all so far as happiness is the result of, or in any way depends on circumstances.

> It is quite certain that honour will not be wanting to disinterested workers
> for the common good ... a man will be respected for what he does for the
> community, not what he gets for himself.
>
> (Unwin, 1886)

In 1887, Unwin, who was never tied to a single tendency or organisation within the
labour movement, became involved with the North of England Socialist Federation
established by the former Socialist League member, John Lincoln Mahon. Mahon
had moved away from Morris's anti-parliamentary approach and was an effective
political organiser, publishing his own Labour programme in 1888. Unwin attended
the Federation meetings in Claycross in Derbyshire and spoke at one meeting. He
was also a regular lecturer at the Sheffield Socialist Society supported by Edward
Carpenter. A lecture given in February 1897 on 'Gladdening v Shortening the Hours
of Labour' to the Sheffield Socialist Education League focused on the potential of
work to be pleasurable, taking the example of the utopian handicraft colonies of
Ruskin and Carpenter.

> We should aim at making all work hobby work. That instead of working a few
> hours a day at drudgery for a living and spending the rest in running a hobby,
> we should all be able to work at a hobby and live by our hobbies, that we should
> in short make our great aim to gladden the hours of labour rather than merely
> to shorten them.
>
> (Unwin, 1897)

Unwin also lectured in Leicester and organised a picnic for the Midlands Counties
Socialist Federation (Miller,1992). In 1891, he welcomed the *Fabian essays* as 'good
from a parliamentary point of view' (cited in ibid., p. 23). In 1893 Unwin subscribed
to Keir Hardie's parliamentary fund. In the later 1890s, Unwin focused on developing
his role as an architect but he was happy to promote his design ideas in political as
well as professional circles, lecturing in 1901 to both the Fabian society and to the
Workmen's National Housing Council. His lecture on 'Light and Air and the Housing
Question' was published the following year as *Cottage Plans and Common Sense* by
the Fabian Society as Tract 109.

The tract was a very practical common sense guide to building new homes. Unwin
argued that it was important that the people must be housed outside the congested
districts, and that as the creation of entirely new towns as advocated by Howard's
Garden City Association was not a practical proposition for municipal bodies,
they should instead use the new power granted them under the 1900 Housing Act
to build cottages outside their boundaries on the town outskirts. Unwin stressed
that the local authorities should 'have regard to the reasonable accessibility from
these houses of places of employment and centres of interest and amusement' (Unwin,
1902, p. 2).

Unwin pointed out that homes should be built for the future rather than the present
and should last for a hundred years:

> As a matter of mere financial justice to succeeding generations this is essential,
> especially in view of the demand for an extension of the time over which payment
> of the buildings can be spread. Obviously it is not fair to borrow on the future

and build for the present only. It is not enough for a municipal authority to copy the house and arrangement which satisfies the average builder or speculator. Only the very best that is known and can be devised today is likely to stand the test of time; and this must be based upon the permanent and essential conditions of life and health, not on passing fashions or conventions established by the speculative builder.

(Unwin, 1902, p. 2)

Unwin then set out the chief purpose of a house and the main challenge for the architect:

It is safe to assume that shelter from inclement weather, protection from predatory neighbours (human or otherwise) and comfort and privacy for family life, were the chief reasons which impelled men in the first instance to live in houses . . . In satisfying this desire for shelter, comfort and privacy, one is at once confronted by a difficulty: the roof and walls which shut out the driving rain, the searching wind and the neighbours' prying eyes, at the same time exclude fresh air and sunlight, the full enjoyment of which is one of the most necessary conditions of a healthy life. Against this difficulty it is a primary duty of the house-builder to be on his guard. The degree both of shelter and privacy must, in fact, be limited to what is compatible with a sufficiency of fresh air and sunlight.

(Unwin, 1902, pp. 2–3)

Unwin then set out in detail, with accompanying sketches, plans, sections and room layouts, designs for each room and provisions for open space. Unwin argued for suburban development, ideally at six homes an acre as developed at Bournville though recognised that such a spreading of development would require 'improvement of transit facilities and the solution of the land question' (ibid. p. 4). He quoted Ruskin's ideal of a house – 'Not a compartment of a model lodging house. Not the number so and so Paradise Row, but a cottage all of our own, with its little garden, its healthy air, its clean kitchen, parlor and bedrooms' (ibid. p. 4) After detailing the requirements for a communal centre with laundry and baths run on a co-operative basis, Unwin's tract concluded with a peroration:

It is along these lines that we must look to for any solution to the housing question in town suburbs which shall be satisfactory from the point of view of health and economy, and at the same time afford some opportunity for the gradual development of a simple dignity and beauty in the cottage, which assuredly is necessary, not only to the proper growth and finer instincts of men, but to the producing of the indefinable something which makes the difference between a mere shelter and a home.

(ibid., p. 15)

In June 1906, Unwin contributed an article on 'Cottage Building in Garden City' to the GCA's *The Garden City* journal. This used some of the earlier material and set out detailed space standards and costings. He did however recognise that the cost of building good quality homes could only be covered by higher rents and he argued that there needed to be a rise in the minimum wage of unskilled labour of 9d per week to cover the higher rent. He argued that 8d to 1s per week represented the whole difference between good and bad:

> With that extra shilling for the rent of the labourer's cottage we may secure that every cottage built upon the Garden City estate shall at least be a decent one; and if Garden City stands for anything, surely it stands for this : a decent home and a garden for every family that comes there. That is the irreducible minimum. Let that go and we fail utterly. And if we succeed utterly, what then? A beautiful home in a beautiful garden and a beautiful city for all!
>
> (*The Garden City*, June 1906, Vol 1, No 6, p. 111)

In 1909, Unwin published *Town Planning in Practice*, a detailed guide to planning and town design, incorporating models from German and American planning as well as from British examples, including his own designs with Barry Parker for Hampstead Garden Suburb and Letchworth. In 1912, he published a more polemical pamphlet for the Garden Cities Association – *Nothing Gained from Overcrowding*. This extended his argument for lower density suburban development as set out in his 1902 tract.

In contrast with Geddes whose main planning activity was overseas, Unwin was in the postwar period to have a significant input into planning in the UK. In 1918 he was the advisor to the Tudor Walters Committee which established the first comprehensive housing standards in the country. In 1927, he was appointed technical adviser to the Greater London Regional Planning Committee and produced two reports in 1929 and 1933, the latter establishing the principle of the Green Belt around London.

Ruskin, Morris and the Arts and Crafts Movement

The influence of Ruskin and Morris on Geddes and Unwin has already been mentioned. One of Geddes's earliest works was a study of Ruskin as economist, while his 1886 essay quoted above owes much to Ruskin. Unwin's favourite quotations kept amongst his papers, included comments by Ruskin, Morris and Carpenter as well as by Lethaby. It was however through the Arts and Crafts Movement and its leading lights, Ashbee, Mackmurdo and Lethaby that the thinking of Ruskin and Morris was to impact on socialist perspectives on the built environment, and proved to be more significant in terms of their impact on architecture than on the development of town planning. Ruskin's influence has been the subject of a detailed study by Swenarton (1989), while that of Morris by Stansky (1985). Swenarton's book includes a chapter on the influence of the Ruskinian tradition on Unwin, as well as a chapter on Lethaby's role in establishing the Central School of Arts and Crafts, and his relationship with the Fabian Society. Stansky's book covers the role of the architect C R Ashbee in the Arts and Crafts Movement and that of Arthur Mackmurdo in establishing the Century Guild. Ashbee has been the subject of a biography by Alan Crawford (2005), while Lethaby has been the subject of a study by Godfrey Rubens (1986).

An American academic, Michael Lang (Lang, 1999), has sought to demonstrate that both Ruskin and Morris had significant impact on the town planning movement in both Britain and the United States. Lang has closely examined the written works of both luminaries to find any comments that could be understood as having a relationship to town planning. He also has reviewed a number of Ruskin's and Morris's projects. For Ruskin, in a chapter curiously titled 'Ruskin's efforts at practical town planning' he considers projects such his attempt to get students to build a road at Hinckley in Oxford to demonstrate the value of muscular labour, his support for Octavia Hill's housing project in Marylebone in London (though he was to disagree with Hill's approach to housing management), his support for the Commons Preservation Society, and his support for working men's colleges and the college settlement movement of Arnold Toynbee and Samuel Barnett. It is however difficult to relate these initiatives directly to the campaigns for housing, land and planning reform considered in the previous chapters, though it could be argued that his focus on medieval styles of architecture and craftsmanship was to act as a reference point for the medievalists within the later guild socialist movement such as C B Purdom.

Lang's work also includes a chapter on 'William Morris and the Town Planning Movement'. Morris's communitarian and medievalist vision in *News from Nowhere* and his hatred of the congestion and smoke of London was to inspire a number of architects and planners. However, as far as I am aware, Morris's extensive works make no explicit reference to town planning, and despite his own early experience in G E Street's architecture practice in Oxford, say little about architecture. In an essay in *Commonweal*, 'How We Live and How We Might Live', reprinted in 1888 in his essay collection *Signs of Change*, Morris set out a vision of a new community:

> When they [the workers] are no longer slaves they will claim as a matter of course that every man and every family should be generously lodged; that every child should be able to play in a garden close to the place his parents live in; that the houses should by their obvious decency and order be ornaments of it; for the decency and order above-mentioned when carried to the due pitch would most assuredly lead to beauty in building.
>
> (Morris, 1888, p. 30)

Morris argued for communal living rather than each family having its own dwelling:

> I console myself with visions of the noble communal hall of the future, unsparing of materials, generous of worthy ornament, alive with the noblest thoughts of our time, and the past, embodied in the best art which a free and manly people could produce; such an abode of man as no private enterprise could come anywhere near for beauty and fitness, because only collective thought and collective life could cherish the aspirations which would give birth to its beauty, or have the skill and leisure to carry them out.
>
> (ibid., p. 31)

Morris did however admit

> that is my opinion as a middle-class man. Whether a working-class man would think his family possession of his wretched little room better than his share in the palace of which I have spoken, I must leave to his opinion . . .
>
> (ibid., p. 32)

Morris's main contribution to discussions on the built environment was his founding of the Society for the Protection of Ancient Buildings (SPAB), known as anti-scrape, which campaigned against what was seen as inappropriate methods of restoration.

Lang refers to a lecture given by Morris, late in his life in 1894, to Charles Rowley's Ancoats Recreation Society in Manchester. The lecture under the title 'Makeshift' was an attack on the design of modern housing, which Morris referred to as 'the worst planned, the most uncomfortable, the most unreasonable: in a word they are idiotic' (Morris, 1894). Morris's polemic continued: 'As for the towns and cities made up of makeshift houses, how could they be anything but makeshift under the circumstances.'

Morris then contrasted the sprawl of Manchester and London with:

> what a city might be: the centre with its big public buildings, theatres, squares and gardens; the zone round the centre with its lesser guildhalls grouping together the houses of the citizens, again with its parks and gardens; the outer zone again, still with its district of public buildings, but with no definite gardens to it because the whole of his outer zone would be a garden thickly besprinkled with houses and other buildings. And at last the suburb proper, mostly fields and fruit gardens with scanty houses dotted about till you come to the open country with its occasional farmsteads. There would be a city for you. What is to hinder such kinds of cities being the type of future dwelling places of aggregated men? Nothing it seems to me, if men shall be free to build them.
>
> (Morris, 1894, cited in Lang, 1999, pp. 85–6)

Perhaps more surprisingly, ten years earlier, Morris had written an article for the SDF journal *Justice* on 'Homes for the Poor'. The article was a critique of the housing management project initiated by Octavia Hill and funded by Ruskin, attacking her 'household paradise of one room' and sought to give ' the philanthropists some idea of what we consider decent housing for the working classes'. It is Morris's proposition that comes as something of a shock –

> It might be advisable, granting the existence of huge towns for the present, that the houses for workers should be built in tall blocks, in what might be called vertical streets . . .This gathering of many small houses into a big tall one would give opportunity for what is also necessary for a decent life, that is garden space round each block.
>
> (Morris, 1884, pp. 4–5)

Morris also proposed each block have communal facilities – common laundries and kitchens and 'a great hall for dining in'. It is a little curious to find the inspirer of the Arts and Crafts Movement and of large Victorian gothic houses for the better off, proposing slab and tower block with communal facilities for the working class – the great medievalist becomes the inspiration for Corbusian modernism!

Lang relies largely for his argument on the role of Philip Webb, friend of and architect for Morris and member of the Socialist League. Webb had briefly worked with the young Morris in the practice of G E Street, but unlike Morris who had quickly moved on to other activities, had stayed in the profession and set up his own practice. Webb was perhaps the leading Arts and Crafts architect and built a number of large homes for well off clients, including Morris himself. Webb shared Morris's interest in gothic architecture and was co-founder with Morris of SPAB (Kirk, 2005). The Arts and Crafts style was however to influence architects and architect-planners, such as Raymond Unwin, Barry Parker, Lutyens, A J Penty, Alan Soutar and Baillie Scott, though as the first generation of LCC architects was to discover, applying such a style within constrained local authority budgets would require some modifications (Beattie, 1980; Rubens, 1986). Any direct or indirect influence of Webb on town planning as opposed to the design of individual buildings is however difficult to discern.

It can be concluded that while the Arts and Crafts Movement inspired by Ruskin and Morris clearly influenced housing design, the influence on the theory and practice of planning and housing policy is more difficult to assess. Of the leaders of the movement it is perhaps Lethaby who had the most direct influence, through his work with Sidney Webb and Quintin Hogg and Hubert Llewellyn Smith on the technical education board of the London County Council and perhaps more indirectly the influence of Webb on the first cohort of architects at the London County Council.

The environmentalism of Alfred Russell Wallace

Planning historians have given rather less attention to the influence of Alfred Russell Wallace. Wallace, co-discoverer of the theory of evolution with Charles Darwin, has already been referred to above in his role as the founder of the Land Nationalisation Society and author of a book on land nationalisation. Wallace's writing was however not limited to the issue of land nationalisation. Wallace had been involved in Mill's Land Tenure Reform Association in 1871. In 1880 he published a number of articles on land reform, before publishing his book in 1882 (Clements, 1983; Fichman, 2004). On reading Bellamy's *Looking Backward*, he moved to a more explicitly socialist position (Wallace, 1908). Though Wallace did not join any socialist organisation, in his campaign for land nationalisation, he collaborated with radicals, socialists and Fabians, though his Land Nationalisation Society with its yellow propaganda vans was to compete with the red vans of the Georgite English Land Restoration League. His socialist position on 'Economic and Social Justice' was set out in his contribution to *Vox Clamantium – the Gospel of the People*, edited by Andrew Reid and published in 1896 .

> I believe that the great work of this century ... is not its well meant and temporarily useful but petty and tentative social legislation, but rather that gradual reform of the political machine – to be completed, it is hoped, within the next six years – which will enable the most thoughtful and able and honest among the manual workers to at one turn the balance of political power, and, at no distant period, to become the real and permanent rulers of the country ... The larger part of the intention that has enriched the country has come from the workers, much of the scientific discovery has also come from their ranks; and it is certain that, given equality of opportunity, they would fully equal, in every high mental and moral characteristic, the bluest blood in the nation.
>
> (Wallace in Reid, 1894, pp. 179–80)

Wallace then set out

> a few principles and suggestions as to the course of legislation calculated to abolish pauperism, poverty, and enforced idleness, and thus lay the foundation for a true civilization which will be beneficial to all.

> That the ownership of large estates in land by private individuals is an injustice to the workers and the source of much of their poverty and misery . . .

> We should recognise no rights to property of the unborn . . .

> To refuse to recognise the right of any bygone rulers to tax future generations . . .

> (ibid., p. 181–6)

While in 1897, his contribution to *Forecasts of the Coming Century* published by the Manchester based Labour Press in 1899 was on 'Re-occupation of the Land' (Wallace, 1897), in 1899, he published a study of the 19th century as *The Wonderful Century – Its Successes and Failures*, which covered a range of mainly scientific subjects. Amongst the failures were Militarism, the Curse of Civilization, the Demon of Greed with his conclusion being entitled 'The Plunder of the Earth'. This was followed by an appendix on 'The Remedy for Want in the Midst of Wealth' (Wallace, 1899). Two further works were published in 1913 – *The Revolt of Democracy*, which was a historical study of 'the labour problem', and a series of essays on *Social Environment and Moral Progress*, with historical and theoretical sections (Wallace, 1913a, 1913b).

Other proponents of garden cities: A R Sennett and Budget Meakin

Howard was not the only writer on garden cities in the first decade of the 19th century.

In 1905, a British engineer, Alfred Richard Sennett, wrote a study of *Garden Cities in Theory and Practice*, which was presented as an amplification of a paper on 'The Potentialities of Applied Science in a Garden City' read before the British Association. This amplification comprised two volumes totalling 1400 pages (Sennett, 1905). Sennett had previously written books on 'horseless road locomotion' and travel books including *Across the Great St Bernard Pass*. He is not mentioned in the standard books on the histories of planning and garden cities (though the volumes are listed in the bibliography to Ashworth, 1954) and no biographical record appears to exist. He does not appear to have been known by Howard or by the other British garden city pioneers, though in his preface, Sennett acknowledges Howard's book as 'opening up a new vista in social, industrial and national welfare' with his own work presented as reinforcement of Howard's propositions. Sennett's starting point seems to have been opposition to concentration of population on the grounds of health and his introductory chapter draws on Richardson's *Hygeia*. His main argument was that new cities should be commercially viable and not dependent on government subsidy. Sennett was strongly opposed to the principles of equality and the role of trade unions. He presented himself as a practical man – 'Were it not wiser . . . to cast aside visions of the millennium, to cease striving for the unattainable, and concentrate on ideas concrete, in the hope of immediate alleviation of pain and suffering?' (Sennett, 1905, p. 35).

Beyond that statement, the volumes are primarily a technical presentation of examples of garden city developments in a range of cities – Sennett draws on British examples, but also schemes in France, Switzerland, the Netherlands, Germany and the United States – with most of his examples taken from employer developed industrial settlements such as Port Sunlight and Bournville and Pullman City in the United States, and the housing developed by the arms manufacturer, Krupp in Germany. Much of the study focused on industrial and artisanal production. Sennett's own contribution focused on sewage systems and transport provision. The volumes contain some 700 illustrations, many of which appear to be drawn by the author, who seems to have had an interest in mechanical devices and city design based on hexagonal forms, which Sennett sees as an improvement on the design concepts of Buckingham and Howard. The book's final section, starting at page 1371, which follows an illustrated note on sewer ventilation, concludes, after denying that his proposals are in any way utopian, with the quote that

> by Commerce are acquired the two things which wise men accompt of all other things most necessary to the wellbeing of a Commonwealth: That is to say, a general Industry of the Mind and Happiness of Body, which never fail to be accompanied with Honour and Plenty.
>
> (ibid., p. 1385)

Budget Meakin presented himself as a lecturer on 'industrial settlement', though it is unclear whether he was attached to any educational institution. His study of *Model Factories and Villages: Ideal Conditions of Labour and Housing* was also published in 1905. Meakin had been editor of the English language newspaper in Morocco, *the Times*, and had written a number of historical studies of the Moors. Meakin's book was a survey of industrial settlements in Europe. He appears to have been inspired by the co-partnership at Guise in France and to have drawn much of his information from the library of the British Institute of Social Service. He may have been associated with the Labour Co-Partnership Association, who published a pamphlet on the Guise project, and which had originated from the Labour Association for Promoting Co-operative Production, established by the Co-operative Congress in 1884. Meakin's book, while containing a wide range of examples of settlements and providing a useful comparative analysis of different components of settlements, such as buildings, communal eating, recreation, education and administrative facilities, is however primarily descriptive. While the concluding section sets out some guidelines for the development of settlements, the work does not set out any novel approach, nor demonstrate radical or communitarian principles.

The New Liberals and the Heart of Empire debate

It is important to recognise the changing political context at the turn of the century within which radical and socialist reformers operated. There had been a significant shift of thinking in the higher echelons of the Liberal Party. The experience of the London progressive alliance which dominated the politics of the London County Council in its early years can be seen as a prefiguration of a wider political shift. The Liberal party had for the last thirty years been moving away from its laissez faire approach as it moved to the more interventionist approach of what was called

'New Liberalism' (which in order to be clear as to our terminology was in many ways the opposite of the free market 'neoliberalism' of contemporary political discourse) (Semmel, 1960; Freeden, 1978; Clarke, 1978). It is also important to recognise that the Conservative governments of Disraeli and Salisbury were also interventionist, strengthening the role of the state in terms of its relationship with local government generally and housing matters more specifically.

Of the New Liberal theorists, it was perhaps Charles Masterman who did most to draw attention to the problems of the inner city (David, 1974; Freeden, 1978). Masterman was a journalist co-editing the *English Review* with Ford Maddox Ford before becoming Liberal MP for West Ham North in 1906. While at Oxford University, Masterman had been influenced by Christian socialism and by Ruskin and was later to publish a biography of Frederick Maurice and a contribution on Ruskin the prophet to a 1920 Ruskin centenary volume. He had then spent some time in South East London, following which he published a series of articles as *From the Abyss*. In 1901 he edited a series of essays under the title *The Heart of Empire: Discussions of problems of modern city life in England*. Masterman wrote the introductory chapter, entitled 'Realities at Home', while a chapter on 'The Housing Problem' was written by Frederick Pethick-Lawrence. Pethick-Lawrence was a suffragist and lawyer who had acted as treasurer for Percy Alden's Mansion House settlement in East London, editor of the progressive *Echo* and the *Reformers Yearbook* before converting to socialism in 1901. He became a Labour MP in 1923, financial secretary to the treasury in 1929 and leader of the opposition in 1942 when the leading Labour MPs joined the war coalition government. Both Masterman and Pethick-Lawrence were to become leading members of the Union for Democratic Control during the First World War.

In his introductory chapter, Masterman set out his reform programme:

> Back to the land, from gigantic mass populations to healthier conditions of scattered industry; housing reforms; temperance reform; a perfected system of national education; the elimination of the submerged; the redemption of women's labour; – all these are immediate necessaries. But all these are but palliatives of the one fundamental malady – attempts in some degree to check the ravages of selfishness, indifference and isolation. Accompanying all these must be whole hearted endeavour to deal with the disease at its very centre.
>
> (Masterman, 1901, p. 50)

In the chapter on housing, Pethick-Lawrence set out a more specific programme:

> Upon municipalities I would urge the importance of looking some way ahead; of making adequate provision to safeguard the growth of our cities where such possibility is in their hands ; of doing their utmost to secure open spaces and broad thoroughfares; of gradually enforcing the demands of the medical officer; of building houses where it seems necessary for the working classes up to the full requirements of sanitary conditions, and charging for them a rent which shall not be a burden on the rates; of demolishing insanitary areas generally , leaving them as open spaces, and frankly recognising that such undertakings must be of an unremunerative character.
>
> (Pethick-Lawrence, 1901)

Other contributors to the volume included R A Bray on 'The Children of the Town', Noel Buxton and Walter Hoare on temperance reform, P W Wilson on the distribution of industry, the economist A C Pigou on charity, F W Head on 'The Church and the People', G P Gooch on imperialism and G M Trevelyan on 'The Past and the Future'.

Masterman's 1906 election manifesto advocated graduated income tax, the rating of land values, farm colonies and public works programmes for the unemployed, small holdings, better housing for the poor, and old age pensions. In 1907 Masterman edited a further volume: *To Colonise England: A Plea for a Policy*. This set out a programme for rural resettlement. It included brief contributions from no less than thirteen other Liberal MPs. Masterman then published in 1909 *The Condition of England*. In 1908, he became undersecretary to John Burns at the Local Government Board, where his attempts to promote land value taxation and strengthen the 1909 Housing and Town Planning Act were frustrated. He supported Lloyd George and Winston Churchill on the 1909 budget crisis, the so called 'Peoples Budget', and in 1911 was to have a key role in steering the National Insurance Act through parliament. In 1920, he published a comprehensive statement of his political views in *The New Liberalism*.

Other New Liberals were to publish volumes on the need for more a more interventionist liberalism to respond to social problems, for example Percy Alden in his *Democratic England* (Alden, 1912). The introduction to this volume was written by Masterman. Alden had been warden of the Congregationalist Mansfield House settlement, a member of the executive of the Christian Socialist League and secretary of the National Unemployed Committee before being elected Liberal MP for Tottenham in 1906. Alden had been deputy Mayor in the ILP dominated West Ham Council in 1898, a co-opted member of the London School Board and a member of the progressive Rainbow Circle, which at one time met at his house, and on the executive of the Fabian Society. Alden also edited the Social Service series of books on social problems in 1908 for the British Institute of Social Service which he helped to found. He wrote three volumes in the series – on housing, poverty and unemployment. He was also an advocate of cooperative labour colonies. He joined the Labour Party in 1919, and was a Labour MP in 1923–4, only to resign from the party in 1927 disillusioned with Ramsay Macdonald's failure to deal with unemployment.

Alden's *Democratic England* included chapters on 'The Problem of Housing the Poor', 'The Land and the Landless' and on 'Municipal Ownership'. In the housing chapter, Alden set out his solution:

> The first remedy then is the destruction of the land monopoly by means of taxation; the second and hardly less important is the provision of cheap rapid transit by means of street railways and electric trains owned by the municipality. Before such railways are constructed, before even the plan of construction is made public, the municipality should be empowered to buy up land on both sides of the roads so that it will get some at least of the increased value of the land, due to the construction of the new street railway and will be able to make provision for the housing of its overcrowded citizens.
>
> (Alden, 1912, pp. 175–6)

Alden and Masterman are both examples of radical Liberals who were prepared to work with socialists and were actively involved in campaigns on housing and related social policy issues, demonstrating a greater interest and commitment than many independent Labour MPs. As shown above, the programmes they promoted in fact adopted many of the proposals of the Workman's National Housing Council and the Land Nationalisation Society and reflected a clear collectivist and socialistic approach to housing, land and town planning.

The politics of the garden city pioneers

Frederic Osborn was the main disciple of Ebenezer Howard and the main proponent of garden cities in England after Howard's death. In the interwar period he was to become the main advocate of new towns. He was to become housing manager of Letchworth garden city and chairman of the Town and Country Planning Association. In a radio interview broadcast in 1967 which is reprinted in Whittick's biography (Whittick, 1987), Osborn recounted how he had been a member of his local ILP branch as well as joining the Fabian Society, where he fell under the influence of H G Wells. He co-edited the *Fabian Nursling*, which was the magazine of the Fabian Nursery, as the Young Fabians were then called. Osborn commented that, as he was clearly 'council school and lower middle class' unlike many of his Fabian nursery colleagues, he was not taken up by the Webbs and had to make his own way in life. One of Osborn's colleagues in the Brixton ILP was Herbert Morrison, who as a conscientious objector also sought haven in Letchworth during World War I, before returning to London to become Mayor of Hackney council, leader of the London County Council, minister of transport under MacDonald and home secretary and foreign secretary under Attlee. Donoughue and Jones, in their biography of Morrison for which Osborn was interviewed, paint a vivid picture of the prewar socialist politics in South London and the wartime politics of Letchworth in which Osborn and Morrison participated (Donoughue and Jones, 1973).

Osborn differed from Howard in that he considered that government intervention was essential if new settlements were to be developed. He advocated this position as early as December 1918 in an article on '*The Public Control of the Location of Towns*' published under the pseudonym of Edward Ormiston in the *Economic Journal* edited by J M Keynes (Whittick, 1987). He was also the main author of '*New Towns after the War*', published in 1918 under the pseudonym 'New Townsmen' on behalf of the National Garden Cities committee.

Osborn's background and beliefs can be contrasted with that of Thomas Adams, who in 1901 became the first secretary of the Garden City Association. Adams brought up on a farm in the Pentland Hills near Edinburgh and first became involved in planning as a member of the West Linton parish council campaigning to remove squatters shacks from the village green. His first career was as a journalist, but he was also involved in Liberal party politics as secretary of the Midlothian Liberal Association, and agent for the Liberal candidate in the 1900 general election. He became chairman of a group of radical Liberals – the Young Scots society, which advocated Scottish self-government. Adams was a traditional laissez faire liberal, having no sympathy for state intervention or for socialism. On moving to London in December 1900, he attended meetings of the Fabian Society, though was clearly not persuaded by the Fabian case, and it was the voluntarist co-operative position of Howard that drew him to the Garden Cities Association (Simpson, 1985).

As secretary of the GCA and editor of its journal, *Garden Cities*, Adams had responsibility for writing papers and articles on a wide range of subjects, and these do show the wide range of influences and his generally pluralist and non-ideological approach. He contributed two extensive articles in the February and March 1906 issues on J S Buckingham's 1848 study, commenting that 'in many of its features it closely resembles the scheme put forward by Howard in 1898'. In an article in May 1906 on 'Model Towns and Communities', he focused on the influence of Carlyle, Ruskin and Emmerson. The June issue included a review of American co-operative communities including the Shakers, the Harmony Society and Zoar. Adams' monthly progress reports also covered contemporary developments in France, Germany, the Netherlands, Japan, America, New Zealand and Karl Lueger's *Ringstrasse* or 'Green Girdle' project in Vienna (*The Garden City*, Vol 1, 1906).

Charles Purdom, the third early pioneer of garden cities, had rather different interests. Purdom authored a 1913 volume on *The Garden City*, which was a study of the early years of Letchworth (and incidentally included an appendix by Unwin on the planning of the town). He was also a member of the National Garden Cities committee of 1918 and claimed to be co-author of the New Townsmen book, despite Osborn's claim to be sole author. Purdom was a literary editor, amateur dramatist and theatre critic, who became president of the actors' union, Equity. He was also a follower and biographer of the Indian mystic, Meher Baba, who advocated silence. Purdom was a member of the Labour Party but let his membership lapse and was elected as an independent councillor on Welwyn Garden City council in 1934. In 1933 he founded the *New Britain* journal, a non-party publication – neither Conservative, Socialist, Fascist or Communist, which sought to ' rouse people to their sense of individual responsibility' and was also involved in a campaign for European federation led by Patrick Geddes. In 1941, he published a book on *The New Order*, arguing for a British revolution and in 1945 a book on *World Organisation*. He continued to publish books on planning, including in 1945 a book on *How to Rebuild London*, and a new edition of his 1925 book on the *Building of Satellite Towns* in 1949. His politics are best described as individualist, voluntarist and federalist.

This review of the influences and politics of the garden city pioneers shows a wide range of influences and significant differences in ideology and political affiliation. It not only raises questions about the extent to which Ebenezer Howard was a synthesiser rather an originator, but also demonstrates the extent to which Howard's so called successors, Unwin, Geddes, Adams, Osborn and Purdom, did not necessarily see Howard as their mentor, but in fact drew inspiration from many earlier thinkers. Moreover, all these pioneers, unlike Howard, had an active engagement with politics and political organisations. This chapter has also sought to place the work of Howard and the other pioneers within their context and to recognise that Howard's work, however seminal, was only one contribution within a wider debate as to the future nature of society. Some previous writers have focused on the influence of Ruskin and Morris, but while these writers clearly influenced the Arts and Crafts Movement and had some influence on the architectural design of the garden cities, their impact on both the theory and practice of planning and civic development has been perhaps overstated (for example MacCarthy, 2014). It is important that the contributions of writers such as Alfred Russell Wallace, H G Wells, Charles Masterman and Percy Alden amongst others, should also be acknowledged.

Primary sources

Alden, P (1912) *Democratic England* (New York: Macmillan)

Branford, V and Geddes, P (1917) *The Coming Polity: A Study in Reconstruction* (London: Williams and Norgate)

Branford, V and Geddes, P (1919) *Our Social Inheritance* (London: Williams and Norgate)

Fabian Society (1896) Tract 70 *Report on Fabian Policy* (London: Fabian Society)

Fabian Society (1900) Tract 101 *The House Famine and How to Relieve It* (London: Fabian Society)

Geddes, P (1886) 'The Capitalist and the Labourer' in *The Claims of Labour* (Edinburgh, UK: Co-operative Printing Company)

Geddes, P and Slater, G (1917) *Ideas at War* (London: Williams and Norgate)

Horsfall, T (1905) *The Improvement of Dwellings and the Surroundings of People. The Example of Germany* (Manchester, UK: Manchester University Press)

Howard, E (1898) *Tomorrow: A Peaceful Path to Real Reform* (London: Swan Sonnenschein)

Howard, E (1902) *Garden Cities of Tomorrow* (London: Swan Sonnenschein)

Industrial Remuneration Conference (1885) *Report of the Proceedings and Papers* (London: Cassell)

Marshall, A (1885) *Where to House the London Poor?* (Cambridge)

Masterman, C (1901) *The Heart of Empire* (London: Fisher Unwin)

Masterman, C (1907) *To Colonise England: A Plea for a Policy* (London: Fisher Unwin)

Meakin, B (1905) *Model Factories and Villages: Ideal Conditions of Labour and Housing* (London: Fisher Unwin)

'New Townsman' (Frederic Osborn) (1918) *New Towns after the War: An Argument for Garden Cities* (London: J M Dent)

Morris, W (1884) 'The Housing of the Poor' in *Justice* 19th July 1884

Morris, W (1888) 'How We Live and How We Might Live' in *Signs of Change* (London: Reeves and Turner)

Morris, W (1891) *News from Nowhere* (London: Reeves and Turner)

Morris, W (1894) *Makeshift*: Lecture given in Ancoats, Manchester

Petavel, J W (1909) 'The Town Planning of the Future' *Westminster Review*, October 1909, Vol 172, pp. 398–405

Petavel, J W (1911) *The Coming Triumph of Christian Civilisation* (London: George Allen and Unwin)

Pethick-Lawrence, Frederick (1901) 'The Housing Problem' in Masterman, C (ed.), *The Heart of Empire* (London: Fisher Unwin)

Purdom, C B (1913) *The Garden City. A Study in the Development of a Modern Town* (London: J M Dent)

Purdom, C B (1951) *Life over Again* (London: J M Dent)

Richardson, John (1894) *How It Can Be Done* (London: Swan Sonnenschein)

Sennett, A R (1905) *Garden Cities in Theory and Practice*. 2 vols (London: Bemrose and Sons)

Simon, A (1893) *Chicago: The Garden City* (Chicago, IL: The Franz Gidele Printing Co.)

Unwin, R (1886) 'The Dawn of a Happier Day' in Creese, W, *The Legacy of Raymond Unwin* (Cambridge, MA: MIT Press, 1967, pp. 42–4)

Unwin, R (1897) 'Gladdening v Shortening the Hours of Labour' in Creese, W, *The Legacy of Raymond Unwin* (Cambridge, MA: MIT Press, 1967, pp. 45–6)

Unwin, R (1902) *Cottage Plans and Common Sense* (London: Fabian Society. Tract 109)

Unwin, R (1909) *Town Planning in Practice* (London: Fisher Unwin)

Unwin, R (1931) 'Edward Carpenter and Towards Democrac'y in Beith, G (ed.), *Edward Carpenter. In Appreciation* (London: George Allen and Unwin)

Wallace, A R (1894) 'Economic and Social Justice' in *Vox Clamantium*, Andrew Reided. (ed.)

Wallace, A R (1897) 'Reoccupation of the Land' in E. Carpenter, ed., *Forecasts of the Coming Century* (Manchester, UK: Labour Press)

Wallace, A R (1899) *The Wonderful Century – Its Successes and Failures* (London: Swan Sonnenschein)

Wallace, A R (1908) *My Life* (London: Chapman Hall)

Wallace, A R (1913a) *Social Environment and Moral Progress* (London: Cassell)

Wallace, A R (1913b) *The Revolt of Democracy* (London: Cassell)

Wells, H G (1902) *Anticipations of the Reaction to Mechanical and Scientific Progress on Human Life and Thought* (London: Chapman and Hall)

Wells, H G (1905) 'A Paper on Administrative Areas' read before the Fabian Society

Wells, H G (1905) 'Utopianisms I – The Garden Cities' *Daily Mail*, 18 March 1905

Wells, H G (1934) *Experiment in Autobiography* (London: Victor Gollanz)

Secondary sources

Aalen, F H A (1992) 'English Origins' in Ward, S, *The Garden City: Past, Present and Future* (London: Spon)

Alston, R (2012) 'Class Cities: Classics, utopianism and urban planning in early twentieth century Britain'. *Journal of Historical Geography*, Vol 30, pp. 1–10

Ashworth, W (1954) *The Genesis of Modern British Town Planning* (London: Routledge Kegan Paul)

Beattie, S (1980) *A Revolution in London Housing: LCC housing architects and their work* (London: Architectural Press)

Beevers, R (1988) *The Garden City Utopia: A Critical Biography of Ebenezer Howard* (London: McMillan)

Beith, G (ed.) (1931) *Edward Carpenter: In Appreciation* (London: George Allen and Unwin)

Bevir, M (2011) *The Making of British Socialism* (Princeton, NJ: Princeton University Press)

Boardman, P (1944) *Patrick Geddes: Maker of the Future* (Chapel Hill, NC: University of North Carolina Press)

Brown, K D (1971) *Labour and Unemployment 1900–1914* (Newton Abbott, UK: David and Charles)

Buder, S (1990) *Visionaries and Planners: The Garden City Movement and the Modern Community* (New York: Oxford University Press)

Cash, A C B Purdom. Biographical Notes at http://cashewnut.me.uk/WGCbooks/Purdom-biographical-details.php

Clarke, P (1978) *Liberals and Social Democrats* (Cambridge: Cambridge University Press)

Clegg, H, Fox, A and Thompson, A F (1964) *A History of British Trade Unions since 1889*, Vol 1, 1889–1910 (Oxford: Oxford University Press)

Clements, H (1983) *Alfred Russell Wallace* (London: Hutchinson)

Crawford, A (2005) *C R Ashbee: Architect, Designer and Romantic Socialist* (New York: Yale University Press)

Creese, W (1967) *The Legacy of Raymond Unwin* (Cambridge, MA: MIT Press)

David, E (1974) 'The New Liberalism of C F G Masterman' in Brown, K (ed.), *Essays in Anti-Labour History* (London: Macmillan)

Donoughue, B and Jones, G (1973) *Herbert Morrison: Portrait of a Politician* (London: Weidenfeld and Nicholson)

Douglas, R (1976) *Land, People and Politics* (London: Allison and Busby)

Fichman, M (2004) *An Elusive Victorian: The Evolution of Alfred Russell Wallace* (Chicago, IL: Chicago University Press)

Freeden, M (1978) *The New Liberalism* (Oxford: Oxford University Press)

Hall, P, Hardy, D and Ward, C (eds) (2003) *Howard, Ebenezer Tomorrow: A Peaceful Path to Real Reform with commentary* (London: Routledge)

Kirk, S (2005) *Philip Webb: The Pioneer of Arts and Crafts Architecture* (London: John Wiley)

Kitchen, P (1975) *A Most Unsettling Person: The Life and Times of Patrick Geddes* (New York: Saturday Review Press)

Lang, M (1999) *Designing Utopia: John Ruskin's Urban Vision for Britain and America* (Montreal: Black Rose Books)

MacCarthy, F (2014) *Anarchy and Beauty: William Morris and his Legacy* (London: National Portrait Gallery)

MacFadyen, D (1970) *Sir Ebenezer Howard and the Town Planning Movement* (Manchester, UK: Manchester University Press)

Mairet, P (1957) *Pioneer of Sociology: The Life and Letters of Patrick Geddes* (London: Lund Humphries)

Marshall, P (1962) 'A British Sensation', in Bowman, S (ed.), *Edward Bellamy Abroad*, ch. 3 (New York: Twayne)

Meller, H (1990) *Patrick Geddes: Social Evolutionist and City Planner* (London: Routledge)

Miller, M (1992) *Raymond Unwin, Garden Cities and Town Planning* (Leicester, UK: Leicester University Press)

Rubens, G (1986) *William Richard Lethaby: His Life and Work* (London: Architectural Press)

Scott, J and Bromley, R (2013) *Envisioning Sociology: Victor Branford, Patrick Geddes and the Quest for Social Reconstruction* (New York: State University of New York Press)

Scott, J and Husbands, C (2007) 'Victor Branford and the building of British Sociology', *Sociological Review*, Vol 55, No 3, pp. 460–84

Semmel, B (1960) *Imperialism and Social Reform* (London: Allen and Unwin)

Simpson, M (1985) *Thomas Adams and the Modern Town Planning Movement* (London: Mansell)

Stansky, P (1985) *Redesigning the World: William Morris, the 1880s, and the Arts and Crafts* (Princeton, NJ: Princeton University Press)

Studholme, M (2007) 'Patrick Geddes: founder of environmental sociology', *Sociological Review*, Vol 55, No 3, pp. 441–59

Sutherland, D (2009) 'Education as an agent of social evolution; the educational projects of Patrick Geddes in late-Victorian Scotland', *History of Education*, Vol 39, No 3, pp. 349–65

Swenarton, M (1989) *Artisans and Architects: The Ruskinian Tradition in Architectural Thought* (New York: St Martin's Press)

Taunton, M (2009) *Fictions of the City* (Basingstoke, UK: Palgrave Macmillan)

Urquhart, G (2003) Patrick Geddes and the Edinburgh Social Union. Accessed 28 March 2016 at http://hodgers.com/mike/patrickgeddes/feature_six.html

Whittick, A (1987) *FJO – Practical Idealist. A Biography of Sir Frederic Osborn* (London: TCPA)

Wright, T R (1986) *The Religion of Humanity: The Impact of Comtean Positivism on Victorian Britain* (Cambridge: Cambridge University Press)

11 The institutionalisation of planning and housing

From theory to practice

Whereas the previous chapter focused on the ideological development of the British planning pioneers, this chapter focuses on the implementation of planning and housing policy in the period before the World War I and the attitudes of progressives – radical Liberals, Labour and planning and housing reformers – to both the 1909 Housing and Town Planning Bill and Lloyd George's land campaign and land enquiries.

Labour and housing reform

The main socialist organisations, the Fabian Society, the ILP and the SDF, appear to have had relatively little input into or interest in the development of housing and planning legislation in the prewar period. It cannot be insignificant that the Fabian Society did not publish a single tract on housing and planning between Unwin's tract on *Cottage Homes* in 1902 and a tract on *Housing* by C M Lloyd in 1920. The Fabians did set up a housing committee in 1905, which was chaired by Edward Pease. This concluded that the real problem was low wages and that a minimum wage of 30 shillings a week would solve the housing problem. A summary of the committee's conclusions in *Fabian News* stated that:

> It would never be possible to tackle the urban problem seriously so long as employers of labour were allowed to transfer the irregularity of their demand for labour onto the shoulders of the wage earners, that in fact the decasualisation of casual employment is as indispensable a factor in urban housing reform as the minimum wage.
>
> (cited in Englander, 1973, p. 212)

The ILP published no further pamphlets on housing and planning and the columns of the ILP's *Socialist Review* do not appear to include any discussion of either the1908 or 1909 Housing and Town Planning Bills. Fred Jowett's 1905 short book on *The Socialist and the City* in the ILPs *Labour Ideals* series, discussed public ownership of land, site value rating, municipal trading, education, public health, poor relief, the unemployed and hospitals, but only made a very brief reference to town planning and housing referring to the experience of German municipalities in directly employing 'architects and others to draw up schemes for developing further building operations' instead of allowing private enterprise to build on the outskirts of the city (Jowett 1905, p. 25). The SDF published one pamphlet on housing in 1900 – *Social*

Democracy and the Housing Problem by Frederick Pickard-Cambridge, a vicar and naturalist, who had travelled to the Amazon and whose main interest was spiders and who was a correspondent of Alfred Russell Wallace. As will be discussed below, the contribution of Labour MPs to the main debates on the new legislation was limited to a short contribution to the debate on the second reading of the 1909 Bill.

The Fabians continued to be interested in the administrative arrangements for local government. In 1903, H G Wells presented a paper on *Administrative Areas* to a Fabian Society meeting (Wells, 1903). Wells' starting point was that the pre-existing local government structures were inefficient and not in a position to take on additional functions. Wells proposed a form of city regional government, going well beyond the London County Council boundary, to include all of what he called the London-centred population', which he based on the Thames Valley, with the addition of Sussex and Surrey and 'the east coast counties up to the Wash': 'You would have what has become, or is becoming very rapidly, a new urban region. A complete community of the new type, rich and poor, and all aspects of economic life together '(Wells, 1903, p. 7).

In 1905, the Fabians set up a committee to consider the reform of local government, under the chairmanship of LCC member W S Sanders. In October 1905, Saunders published a tract on *Municipalization by Provinces*, in which he argued for a system of city regional government. Saunders reviewed the range of municipal services – tramways and light railways, electricity and industrial progress, and housing. He argued against the voluntary federation of local authorities as this would only be adopted in a few cases – 'where all the districts represented on the committee would be equally benefited by co-operation'. He concluded that 'it is hopeless to expect an effective linking up of areas except by legislation, which will not make allowance for purely parochial considerations' (Sanders, 1905, p. 8). The paper then went on to set out details for the election funding and management of these new provincial bodies.

The genesis of the 1909 Housing and Town Planning Bill

The advocacy of housing and planning legislation came from three main sources – from the Garden Cities Association and the promoters of garden cities and suburbs, such as Letchworth, Hampstead Garden Suburb and Brentham Park in Ealing; from the National Housing Reform Council led by William Thompson and Henry Aldridge, and from the municipalities themselves, lobbying through the Association of Municipal Corporations, led by midlands and northern councils such as Birmingham, Manchester and Leeds. The Co-Partnership Housing Association also had a significant role. There was overlapping membership between these groups, the significant fact being that these were largely Liberal MPs and councillors, not Lib–Labs or independent Labour. The Workmen's National Housing Committee also continued to promote legislation, largely independently of the other bodies, given its focus remained on the provision of municipal housing. In addition, the Land Nationalisation Society and the English Land Restoration League and its offshoots advocated a series of Bills for land taxation and public ownership of land.

The most effective lobby for housing and planning reform was from the municipal authorities themselves, lobbying through both the Association of Municipal Corporations and the National Housing Reform Council. The first organisation had been formed in 1873 at a conference attended by representatives of forty-eight cities and boroughs and fifty-eight members of parliament. It had by been initiated by Manchester Corporation to organise opposition to protect the interests of municipal corporations as they might be affected by national legislative proposals; the initial concern being with the 1872 Borough Funds Act, which restricted a corporation's ability to incur expenditure in opposing legislation (Bellamy, 1988).

The AMC had eighty-three municipal corporations as members, with an executive committee of representatives from fourteen corporations, extended to a council of fifty in 1889. The town clerks of Manchester, Birmingham and Liverpool were honorary secretaries, with the Lord Mayor of London as honorary treasurer. Between 1890 and 1906, the chairman was Sir Albert Rollit, a lawyer and ship owner who was Mayor of Hull between 1883 and 1885 and from 1886 to 1906, the Conservative MP for South Islington, and at one time also president of the Law Society as well as founding the Associated Chambers of Commerce. He had also served as the chairman of the National Union of Conservative Associations. Rollit was a fervent advocate of the rights of municipal corporations. His view was that municipal collectivism was a safeguard for private property and that public works were an embodiment of virtue (Offer, 1981). In 1889, in a speech to the National Union of Conservative Associations, Rollit argued that:

> Men must meet Socialism itself. It stalks abroad and we must look in its face not shirk from it as a spectre only to be avoided. In its one sense of the State, the Municipality or public bodies, doing what men cannot do, or do so well, for themselves, its principle has been adopted in many of those statutes which are our own work, and of which our party has no reason to be ashamed.
>
> (cited in Offer, 1981, p. 223–4)

In a speech in 1895 on Municipalisation, in defending public works, Rollit commented that 'if it be said that such a programme is socialistic, I reply that as in all else, there is both good and bad in Socialism, that the adoption of what is good is the best preventative of what is bad' (ibid.).

In a speech in 1898, in response to the question 'What is the Ideal State?' Rollit responded:

> One in which the rich are not too rich nor the poor too poor. Danger, political and social, still lurks in each of these extremes, and they may best be modified by a wise and enterprising appreciation and application of the municipal spirit.
>
> (ibid.)

Under Rollit's leadership, in 1894 the AMC endorsed the principle of betterment as proposed in Bills by the London County Council and the Birmingham Corporation. Rollit demanded a wider extension of municipal powers, as 'the municipalities would soon practically solve for themselves the question of Betterment and Worsement much better than Parliament has yet shown its ability to do so, which would remove the great obstacle to local improvements' (cited in Offer, 1981, pp. 227–8).

In 1903, Rollit also defended the municipal corporations in parliament against the attacks made on 'municipal socialism' by *The Times*, which focused on West Ham, the first Labour controlled municipality and on Glasgow and Halifax. Rollit contrasted local government positively with the 'excesses of private enterprise' (Offer, 1981, p. 238).

It is therefore not surprising that the AMC also promoted an enhanced role for municipal corporations in housing and planning and in 1908 submitted a draft Housing and Town Planning Bill to the President of the Local Government Board.

Most prominent among the municipal corporations promoting housing and planning reform was the City of Birmingham. Birmingham had extensive experience of planning schemes, garden suburbs and housing development. Birmingham promoted its activity as a precursor for national legislation – J S Nettlefold, the chair of Birmingham's housing committee, published a series of books promoting housing and planning reform: *Practical Housing* in 1904; *Slum Reform and Town Planning: The Garden City Idea Applied to Existing Cities and Their Suburbs*, in 1906 and *Practical Town Planning* in 1914 (Gaskell, 1981). George Cadbury, member of the family which had developed the garden suburb at Bournville, became a member of Birmingham Council's planning committee. A land reformer, he co-authored the 1907 volume on *Land and the Landless* in Percy Alden's social service series. In 1915 he was to publish *Town Planning*, based on the experience of the Birmingham schemes.

The role of Manchester should also be recognised. The city had a record of housing and amenities improvements dating from the work of Charles Rowley's Ancoats Brotherhood of the 1880s. Thomas Coglan Horsfall, who had been active in the Brotherhood and who had campaigned for public parks, fresh air and museums for the working people of the city in 1905 visited Germany to study their experience of town planning and garden suburbs, and on his return published *The Improvement of Dwellings and the Surroundings of People. The Example of Germany* (Horsfall, 1905; Harrison, 1981; Ward, 2010).

Some recognition also needs to be given to the role of Leeds, which also had a history of promoting housing improvements, with the work of James Hole in the 1860s and 187's. In 1909, a plan was drawn up for the Fearnville Park garden city at Roundhay (Hole, 1866; Harrison, 1954; Gaskell, 1981).

At the AMC conference in Manchester Town Hall in October 1906, the Lord Mayor of Manchester proposed that the Association of Municipal Corporations promote a Bill. The conference agreed that:

> it was necessary for the safeguarding of the health and welfare of the inhabitants of our towns that Parliamentary powers should be conferred on town councils and other local authorities to enable them to control, by means of town extension plans, the laying out of all land within the boundaries of the towns or which may hereafter be incorporated; that in the opinion of this Conference, it is desirable that some central authority should be empowered to confer with town councils and other local authorities in regard to the plans contemplated building upon the areas between contiguous towns.

The Conference appointed a committee to draft a Bill, which was then submitted to the President of the Local Government Board (report in *The Garden City*, 1906, Vol 1, No 10, p. 236).

The first planning provisions to be included within legislation appear to have been in the Hampstead Garden Suburb Act of 1906 (Jackson, 1985). These were based on proposals from Raymond Unwin, the architect for the scheme, who was already involved in Joseph Rowntree's scheme at New Earswick in York and the garden city scheme at Letchworth. Unwin proposed a low density development with green spaces and allotments and with variable road widths and an ability to set houses back from road frontages. In order to overcome existing bye-law restrictions, which had proved an obstacle to Cadbury's scheme at Bournville, the Hampstead Garden City Trust, under the leadership of Henrietta Barnett, promoted a private Bill. This included a number of novel provisions:

1   that density of the development should on average be no greater than eight homes to an acre;
2   there should be at least fifty feet between homes on opposite sides of any road;
3   the trust had the power to make bye-laws relating to gardens, recreation grounds and open spaces;
4   existing bye-laws were suspended;
5   cul-de-sacs could be designed on different principles from through roads.

The Bill was promoted by the Liberal MP, Henry Vivian, one of the Trust directors and was enacted without any controversy. Some of these design provisions were to be included in the draft 1908 Bill by the Association of Municipal Corporations and the proposals put forward by the Garden Cities Association, and would appear in the final 1909 Act.

The main promoter of housing and planning reform was the National Housing Reform Council, which was to change its name to the National Housing and Town Planning Council in 1909, to reflect the enactment of the Housing and Town Planning Bill.

The National Housing Reform Council had been initiated in 1900. Peacock (1961, p. 142) argues that the organisation was initiated by the Land Nationalisation Society and that the organisation actually grew out of a series of provincial housing conferences organised by the LNS supporters in the co-operative and trade union movements culminating in a meeting in Leicester. The NHRC focused on parliamentary work and by 1906 had 130 vice-presidents in parliament. Its policy was that all insanitary dwellings should be destroyed without compensation, and that local authorities should implement the 1890 Housing Act, including using compulsory purchase powers to acquire unfit property. Its policy on land acquisition was based on rateable value – 'not on the basis of extortionate demands by landlords'. The NHRC however soon became independent of the LNS and developed a broader base of support, with its chairman, the housing reformer William Thompson of Richmond, and its secretary, Henry Aldridge, becoming prominent in debates over housing reform.

In 1906, the NHRC took a delegation to meet the prime minister, Henry Campbell-Bannerman and the President of the Local Government Board, John Burns. The delegation led by William Thompson, the chairman, had eighteen members, including the secretary, Aldridge, Horsfall, Cadbury, the Bishop of Wakefield, Sybella Gurney who was secretary of the Co-Partnership Housing Association, and councillors from Sheffield, Newcastle and Hull (Aldridge, 1914). The delegation presented a twelve-point programme – in effect a draft Bill:

1   Local Authorities should be stimulated to carry out their duties under the Health and Housing acts
2   Amendments to Public Health Acts

3 Closing and demolition of unhealthy dwellings
4 Clearance of slum areas
5 The creation of model suburbs
6 Acquisition of land by agreement
7 Compulsory purchase of land
8 Establishment of a national town and village development commission
9 Rural housing, smallholdings and other village development
10 Town extension planning
11 Cheaper money
12 Revision of bye-laws

(Aldridge, 1914, pp. 161–6)

Thompson gave an introductory presentation on the case for reform:

> Intemperance, lunacy, physical deterioration, unemployment, poverty and hooliganism followed in the train of other evils arising largely from bad housing conditions, although these by no means exhausted the consequences of the body-blighting, soul-destroying conditions of overcrowding and the slums. The cost of the products of bad housing conditions was also a serious matter for the ratepayers and taxpayers. . . . Local authorities had failed to do what was necessary under the Health and Housing Acts, partly because of apathy, ignorance, prejudice, and vested interests, but even more largely perhaps because of costly and difficult procedure or the inadequate powers contained in those Acts, while so far as sanitary improvements in existing dwellings were concerned, the scarcity of other suitable accommodation resulted in the penalising of the tenants by increased rents following on execution of sanitary repairs.

(ibid., p. 166)

Thompson claimed that many of the proposals were similar to those of the 1886 Royal Commission and that the overall reform package had been endorsed by the recent Trades Union Congress. One of the more novel proposals was for

> A central Town and Village Developments Commission acting through local bodies, such as county or borough councils, or special statutory committees established for suitable areas, should have large powers over land, housing and transit, the three great factors in town and village growth, and also a special fund and borrowing powers if necessary for doing this work effectively . . . Special powers for securing land for main roads, recreation grounds, sites for public buildings and workman's dwellings, together with facilities to encourage the provision of small holdings, the promotion of agricultural co-operation, and the improvement of transit might be conferred on these central and local authorities. It was therefore, essential to have improved facilities for compulsory purchase of land, which should be based upon the amount at which it was assessed for rates and taxes.

(ibid., pp. 167–8)

George Cadbury followed Thomson, and focused on the creation of garden suburbs. He suggested that each city should set up a development board to control development of the surrounding area from five to twenty miles around it, with the board controlled by representatives on the pre-existing developed area. Horsfall then spoke on the case for town planning powers to be given to local authorities, following the example of Germany and other European countries –

> the power to make extension plans for all land within the town boundaries, no matter to whom it belongs, the arrangements indicated in which all owners of land and all builders on it are compelled to comply with. . . The plan indicates the direction and width of every street; care is taken that some streets shall be pleasantly curved, that the new districts shall be beautiful as well as conveniently arranged and wholesome; that a sufficient number of playgrounds, planted open spaces, tree-planted streets, sites and schools and other public buildings shall be provided. The plan and the building regulations together can create districts of different character, some for dwellings, some for manufacture, and, in the districts of dwellings, prevent the erection of long rows of monotonous houses, and the covering of to large a portion of each site with buildings.
>
> (ibid., p. 169)

After a further eight presentations, Burns had the opportunity to reply. He quoted from Robert Burns whom he claimed to be a housing reformer

> To mak' a happy fireside clime-
> For weans and wife –
> That's the true pathos and sublime
> Of human life.

He then said that he accepted that 'the moment for practical ameliorative achievement was nearer to hand than it was some years ago'. He disputed claims that continental countries had more comfortable cities, even if they appeared to be better planned. Burns was not convinced that new powers were needed and that local authorities already had the powers to achieve most of what the NHRC wanted. Campbell Bannerman was similarly reluctant to give a commitment to bringing forward new legislation, commenting only that 'I hope we may find some time within a very few months to do something at least towards carrying out the object you have in view', a comment which the NHRC deputation seems to have taken as a firm commitment (ibid., pp. 177–82).

It is also necessary to refer to the work of the Co-Partnership Housing Association. The co-operative movement had been involved in previous projects for housing and new settlements, some of which have been discussed in earlier chapters. In 1881, the co-operator, E O Greening had proposed housing societies should share profits with the tenants. Benjamin Jones had presented this idea to the 1885 Industrial Remuneration Conference and in 1887 had set his proposals out in a pamphlet. The initiative was also inspired by Godin's project at Guise in France (Gaskell, 1981; Birchall, 1995). The Labour Co-partnership Association was established in 1884 – the chair in 1901 was the lawyer and former Liberal MP, Ralph Neville, who was later to chair the Garden City Association. In 1901, a co-partnership housing project was established in Brentham, Ealing with the support of Henry Vivian, the promoter of the Brentham Park garden suburb, who in 1906 was elected Liberal MP for Birkenhead. A former trade union organiser for the Society of Carpenters and Joiners, Vivian was a member of the Central Board of the Cooperative Congress for the London region, edited the journal *Labour Co-Partnership* and founded the Labour Co-partnership Association. The Ealing project was also supported by Neville and by the elderly former registrar of friendly sites, the Christian socialist, J M Ludlow. Following the Ealing initiative, the movement spread with projects being initiated by the economist Professor Stanley Jevons in South Wales, by Nettlefold in Harborne in Birmingham, as well as other projects in Sevenoaks, Letchworth, Hampstead Garden Suburb, Oldham, Manchester, Warrington, Liverpool, Knebworth and a number of other towns – in all there were thirty-six schemes before 1914. In 1905, Unwin was employed as consulting architect to the Co-partnership Tenants Housing Council. Vivian, Howard, Lever and Cadbury all sat on the executive together with representatives from each project. There was a close relationship with both the Garden Cities Association and the NHRC/NHTPC (Birchall, 1995).

As mentioned above, the Garden Cities Association was established in June 1899 by Ebenezer Howard. The first meeting with twelve sympathisers was held in the office of Alexander Payne, an accountant who was treasurer of the Land Nationalisation Society. The meeting was chaired by Alfred Bishop, who also supported land nationalisation, and in fact six attendees were members of the LNS. The meeting was also attended by Bruce Wallace of the Brotherhood Church. The other attendees were George Crosoer, Joseph Johnson, George King, Joseph Hyder, Herbert Mansford, W Charter Piggott, W Sheowring, A H Singleton, and Francis Steere. It is significant that this group did not include any of the Liberal MPs on whom Howard and the GCA were later to depend, nor were any involved in the Georgeite groups. Bruce Wallace was the only attendee with a record in socialist communitarianism (Marshall, 1962; Buder, 1990; Hardy, 1991).

The GCA was initially based in the LNS office. Fishman commented that

> At first the Garden City Association seemed little more than an adjunct of the LNS. A corner in the LNS office was designated as the headquarters of the Garden City Association, and a majority of its members were prominent in the older body.
>
> (Fishman, 1977, p. 56)

Buder comments that Howard was not only sympathetic to Wallace's views on land reform, but had actually been employed in the past by the LNS to take notes of its meetings (Buder, 1969, p. 392).

The first chairman of the GCA was H W Idris, a Liberal member of the London County Council. The first secretary was Francis Steere, a barrister, who was already secretary of the LNS, though within a few months this role had been taken over by another barrister, C M Bailhache. Payne, the LNS treasurer, became GCA treasurer, reinforcing the links between the two organisations (Hardy, 1991). Howard however quickly sought to broaden out the membership of the organisation from its LNS sponsorship and claimed that it had amongst its members 'manufacturers, cooperators, architects, artists, medical men, financial experts, lawyers, merchants, ministers of religion, members of the LCC, moderates and progressives, socialists and individualists, radicals and conservatives' (Howard, 1902, cited in Hardy, 1991, p. 19).

In July 1903, the GCA decided to extend its role beyond the promotion of the ideas in Howard's book to the general promotion of the relief of overcrowded areas and the achievement of a wider distribution of the population. A resolution was passed setting up a number of subsidiary objectives: encouraging manufacturers to remove their works from congested areas of the country, co-operating with or advising firms, public bodies and other associations to secure better housing for workers near to their place of employment; taking steps to promote effective legislation and generally advocating the ordered design of and development of towns and promoting the practice of well-designed houses with gardens (Culpin, 1913; Hardy, 1991). Culpin claimed that this statement represented an endorsement of municipal planning – Howard's original vision having focused on the role of entrepreneurs and philanthropists rather than the municipalities. The shift of position clearly reflects the influence of the LNS and municipal practitioners such as Nettlefold and the LCC progressives.

In September 1903, the GCA established the First Garden City Association to develop the land they had acquired at Letchworth in Hertfordshire. Ralph Neville, who had taken over as GCA chair, became chair of the Board of Directors. Thomas Adams was employed by both organisations. The first issue of the GCA journal, *Garden Cities*, published in October 1904, sought to distinguish between the two organisations 'The Association is entirely educational; The Company entirely practical' (quoted in Hardy, 1991, p. 43).

In March 1906, the Garden Cities Association held a conference at the Criterion restaurant in London on Garden Cities and Agriculture. This was chaired by the Liberal MP, James Bryce. Bryce argued that

> cities in England, more than anywhere else in Europe, had been growing too large, and steps were urgently needed to check their growth. London was practically annexing other towns by the extension of electric tramways. Few realised the enormous economic waste caused by people living at a great distance from their work; and though much had been done to accelerate the conveyance of working men to and from their work no very great acceleration would now be possible without gigantic expense. If people could do their work close to their own homes, there would be a great increase, not only in the comfort of the people, but in the wealth-producing power of the country.

Bryce argued that if a city was bigger than 200,000 to 300,000 people, few people got access to the countryside and fresh air. He also considered that the overgrowth of cities led to the evil of the segregation of classes. After Thomas Adams had read a paper by Ralph Neville on 'Garden cities as a solution to the housing problem from an industrial point of view', Geddes proposed that

> the housing problem can be solved and the congestion in crowded centres relived by a concerted movement of manufacturers, co-operators and others to new areas, arrangements being made for securing to the people the increased value which their presence will give to the sites, and the areas being carefully planned so as to make adequate provision for the individual and social needs of the people, especially with a view to securing for all time, the combined advantages of town and country life.

In the afternoon session of the conference, which focused on the role of garden cities in countering the trend towards rural depopulation, speakers included the author, Rider Haggard, who was a farmer and active in rural reform campaigns, the radical Liberal MP, Percy Alden and Henrietta Barnett, who spoke on the Hampstead Garden Suburb. A representative of the Social Democratic Federation, Mr Webster, proposed 'the abolition of monopoly in the possession of land', a proposal which though rejected, won the support of thirty-three attendees (Report of conference in *The Garden City*, April 1906, Vol 1, No 3, pp. 70–3).

After this conference, the Garden Cities Association focused on pressing for planning legislation. Nettlefold, who led on planning issues for the NHRC, was also involved in the GCA and in February 1907 a GCA conference adopted a resolution he had proposed that town planning powers should be granted to local authorities. In October, the GCA held a town planning conference on Town Planning in Theory and Practice at the London Guildhall at which over a hundred local authorities were represented (GCA, 1907). Representatives attended from a wide range of organisations including the Association of Municipal Corporations, the Housing Reform Council, First Garden City (Letchworth), Hampstead Suburb Trust, RIBA, the Engineers Institute, the Surveyors Institute, the Land Nationalisation Society and Geddes's Sociological Society. Neither the SDF nor the WNHC appear to have been represented and the conference passed without any dissent to the position of the GCA being expressed.

The GCA was aware that the government was already drafting legislation. The GCA submitted for discussion a memorandum which promoted the garden city concept but also acknowledged the case for town planning legislation following the German model. It also included in the conference report, extracts from the 1906 Hampstead Garden Suburb Act, as well as notes on town planning at Harborne in Birmingham and a brief history of the GCA's previous work on town planning.

The memorandum, after referring to the evil of slums and overcrowding, stated that its object was

> to draw the attention of local authorities to the inadequacy of their powers in dealing with the Housing question; to invite their suggestions and co-operation in stimulating both public opinion and the Legislature, and to assist the Association in its modest but earnest endeavours towards the prevention of the growth of the above mentioned evil and the creation of happier communal conditions of public health and social environment.
>
> (ibid., pp. 68–9)

The main conference resolution was introduced by Nettlefold:

> That this meeting of municipal and local authorities and societies and others interested in housing reform and town planning, affirms its belief that the present planless and haphazard extension of towns is detrimental to the best interests in the nation, inasmuch as, by the creation of new slums and overcrowding, it produces mental, moral and physical degeneration, and is also burdensome to the ratepayers; it therefore calls on all parties to welcome the Government's promise of legislation upon the matter. This meeting urges, also, the great advantages which should result if, wherever possible, a belt of agricultural land

could be retained around the neighbourhood of any new suburb or town which may be built to relieve the congestion of the urban population. It would further urge the importance of dealing with the problem of rural housing.

(ibid. p. 13)

The memorandum then set out its programme for inclusion in legislation as:

a) General development schemes for the increase of existing towns and planning of new towns;

b) Powers for Local Authorities to Acquire Land for the creation of new towns; and

c) Money loans – that the Government should lend money for housing purposes to public bodies.

(ibid., p. 71)

Howard and the GCA had in the past been ambivalent about a government controlled planning system, preferring self-supporting philanthropic and co-operative initiatives. Nettlefold claimed that town planning was the 'application of the garden city idea to existing cities and their suburbs ... and the application of business principles to the solution of the housing problem'. As Sutcliffe rightly points out, the second statement is questionable, given the town planning causes of the 1909 Act were not in any way based on business principles (Sutcliffe, 1981, p. 78). It could also be argued that the first statement represents a significant adaption of Howard's position.

The cost of acquiring land was much discussed at the conference, though there is no record of the representative of the Land Nationalisation Society contributing to the debate. Thomas Adams however made the significant point that it was a landowner's ability to develop at high densities that pushed up land values –

the law allowed the putting up of more houses to the acre than was good for the health of the people; and if there were a law restricting the number of houses to the acre in accordance with the dictates of common sense and with the necessities of health, that law would make it much more easy for the public to purchase.

(ibid., p. 50)

The conference report states that the resolution proposed by Nettlefold was carried unanimously.

The conference represented a significant shift in the GCA's position to recognise the establishment of planning as a statutory function of government, and after the conference, the GCA changed its name to the Garden Cities and Town Planning Association.

The Land Nationalisation Society and the English Land Restoration League in the early 1900s

The LNS, while supporting the work of the National Reform Council, initiated its own municipal housing campaign in 1902. It held a conference in May at the Essex Hall in London, with delegates from ninety-two progressive organisations – Liberals, socialists, co-operatives and trade unions. Local authorities and the single-taxers did not participate. The conference was attended by Charles Macnamara MP and also by Randal Cremer, who had been involved in the Land Tenure Reform Association in the early 1870s. The LNS had realised that the chances of getting a comprehensive land nationalisation measure through parliament were minimal, so Cremer suggested that the best way of getting land into public ownership was by legislating for local authorities to have the power to compulsorily acquire land for any purpose. As a concession to the Georgite single-taxers, the Bill they proposed, which became known as the 'Tax and Buy Bill', included provisions for a local authority levy of 1d in the £1 of capital value of both developed and undeveloped land (equivalent to 2 shillings in the £1 of annual value – ie 10 per cent), as well as a power for local authorities to acquire any land on a compulsory basis. Any tenants would have security of tenure. The proposals were supported by local authorities and by a wide range of Liberal and Labour MPs. The Bill was introduced into parliament in 1904 and in 1905, with support from Keir Hardie, Will Crooks and Richard Bell. A conference on metropolitan borough councils was arranged to publicise the Bill (Peacock, 1961, pp. 142–6).

While the LNS concentrated on work in parliament, the ELRL focused on a propaganda campaign in rural areas – known as the 'red van' campaign, undertaken on a similar basis to the earlier 'yellow vans' of the LNS. The campaign focused on the issue of rural depopulation and obtained support from trade unions whom were concerned not just at the position of agricultural workers, but the fact that the move of unemployed rural labourers to the towns was supplying cheap labour which jeopardised the wages of urban trade unionists such as the London dockers. These campaigns were often supported by ILP members, though the campaigns also served to help the Liberal party in rural areas in the general elections (Peacock,1961, pp. 152–78).

Both the LNS and the ELRL were active in the 1906 election. Peacock notes that thirty-seven supporters of the LNS's 'tax and buy bill' stood as candidates for either the Liberal party or the Labour party (Peacock, 1961, p. 179). After the election, with the Liberals in government, the LNS focused on promoting a Smallholders Bill to give Local Authorities the power to compulsorily purchase land for smallholdings, with the Board of Agriculture having the power to do so where a local authority was reluctant – legislation which was enacted in 1907. The LNS continued to pursue their 'Tax and Buy' proposals, with the bill reintroduced in 1906, 1907 and 1908. The LNS however withdrew their measure in 1909 in favour of a new motion of the taxation of land values proposed by the Labour MP, James O'Grady. There was disagreement between the Georgites and the LNS on the basis for valuing land for taxation purposes. Asquith in 1907 indicated that the government would itself bring forward a land taxation Bill (Peacock, 1961, pp. 179–84). The advocacy of both the LNS and the ELRL prepared the way for Lloyd George's Peoples Budget, which will be discussed below.

The Workman's National Housing Council and the Housing and Town Planning Bill

The Workman's National Housing Council carried out its own lobbying on the new Bill, seeking to revisit some of the issues raised in its previous attempts to revise housing legislation. They were disappointed that the extension of the loan repayment period in the 1903 Act, was of little use to London councils. In practice the president of the Local Government Board, Walter Long, was refusing consent for any loan with a repayment period over fifty-five years. The WNHC argued that the interest rate should be subsidised and tried to get London Labour by-election candidates to endorse this position. The WNHC was concerned that the 'town planning movement' had in 'informed circles' at least eclipsed the housing movement. They also found divisions within their own ranks – at a housing conference in London on 3rd December 1904, Macnamara turned up and persuaded the delegates, by a majority of 162 votes to 160, to oppose the levying of a direct rate by councils to fund their housing schemes (Englander, 1973, p. 223).

The WNHC focused its attention on the London County Council. Robert Williams was elected to the LCC for Lambeth and together with the ILPer Frank Smith fought to maintain the standards of the LCC housing schemes. The LCC, now under control of the Moderates, had reduced the standards for the scheme in Tottenham from those adopted for the Boundary Street estate, the reduction of standards being supported by John Burns. The LCC moderates then decided to sell off the undeveloped sites. The main controversy was over a site at White Hart Lane, Tottenham. After WNHC protests, John Burns at the Local Government Board intervened to stop the sale of part of the site. The WNHC also tried to get the ILP and the SDF to agree joint candidates for the 1907 LCC elections, but the Moderates retained control. Steadman did however return to parliament in the 1906 general election. Nationally some thirty Labour MPs endorsed the WNHC policies. The radical Liberal, Percy Alden, tried to set up a parliamentary housing lobby group (Englander, 1973, p. 265).

At the Local Government Board, Burns focused initially on rural housing. He set up a select committee on rural housing, to which Knee gave evidence. The committee endorsed the WNHC's case for government subsidy. Knee was concerned that the organisation was being marginalised by Thompson and Aldridge of the National Housing Reform Council, who were working closely with Burns, as shown by the Prime Minister's reception of their delegation discussed above. Macnamara, now disaffected from the WNHC, became parliamentary secretary at the Local Government Board. Knee reported to the WNHC in 1907 that 'there is too much talk of land just now and too little of housing' (ibid., p. 373).

As discussed above, Campbell Bannerman and Burns had indicated to the NHRC that they would consider bringing forward some housing and planning legislation. In June 1907, the prime minister announced that this would now be deferred. Knee attacked the NHRC for being too timid:

> We played our part as a workman's organisation in kicking and prodding the Conservative government of 1900 and 1903 and legislation ensued; but if the policy of the NHRC ... is to continue to express unwarranted confidence in the premier and Mr John Burns, and to persuade the latter that housing is after all only a speculative fad of 'town planning' (a play term which signifies nothing, and can wait till all the other fads have been dealt with), then they are playing directly against the interests of the workers and against the housing problem being solved ... through the action of professional housing reformers, the slum dweller, the overcrowded, the rack rented have been sold once more.
>
> (*Housing Journal*, July 1907, cited in
> Englander, 1973, p. 275)

Englander rightly comments that the Labour Representation Committee established in 1900 had shown little interest in housing, with Keir Hardie focusing on the issue of unemployment and defence of the Labour-trade union link (in the aftermath of the Taff Vale judgement of 1901). The only Labour MPs actively supporting the WNHC were Will Thorne and Charles Bowerman. Knee commented that the ILP leadership did not understand the difference between the government's position and that of the WNHC. The Labour Party conference in 1908 did however support the WNHC's criticism of the government's draft Bill (Englander, 1973, pp. 279–82).

Knee's main criticism of the government's initial proposals was that 'the measure lacks the one thing necessary to a national scheme of housing, that is money' (*Housing Journal*, April 1908). In *Justice* the following month, Knee's criticism was more severe. It was a:

> Bill of mere machinery clauses and with a theatrical bundle of nebulous town planning proposals, borrowed from slummy Birmingham . . . Unless he (Burns) and his friend Asquith put some money into this business, they will be as the jerry builder of commerce who use mud for mortar.
>
> (*Justice*, 4th April 1908)

In May, the WNHC held a conference at the Westminster Palace hotel, to discuss their amendments to the legislation. Knee then approached Henderson to lobby for their proposals, and Henderson agreed that the Labour Party support the WNHC position.

Fred Jowett spoke on behalf of the Labour Party in the second reading debate on 12 May 1908. Jowett first made positive comments about the 1890 Housing of the Working Classes Act before pointing out that 'the condition of affairs had remained practically untouched, so far as the large towns were concerned' and that the proposed new legislation 'would not touch vitally the problems of housing in large towns'. Jowett then drew attention to Labourers (Ireland) Bill, in which the government had provided £4.5 million at 3 1/2 per cent interest to fund 25,000 cottages in Ireland and questioned why England, Scotland and Wales should be treated differently. 'He despaired of any substantial improvement being made until the question of the provision of means by the State was boldly and fearlessly dealt with.'

He argued that the cost of acquiring land had been the main obstacle to councils using the powers granted by the 1890 Act. He was concerned that councils had to pay commercial value for development land, but argued that it was a council decision to develop land for housing which gave the land increased value, not any action taken by the landowner – 'the difference between the value of land as a site for houses and its value as a site for warehouses or other purposes ought to belong to the community'.

Jowett challenged Burns 'in view of his own record and previous associations why he had made no provision for purchasing the land on terms such as he was sure the right on Gentleman in his heart of hearts must favour'. Rather tactlessly, Jowett then followed up his appeal with an attack on the performance of the Local Government Board, of which Burns was the president. Jowett saw the Board as the main obstacle to housing reform rather than a 'great reforming agency of the State' – 'it seemed to be assumed that the Ethiopian was to change its skin and the leopard its spots'. In response to his comment that 'there was work for the Local Government Board to do', Burns responded 'hear, hear' which led Jowett to quip 'Yes, but he would like to see it do it, it had not yet done it'. Jowett argued that there should be a much tougher inspection regime, that Inspectors should collect information on death rates in different kinds of property, hold a public enquiry and 'bring the force of publicity to bear on the local authority'. Burns responded 'That is what these Inspectors will do'. Jowett concluded that 'The Labour Party thought that this Bill ought to go much further, and it would therefore be their duty as far as they could to make every effort to strengthen its provisions and make it better than it now was' (Parliamentary Debates, May 1908).

The Labour Party, betterment and land nationalisation

There is little evidence that the Labour Party followed through on Jowett's promise. With the conclusion of the second reading debate, the Bill was then sent to standing committee, which was chaired by Sir F Channing and held twenty-three meetings between 14 July and 3 December. The Labour Party did not nominate either of their two housing experts, Bowerman and Jowett, to the Bill committee and were instead represented by four MPs – Pete Curran, A H Gill, G D Kelley and J W Taylor, none of whom had showed much interests in housing or planning. In fact, Taylor, who was supposed to be the lead Labour Party representative, missed many committee meetings, apparently on union business, and though eventually replaced by Jowett, it was too late for the latter to have much impact (Englander, 1973, p. 289). Burns told a WNHC delegation that he sympathised with the WNHC positon on the need for subsidy, and apparently considered using part of the unemployment grant budget for housing, but Asquith then announced that there was no time to take the Bill as amended by committee back to the full House of Commons for enactment, and the Bill was deferred to the following session.

On its return on 5th April 1909, the Bill was not significantly modified. This time Jowett did manage to contribute to the debate. His main point was the cost to local authorities in buying land and undertaking housing schemes was excessive and that the Bill did not include any provisions to mitigate this. He then spoke in favour of the clause requiring local authorities to carry out surveys of housing conditions (a clause inserted in standing committee apparently against Burns' wishes). Jowett also expressed concern at the possibility that landowners would benefit from the increased value of land arising from it being allocated for housing in a council plan, arguing that a landowner should only be paid on the basis of its pre-existing value. He was also concerned that houses built by public utility societies in locations such as Letchworth and Hampstead were too expensive for most working class households (*Hansard* 5th series, Vol 2, 5 April 1909). Booth and Huxley (2012) have pointed out that when the Bill went back into committee, Keir Hardie, with support from George Barnes and Fred Jowett, proposed an amendment, following Jowett's earlier representations, to introduce clauses

> providing for the separate valuation and assessment of all lands and buildings acquired or created in connection with any scheme carried out under the provisions of the this Act, and for acquiring for the local authority all increments of value in lands which can be traced to the improvements or schemes carried out under the provisions of this Act.

Booth and Huxley note that the Speaker ruled this amendment as out of order as introducing clauses which went beyond the original objectives of the Bill (ibid., pp. 278–9).

It should however be noted that the enacted legislation did nevertheless include a betterment clause – Clause 58(3) reads:

Betterment charges for property increased in value by town planning schemes

Whereby the making of any town planning scheme, any property is increased in value the responsible authority, if they make a claim for the purpose within the time (if any) limited by the scheme (not being less than three months after the date when notice of the approval of the scheme is first published in the manner prescribed by regulations made by the Local Government Board, shall be entitled to recover from any person whose property is so increased in value one half of the amount of that increase.

When this clause, which had not been in the draft Bill but which had been inserted by the government at standing committee stage, was debated in the Committee stage in the full House of Commons, it was opposed by the Conservatives. No Labour MP spoke in the debate. The debate over the Housing and Town Planning Bill clause was paralleled by a debate over a clause in the Finance Bill that local authorities should recover the full increase in the value of property arising from redevelopment. This Bill was rejected which led to a constitutional crisis and a reform of the powers of the House of Lords, before the Bill was enacted in 1910, including provisions for a tax of 20 per cent on the increase in value of all land (not just development land) on resale (Douglas, 1976; Murray, 1980). Although the Finance Bill provisions generated significant political opposition, the debate over the Housing and Town Planning Act clause was more muted. References were made to the report of the House of Lords select committee on betterment which had concluded that:

The principle of betterment, in other words, the principle that where persons have property which has clearly increased in value by an improvement effected by the expenditure of public funds, is not in itself unjust, and such persons can equitably be required to contribute to the cost of the improvement.

(House of Lords, 1894)

As discussed earlier, the principle of betterment had also been accepted by the Royal Commission on Housing of the Working Classes in 1885.When the new clause was put to the vote it was carried by a majority of 184 votes to 36.

For the radicals, including the more radical members of the 1906–1914 governments, the debate over the planning clauses of the Housing and Town Planning Bill was part of the wider campaign against private landlords, which was linked to the attack on the power and wealth of the aristocracy, which had been central to radical ideology over the previous century. The Liberal party position on land in the prewar period was dominated by the single-taxers of the English Land Restoration League, who followed the economic ideas of Henry George. This marginalised both the land nationalisers in Russell Wallace's Land Nationalisation Society, and their allies in Knee's Workman's National Housing Council, who saw municipal ownership of land

and development as a better approach than private and philanthropic led development. It is significant that the Garden City Association kept out of the land tax and land nationalisation debate – the economic viability of garden city development as promoted by Howard relying on the trustification of land value and reinvestment in the community. Proposals for the nationalisation of land or the payment of land value increments to the Treasury would both obstruct the garden city economic model.

Some form of betterment taxation had been long promoted by Fabians such as Sidney Webb and the Georgite single tax position, long promoted by the Christian socialist wing of the party including Stuart Headlam and Frederick Verinder, and was supported by leading members of the parliamentary Labour Party such as George Barnes, who published a pamphlet biography of George in 1906 for the ILP. Tichelar (1997), however, referring to correspondence between Keir Hardie and the American single-taxer, Joseph Fels in 1910, suggested that the ILP as a whole favoured the position of the Land Nationalisation Society of a combination of municipalisation and taxation and was opposed to the single-taxers. Pat Thane quotes an early manifesto by Ramsay MacDonald in 1892 that the land monopoly be solved by a combination of taxation of land values and rents by county and town councils and council ownership of land (Thane, 1991). Packer notes that thirty of the thirty-seven Labour MPs sitting in the 1914 parliament were LNS vice presidents (Packer, 2001). However, thirty-six of the forty-two Labour MPs elected in December 1910 signed the single taxers land memorandum of 1911, and in 1914, Labour supported the introduction of site value rating in the 1914 budget (Packer, 2001). There is therefore evidence that most MPs managed to support both nationalisation and site value rating rather than seeing them as alternatives.

Support for the LNS was not confined to the Labour Party. In 1909 at the time of the budget controversy, the LNS claimed to have a total of 112 supporters in parliament. This did not necessarily mean that the seventy or so Liberal MPs listed actually supported comprehensive land nationalisation. The LNS was active in campaigning to support Lloyd George's budget proposals, participated in two rallies in Hyde Park in July and December 1909 and distributed some two million leaflets in the 1910 general election campaign (Barry, 1965).

It was the Georgites who were to have the most impact on land reform legislation. Their most prominent parliamentary advocate was the radical MP, Josiah Wedgwood, who was president of the English League for the Taxation of Land Values. Wedgwood led a group of radical MPs which included Philip Morrell, Charles Trevelyan and the Scottish Lord Advocate, Alexander Ure. In 1908, the House of Lords threw out the Land Values (Scotland) Bill which would have allowed for site value rating, with the consequence that Asquith reneged on his earlier promise to Wedgwood to introduce a similar measure for England. Wedgwood was furious – at the annual Henry George commemoration dinner in November 1908, Wedgwood stated that 'On my part I refuse to belong to the Liberal party. I don't care from what platform I speak in the future – whether Liberal, Conservative, or Socialist – but the only platform worth speaking from is the land platform' (*Land Values*, June 1908, cited in Mulvey, 2010).

The land taxers maintained the pressure on the government. A petition signed in February 1909 by 245 Liberal and Labour MPs argued for valuation and land tax to be included in the next budget. According to Mulvey (2010, p. 22), Asquith confirmed to Wedgwood that he was intending to do this. Lloyd George as Chancellor of the Exchequer had considered introducing a tax of a penny in the pound on all land, which Wedgwood had suggested would raise £23 million a year. However, he was dissuaded by the more moderate members of the government who were concerned at the impact on existing leases and property prices. Lloyd George therefore modified his proposal to limit a tax of a halfpenny in the pound to mining royalties, ground rents and vacant non-agricultural land, with a transfer tax of 20 per cent on capital gains over the valuation price, and a duty of 10 per cent on lease reversions. These more modest taxes were expected to raise some £500,000 a year. The Georgites nevertheless welcomed the modified budget proposals as they established the principle of land taxation (Mulvey, 2010, pp. 22–3).

The Labour Party, land tax and the budget crisis of 1909–10

In 1907, Philip Snowden set out the Labour Party's position on taxation in *The Socialist's Budget*, a small book published in the ILP's *Labour Ideal* series. This set out the party's support for direct taxes, including a progressive income tax and its opposition to indirect taxes. Snowden opened the book with three statements that set out a position which was distinct from that of the new Liberal administration: 'Socialists look to the Budget as a means not only of raising revenue to meet unavoidable expenditure, but as an instrument for redressing inequalities in the distribution of wealth' (Snowden, 1907, p. 1).

Snowden also restated the party's position on state ownership:

> Socialists aim at the transfer to public ownership and control of such industrial concerns as can be managed better by the Municipality or the State. They maintain that experience justifies the claim and that public management is more efficient and more economical than private control.
>
> (ibid.)

This was followed by a statement on the mechanisms for achieving these objectives:

> The purpose of Socialism is to transfer Land and Industrial Capital to the people. There are two ways in which, simultaneously, this object may be carried out. The one way is by the municipal and national appropriation (with such compensation to the existing owners as the community may think fit to give) of the land and industrial concerns. . . The second method is by Taxation. Taxation has its special sphere of usefulness in helping the community to secure some part of its own, by diverting into the national purse portions of Rent, Interest, and Profit which now go to keep an idle class in luxury at the expense of the industrious poor.
>
> (ibid., p. 2)

On taxation of land values, Snowden stated:

> Land values are so obviously not created by individual effort, that the justice of taking the increment for the use of the community appeals to those who may

have some difficulty in grasping the working of the 'Unearned Increment' in commercial concerns, where, however, it operates just as truly though not so obviously.

Snowden then proposed as an initial measure an annual tax of one penny in the pound on the capital value of land, as 'a beginning but by no means the end of the process of diverting socially created rent of land into the public exchequer', before commenting that

> Taxation will do something towards this end; but taxation would be a long, irritating and untrustworthy way of trying to secure the whole annual value of land for the community... But to get the full value of land for the community, there is no way but for the State to own the land.
>
> (ibid., pp. 83–4)

In January 1909, the Labour Party held a special conference in Portsmouth, chaired by Snowden to decide their policy on taxation (Daunton, 2001; Whiting, 2001). Snowden summarised the new party policy in an article in the *Socialist Review* on 'Socialism and the Coming Budget'. The party agreed the principle that national taxation 'should be raised from those best able to pay for it and who receive the most protection and benefit from the state'. Indirect taxation fell 'most oppressively on the industrious classes' and should be abolished. The party agreed that there should be 'a super-tax on large incomes, special taxation of State-conferred monopolies, increased estate and legacy duties; and a really substantial beginning with the taxation of land values.' In contrast with those radicals who thought that social reform required a retrenchment of national expenditure, Snowden argued that 'social reform is the better distribution of national wealth and that taxation is one of the two ways in which that can be brought about'. Snowden welcomed the commitment of the Liberal government to taxing land values: 'There is a strong public opinion in favour of this reform. The scandal of the ground landlord appropriating unearned increment is so glaring that its dishonesty appeals to even the man in the street' (Snowden, 1909, p. 17).

The debate about the best means to deal with the 'land problem' continued after the 1909 Finance Bill was eventually enacted in April 1910. The ILPer, Charles Smith wrote an article on 'Land Nationalisation: Its Present Position' in the *Socialist Review* of October 1911. He was critical of the Georgites' proposal for an annual tax on land value. Instead, he welcomed the provisions in the 1909 Act on the taxation of the increased value of land arising from development. His main argument was that measures were needed to bring land under municipal control. He supported the case for planning. His proposal was that local authorities should be given the power to purchase land 'where and when desired, without specifying the purpose for which it is required'. He suggested that

> Local authorities may be relied upon only to acquire land which they believe can be put to better purpose than the present proprietor. They will not buy for the fun of the thing, or because they believe in land nationalisation in the abstract, but because they think they can work it at less expense, and more in the common

interest than Lord A or Squire B. Effective use is still the best credential for possession.

(Smith, 1911, p. 116)

The ILP treasurer, T D Benson wrote an article in *Socialist Review* in October 1912 on the single tax. Benson attacked the concept of the single tax – replacing taxation of income and wealth with a single tax on land, pointing out that the single tax proposal related only to the value of unimproved land and would not apply tax to the value generated by the physical development of a site. Benson argued that taxing agricultural land would hit agricultural production and agricultural workers, and that taxing urban land would not necessarily increase the availability of land for housing development and the main constraint was the lack of funding for the building of homes. He argued that

> One effect of the taxation of land values, which should condemn it utterly in the eyes of every socialist and housing reformer, is that it gives a premium to the owners of congested areas in towns, and places a burden on the more open areas. The contention of the Single Taxers is that it compels land to be put to its full economic use. This means that it puts economic pressure on the owner of land to build as many slums, or at any rate as many cottages or tenements, on the land as the bye-laws permit.

(Benson, 1912, p. 106)

In the following year, Benson published a pamphlet promoting land nationalisation as the most effective approach.

The Liberal Land Enquiry reports and the Labour response

The Liberal Land Campaign launched by Lloyd George in Autumn 1913 was primarily an attack on rural landowners. In August 1912, the Labour Party executive had established a Land committee to parallel the Liberal committee that Lloyd George had established. The Labour Party was concerned that the Liberal attack on land-lordism would lead to the Liberals capturing the votes of potential Labour supporters in the agricultural areas – this was after the collapse of the Lib-Lab pact, and many Labour politicians thought this was the main purpose of the Liberal's new policy. The Labour committee was chaired by George Roberts, Labour's agricultural spokesman, and included George Barnes and George Lansbury, both supporters of the taxation of land values (Tichelar, 1997).

The Liberal government then established a Land Enquiry Committee. This was chaired by Arthur Acland, with Charles Rhoden Buxton as honorary secretary and with Seebohm Rowntree amongst its members. Two separate groups were established – an urban enquiry serviced by H E Crawford, and a rural enquiry serviced by R L Reiss, later to be a leading housing reformer and chairman of the Garden Cities and Town Planning Association and member of the postwar committee on unhealthy areas established in 1921 by Neville Chamberlain.

The Labour committee published an interim report in May 1913 advocating a minimum wage for agricultural labourers, fair rent courts, the extension of the

Smallholdings and Allotments Act, the establishment of rural credit banks and support for co-operative agriculture. The report of the Liberal government's rural enquiry focused on the need to raise the wages of agricultural labourers and proposed the establishment of local wages boards. Reiss and Buxton had advocated housing subsidies for agricultural workers. Burns had however opposed the Conservative proposals for subsidies in their 1912 Bill as 'doles' and 'charity rents' and a 'bonus to employers in aid of low wages', so the report rejected subsidies, proposing instead that the wages board should have regard to housing costs (Packer, 2001).

The final Labour Party report in January 1914 – *The Labour Party and the Agricultural Problem*, argued the case for taxation of land values in the longer term and public ownership of smallholdings (Labour Party, 1914). Tichelar comments that there was little difference between the Labour and Liberal reports. The Liberal report had actually been published in October 1913, and had been welcomed by MacDonald and Henderson, and the final Labour report appeared to be in effect endorsing the government's position, rather than setting out any alternative, though the ILP did argue that the proposals for land nationalisation should still be pursued (Tichelar, 1997).

The Liberal government's Land Enquiry urban report was published at the same time as the rural report. The report considered that the pre-existing system of rating was 'an obstacle in the way of providing good working class houses at reasonable rents'. It argued that:

> in many cases where a town is rapidly expanding, land, which could be built upon if offered at a reasonable price, is kept out of the market, either because the owners take a more sanguine view of its probable increase in value. Or because they prefer to keep it in its present condition for personal or sentimental reasons. The present rating system encourages this proceeding.
>
> (Land Enquiry Committee Report, 1914, Vol 2, pp. 673–4)

The report also made an interesting comment on the impact of recent urban growth:

> The recent development of the means of transport and the rapid growth of certain towns has resulted in the geographical separation from each other of the population who really belong to the same community (e.g., the separation of industrial from residential districts, and of districts where the poor live from those occupied by the rich). The difficulty of expanding the boundaries of local authorities has prevented the adjustment of local government areas to meet these changing conditions. The inequality of rates is thus aggravated.
>
> (ibid., pp. 675–6)

The report also noted the conflict between urban and rural ratepayers within a local authority.

The main proposal in the report was to introduce a system of site value rating and that 'all future increases in local government expenditure that are chargeable on the rates should be met by a rate on site values' (ibid., p. 678). Lloyd George had already indicated his support for site value rating, and Seebohm Rowntree had advocated such an approach in his book *Land and Labour: Lessons from Belgium*

(Rowntree, 1911). The report's proposal was informed by a site value rating exercise carried out by the Inland Revenue. The report proposed an incremental system of transferring part of the existing rate system to the new site value basis. It was recognised that changing the rating system would not necessarily significantly increase local authority resources, so the report also recommended a £5 million increase in the level of state grants to local authorities. Cross had proposed a national land tax, but while the committee accepted the logic of the proposal, the report did not include this proposal as it was considered that it would be seen as predatory and cause divisions within the government and the Liberal Party. While half Liberal MPs supported a national system of land taxation, the other half did not and a small group of Liberal MPs, led by A C Murray, had campaigned vigorously against a national land tax (Packer, 2001). Focusing on a local system of site value rating was a perhaps inevitable compromise, if an unsatisfactory one. The report's conclusion on this sensitive issue was:

1   The principle of a national site tax as a weapon in the fiscal armoury is one that can be fully justified, and unless a very substantial measure of rating reform in the direction of rating site values were carried, we should regard the adoption of a national site tax as essential.
2   As to the immediate practicability of imposing such a tax concurrently with a compulsory transference of at least ten millions of local rates to site values, and the grant of power to make, if they so incline, a substantial further transference, the case is by no means as clear;
3   In view, therefore, of these considerations, we are unable, with the limited information at present at our disposal, to make any recommendation for the immediate imposition of a national tax on site values, at the same time as the transference of part of the burden of the rates from the composite hereditament to the site.

(Land Enquiry Committee Report, 1914, Vol 2, pp. 635–6)

The report seems to have been successful in that unity in the Liberal party had been maintained. The LNS welcomed the report while English League for the Taxation of Land Values declared that they were satisfied with the report. The purist single-taxer Josiah Wedgwood remained unreconciled but could not secure wider support. Packer (2001) comments that in dropping land taxation as the basis for urban policy reform, the government was in fact relying on town planning, grants to local authorities and increased land acquisition by local authorities to deliver the housing programme, while avoiding contentious increases in local rates. As Packer (2001) argues, this was significantly increasing the role of the state in welfare provision for the working class.

Labour's response was also fairly muted. The ILP and Fabians welcomed the minimum wage proposals in the rural report. The Labour Party generally welcomed the proposals on site value rating, planning and local authority land acquisition. The Labour Party was divided on the issue of state subsidy to housing. George Barnes, the leading single-taxer in the Labour leadership led a group of eight MPs, including Charles Bowerman, to oppose the subsidy proposals, although they were supported by McDonald and Henderson and the majority of the Parliamentary Labour Party. Barnes claimed that subsidies would benefit landlords and perpetuate low rents and therefore low wages. He opposed the use of national taxation to subsidise individual areas and individual households. Jowett argued the opposite position – only state aid could achieve a significant municipal housing programme and better housing stimulated workers' self-respect and aspirations, rather than generating dependency (Packer, 2001). This is an issue which remains vigorously contested a hundred years later!

Jowett's position did however prevail. It was endorsed at the Labour Party Conference and when the Unionist Social Reform Council promoted their 1914 Bill to subsidise agricultural workers' housing in England, following the Irish precedent, this was supported by Labour MPs, only to be defeated by the Liberal's parliamentary majority (Packer, 2001). The Labour Party however having tail-ended the Liberals on land reform ended up tail-ending the Conservatives on housing reform. Given the divisions within the Labour Party on both issues, and the inability to form cohesive alliances with either the Land Nationalisation Society or the Workman's National Housing Council, the Labour Party actually failed to take a distinctive stand on either land or housing. It was only in the postwar period, that the Labour Party was able to formulate a more coherent and distinctive position.

The professionalisation of housing and planning

With the passage of the 1909 Housing and Town Planning Act, a new professional discipline was established. This was not an easy process as there were a number of disciplines involved in urban development, with competition between architects, surveyors and engineers as to which profession should have the co-ordinating role. It was the Royal Institute of British Architects (RIBA), originally established in 1834, that took the lead, with their establishment of a Town Planning committee and the organisation of a major international planning conference in 1910. Many of the leaders of professional movement for planning were architects – for example Raymond Unwin, Aston Webb, Stanley Adshead, Edwin Lutyens, Thomas Mawson and H V Lanchester. Mawson as a landscape architect saw that sub-discipline as the basis of a town planning profession. This was contested by the Institute of Civil Engineers as the oldest Institute founded in 1816 and the Surveyors Institute, founded in 1868, both of whom represented existing senior professionals within the local government structure actively engaged in the development process – city engineers and city surveyors. Patrick Geddes and his Sociological Association, founded more recently in 1904, also claimed a role in the new town planning discipline. Cherry (1974) recounts the story of the inter-relationship of the competing groups which eventually led to the establishment of a Town Planning Institute. The process was far from easy. At the 1910 RIBA planning conference, the architect Beresford Pike claimed that: 'The town is too precious a possibility if not already a possession of beauty, to be entrusted to the consideration only of its expert surveyors and engineers. The problems are architectural and will ultimately be judged as such.'

Henry Stilgoe, the City Engineer of Birmingham, an authority which already had considerable experience of town planning, commented that

> I think the people who administer it [the 1909 Act] will be the borough engineers and surveyors of this country. It is their right. They are the officials, the statutory officials, appointed under the Public Health Act, and without their co-operation

and in fact, without their intimate knowledge of their districts, this Act cannot be put into proper and efficient working order, leaving the little matters, good as they are, the small garden suburbs, to develop of themselves.

In case this message was not sufficiently blunt, Stilgoe concluded 'Those people who talk so much about town planning do not know what they want; would not know what to do with it if given the opportunity' (cited in Cherry, 1974, p. 46).

The Engineers Institute actually held their own conference on Housing and Town Planning in West Bromwich in July 1911 (Institution of Municipal and County Engineers, 1907). The Institute had established a Town Planning Committee, comprising thirteen borough engineers and surveyors, led by the Institute's president, Albert Greatorex, the borough surveyor of West Bromwich. The conference received some seventeen papers on aspects of town planning, many of which included plans of housing development, roads and drainage systems, including plans for garden suburbs in towns such as Northwood and Ruislip, Great Yarmouth, Sheffield and Warrington.

In his presidential address, Greatorex commented that

> Expressions of opinion have been given to the idea that municipal engineers and surveyors are not the proper persons to be entrusted with the carrying out of this Act, but the members of other professional bodies are more competent to do the work.

The purpose of the conference was

> to show the general public and especially the members of the various local authorities, that the engineer and surveyor was fully alive to his added responsibilities and well able to perform the extra duties placed upon him by the Act when called upon, and, at the same time, to show that on account of the peculiar position in which he was placed no one was better able to deal with the subject.
>
> (ibid., p. 4)

The Garden Cities Association responded to the 1909 legislation by renaming their organisation as the Garden Cities and Town Planning Association and relaunching their *Garden Cities* journal as *Garden Cities and Town Planning*. In the first issue published in February 1911, the TCPA secretary, Ewart Culpin, celebrated the advances of the movement.

> When this journal first made its appearance in 1904 it was alone in the promulgation of these principles which are to-day accepted everywhere. Town planning was almost unheard of outside the pioneer Association, and Garden City was still a project of dubious import save among the few. In the first issues out contributors told forth their visions of the things to be, and the happenings in the tiny colony springing up at Letchworth occupied a prominent space. We were still fighting against prejudice and misconception; pleading for a broader view of the problem of the city. Today we are confronted with a totally different set of conditions. Garden cities and suburbs have come to stay; the principles

are recognised as essential to proper development, and schemes of various proportions are being launched in every direction. Town planning is passing to the realm of the practical, and the engineer, the architect, and the surveyor are succeeding to the work of the propagandist. The State has adopted an important part of our principles, and the municipalities have taken in hand the putting of them into practice.

(*Garden Cities and Town Planning*, Feb 1911,
Vol 1, No 1, pp. 1–2)

In the same issue a list was published of the garden city, village and suburb schemes under development in England. In addition to Letchworth, the list included garden suburbs at Northwood and Ruislip, East Hyde, Romford, Fallings Park, Glyn Cory (Cardiff), Hampstead, Wavertree (Liverpool), Anchor Tenants (Leicester), Ealing and Harborne (Birmingham). The list of garden villages comprised Knebworth, Bournville, Port Sunlight, Woodlands, Earswick (York) and Hull. The schemes involved a total of 9577 acres, of which Letchworth comprised 3818 acres (ibid., p. 12).

The National Housing and Town Planning Council established an Advisory Committee on Planning. Its purpose was to advise Local Authorities 'in the work of practical administration of the Town Planning clauses' of the 1909 Act. The committee held a number of conferences, with an initial conference being held in Liverpool in February 1911. Three hundred local authorities were represented with a total of nearly 600 delegates. The conference was organised by Henry Aldridge. Alderman Thompson gave a presentation on the Northwood garden suburb, Thomas Adams and Raymond Unwin both gave presentations. The Council then held a conference in Newcastle on the housing clauses of the Act, chaired by William Straker of the Northumberland Miners Association, with Henry Aldridge as the main speaker. The advisory committee announced a list of experts including Prof Adshead of Liverpool University, W H Lever, George Cadbury, Seebohm Rowntree, Raymond Unwin, Patrick Geddes, T C Horsfall, T H Mawson and George Pepler, together with a number of French and German planners. The group also established a Greater London Town Planning committee with the object of 'bringing together the Local Authorities in the area of unbuilt-upon land around the central zone of London and the evolution of a wise policy of Garden Suburb development' (*Garden Cities and Town Planning*, April 1911, pp. 52–3; May 1911, pp. 102–3). In the May issue, George Pepler, who had recently argued for a Green Girdle around London together with an orbital Ringway road, argued the case for a central authority for the Greater London area. The article concluded that

> Some people think that London has nearly reached its bounds in population. Supposing it has; while some parts are so unhealthily crowded, the hospitals so crammed with the results of both disease and accidents, and the streets as congested as they are now, it is clear that there is ample scope for present London to spread itself a little and for its population to regain health and vigour among green fields and pastures new.
>
> (Garden Cities and Town Planning, May 1911, pp. 86–7)

When in November 1913 the Town Planning Institute was eventually established, its provisional committee comprised eleven architects, four engineers, four surveyors and the sociologist Geddes. Thomas Adams, a surveyor, was elected president, with J W Cockrill, an engineer, and Raymond Unwin, an architect, as vice presidents. Geddes was appointed honorary librarian, though as Cherry points out, the Institute did not have a library.

It is interesting to note that the three main pressure groups which had pushed for the legislation, the National Housing and Town Planning Council, the Workman's National Housing Council and the Garden Cities and Town Planning Association, do not appear to have played any role in the establishment of the Institute, though Thomas Adams had been secretary of the original Garden Cities Association. The founders of the town planning movement, not having the appropriate professional qualifications, all appear on the list of associate members of the new Institute – Ebenezer Howard, John Burns, George and Edward Cadbury, Henrietta Barnett, Thomas Horsfall, Ralph Neville, Henry Vivian, Seebohm Rowntree and Aneurin Williams. Henry Aldridge and Ewart Culpin were also given the status of associates. Fred Knee, William Thompson and J S Nettlefold appear not to have been recognised by the new Institute. The Institute had one foreign member, Dr Stubben, the German planner from whom Horsfall, Unwin and many other 'founders' of the British planning movement got their ideas, though he appears to have been expelled when the war was declared.

The period after the passage of the Housing and Town Planning Act also saw the development of a literature of planning practice and the first attempts to establish a history for the new discipline. There had been previous collections of plans, such as Sennett's monumental *Garden Cities in Theory and Practice* and Budget Meakin's *Model Factories and Villages* discussed in the previous chapter. There were also a number of guides to housing, of which Thompson's *Housing Handbook* and Nettlefold's *Practical Housing* were perhaps the most significant. William Thompson and W A Willis both produced guides to the new Act. Raymond Unwin was the first to provide a text book for site planning with his *Town Planning in Practice*, published in 1909, which drew on a wide range of examples including Bournville, Letchworth, Hampstead Garden suburb and German town extensions.

In 1909, the architect Inigo Triggs also published *Town planning, past, present and possible* (Triggs, 1909). This work, less well known than Unwin's classic work, after an introductory chapter comparing the development of London with New York, Paris, Berlin and a number of other German cities, provides a history of urban planning since the Babylonians, before giving guidance on the circulation of traffic, town expansion, the planning of streets and the planning of squares and open spaces.

Like Unwin's book, Trigg's volume was lavishly illustrated with photographs and site plans from Britain, Europe and the United States, drawing heavily on the work of Stubben, Camillo Sitte, Eugene Henard and Charles Robinson. In his preface, Triggs comments that

> In England, until last year, when Mr John Burns introduced the Housing and Town Planning Bill, any idea of a systematic treatment of the subject was practically unknown outside aesthetic coteries, and although such matters as public health and restrictive building have for many years received great attention, we have yet very much to learn on the subject of the laying out and development of town areas. . . We are beginning to. . . gradually realise that a city is not, and

ought not to be, a chance aggregation of so many houses ...The technical literature dealing with town planning is comparatively small and is almost entirely confined to Germany and France. The present work is the outcome of several years spent on the continent ... It is hoped that the result will be of use, as a means of reference, not only to those who are called on to act as advisors on projecting schemes of city improvement, but also to members of town councils, who have so great a responsibility for determining what is to be the future of our city development.

(Triggs, 1909, pp. v–viii)

It is perhaps not surprising that 'town planning' struggled to establish itself as a distinct discipline. Unwin and Triggs were both architects. The founders of the TPI recognised that 'town planning' involved the collaboration of a range of professional disciplines. The first distinct town planning course was established at Liverpool University with funding from W H Lever with S D Adshead as professor, supported by Patrick Abercrombie and Thomas Mawson. In 1912, Unwin was appointed as a part time lecturer in town planning at Birmingham University and gave lectures on 'civic design and town planning' and 'social origins and economic bases of towns', the initiative being funded by George Cadbury. In 1914, a department of planning was created within the Bartlett School of Architecture at University College, London, to which Adshead transferred from Liverpool. The first TPI examination syllabus was not drawn up until 1916 (Cherry, 1974, pp. 218–19). The first students to qualify in 1920 were already qualified as surveyors, architects and engineers, and entry to the examination required a relevant prior professional qualification.

Town planning as a separate professional qualification was therefore not in effect until after the World War I. The prewar town planning schemes, carried out under the 1909 legislation, were therefore generally supervised by the pre-existing civic engineers, much as Stilgoe had anticipated. In fact, as has been shown by Hawtree (1981) several of the early schemes were carried out by Stilgoe's own department in Birmingham. Local authorities did not directly employ 'town planners' and few brought in external 'town planning consultants'. The new profession was dominated by individuals who saw themselves primarily as engineers, architects or surveyors.

Nevertheless, the reforms introduced by the Act did create a new role for local authorities and represented a significant extension of the role of the state. The planning of new settlements was no longer the preserve of individual philanthropists such as the Rowntrees, the Cadburys or Lever, but was the responsibility of the state at both central and local levels.

With the 1909 Act and the recognition of the need for housing subsidy in the 1914 Housing Act, the housing and planning reformers of the 1890s and 1900s had largely achieved their objectives. The war brought new challenges, with the demand for rent controls and the government developing a programme of subsidised housing for munitions workers, largely designed by Unwin. The postwar period brought the Homes for Heroes campaign, the 1919 Housing and Town Planning Act and eventually the 1924 Wheatley Act with its subsidy regime. These reforms owed much to the campaigns of the reformers, not just those of the immediate prewar period, but also the generally forgotten radical and socialist campaigners of the mid-and late-19th century.

Primary sources

Alden, P and Hayward, E (1907) *Housing: Social Services Handbooks* No 1 (London: Headley Brothers)

Aldridge, H (1915) *The Case for Town Planning* (London: National Housing and Town Planning Council)

Aldridge, H (1923) *The National Housing Manual* (London: National Housing and Town Planning Council)

Barnes, G (1906?) *Henry George* (London: Independent Labour Party)

Benson, T D (1912) 'The Single Tax', *Socialist Review*, Vol 10, No 56, October (London: Independent Labour Party)

Benson, T D (1913) *Land Nationalisation* (London: Independent Labour Party)

Cadbury, G (1915) *Town Planning with special reference to Birmingham* (London: Longmans, Green)

Cadbury, G and Bryan, T (1907) The Land and the Landless (London: Headley Brothers)

Culpin, E G (1913) *The Garden City Movement Up to Date* (London: GCTPA)

Garden City Association (1907) *Town Planning Theory and Practice* (London: Garden City Association)

Garden City Association (1906) *The Garden City* Vol 1 (London: Garden Cities Association)

Garden City and Town Planning Association (1911) *Garden Cities and Town Planning*. New series. Vol 1 (London: Garden Cities and Town Planning Association)

Horsfall, T C (1905) *The Improvement of Dwellings and the Surroundings of the People* (Manchester, UK)

House of Lords (1894) *Report on Select Committee on Town Improvements (Betterment)* (London: Eyre and Spottiswoode)

Institution of Municipal and County Engineers (1907) *Report of Housing and Town Planning Conference* (London: E and F N Spon)

Jowett, F (1905) *The Socialist and the City* (London: George Allen for Independent Labour Party)

Labour Party (1914) *The Labour Party and the Agricultural Problem* (London: Labour Party)

Land Enquiry Committee Report (1914) Vol 1, *Rural*; Vol 2, *Urban* (London: Hodder and Stoughton)

Nettlefold, J S (1906) *Slum Reform and Town Planning* (London: Hudson and Sons)

Nettlefold, J S (1908) *Practical Housing* (Letchworth, UK: Garden City Press)

Nettlefold, J S (1914) *Practical Town Planning* (London: St Catherine's Press)

Neville, R (1904) *Garden Cities. A Warburton lecture* (Reprint: Kessinger Publishing 2009)

Parliamentary Debates (1908) *Housing and Town Planning Bill*, 12 May 1908, Second Reading 4th series, Vol 188, cc 947–1063

Parliamentary Debates (1909) *Housing and Town Planning Bill*, 5 April 1909, Second Reading 5th series, Vol 3, cc733–98

Rowntree, S (1911) *Land and Labour: Lessons from Belgium* (London: Macmillan)

Sanders, W S (1905) *Muncipalization by Provinces*. Fabian Tract No 125 (London: Fabian Society)

Smith, C (1911) 'Land Nationalisation: Its Present Position', *Socialist Review*, Vol 6, No 44, October (London: Independent Labour Party)

Snowden, P (1907) *The Socialist's Budget* (London: George Allen)

Snowden, P (1909) 'Socialism and the Coming Budget', *Socialist Review*, Vol 3, No 13, March (London: Independent Labour Party)

Thompson, W (1903) *The Housing Handbook* (London: National Housing Reform Council)

Thompson, W (1907) *Housing Up to Date* (London: National Housing Reform Council)

Thompson, W (1910) *Handbook to the Housing and Town Planning Act* (London: National Housing Reform Council)

Triggs, I (1909) *Town Planning, Past Present and Future* (London: Methuen)

Unwin, R (1909) *Town Planning in Practice* (London: Fisher Unwin)

Wells, H G (1903) *A Paper on Administrative Areas* read before the Fabian Society. Published as an appendix to Wells, H G, *Mankind in the Making* (London: Chapman and Hall)

Willis, W A (1910) *Housing and Town Planning in Britain* (London: Butterworth)

Secondary sources

Ashworth, W (1954) *The Genesis of Modern Town Planning* (London: Routledge and Kegan Paul)

Barry, E Eldon (1965) *Nationalisation in British Politics: The Historical Background* (London: Jonathan Cape)

Bellamy, C (1988) *Administering Central-Local Relations. 1871–1919: The Local Government Board* (Manchester, UK: Manchester University Press)

Birchall, J (1995) 'Co-partnership housing and the garden city movement', *Planning Perspectives*, 10, pp. 329–58

Booth, P and Huxley, M (2012) '1909 and all that: reflections on the Housing, Town Planning Act 1909', *Planning Perspectives*, Vol 27, pp. 267–83

Bowman, S E (1962) *Edward Bellamy Abroad* (New York: Twayne)

Brittain, I (1982) *Fabianism and Culture: A Study in British Socialism and the Arts 1884–1918* (Cambridge: Cambridge University Press)

Brown, K (1977) *John Burns* (London: Royal Historical Society)

Buder, S (1990) *Visionaries and Planners: The Garden City Movement and the Modern Community* (New York: Oxford University Press)

Cherry, G (1974) *The Evolution of British Town Planning* (Leighton Buzzard, UK: Leonard Hill Books)

Daunton, M (2001) *Trusting Leviathan. The Politics of Taxation in Britain 1799–1914* (Cambridge: Cambridge University Press)

Day, M (1981) 'The contribution of Sir Raymond Unwin and Barry Parker to the development of site-planning theory and practice', in Sutcliffe, A (ed.), *British Town Planning: The Formative Years* (Leicester, UK: Leicester University Press)

Douglas, R (1976) *Land, People and Politics* (London: Allison and Busby)

Englander, D (1973) The Workman's Housing Council (unpublished MA dissertation, University of Warwick)

Fishman, R (1977) *Urban Utopias in the Twentieth Century* (New York: Basic Books)

Gaskell, M (1981) '"The Suburb Salubrious": Town Planning in Practice', in Sutcliffe, A (ed.), *British Town Planning: The Formative Years* (Leicester, UK Leicester University Press)

Gehrke, J Georgist Thought and the Emergence of Municipal Socialism in Britain 1870–1914. Accessed 28th March 2016 *http://schalkenbach.org/scholars-forum/Municipal-Socialism-in-Britain-J-Gehrke.pdf*

Gehrke, J (2006) Municipal Anti-Socialism and the Growth of the Anti-Socialist Critique in Britain 1873–1914 (unpublished PhD thesis, University of Minnesota, MN)

Hardy, D (1991) *From Garden Cities to New Towns* (London: Routledge)

Harrison, J F C (1954) *James Hole and Social Reform in Leeds* (Leeds, UK: Thoresby Society)

Harrison, M (1981) 'Housing and Town Planning in Manchester before 1914', in Sutcliffe, A (ed.), *British Town Planning: The Formative Years* (Leicester, UK: Leicester University Press)

Hawtree, M (1981) 'The Emergence of the Town Planning Profession', in Sutcliffe, A (ed.), *British Town Planning: The Formative Years* (Leicester, UK: Leicester University Press)

Jackson, F (1985) *Raymond Unwin: Architect, Planner and Visionary* (London: Zwemmer)

Kent, W (1950) *John Burns: Labour's Lost Leader* (London: Williams and Norgate)

Malpass, P (2000) 'Public utility societies and the Housing and Town Planning Act,1919', *Planning Perspectives*, Vol 15, No 4, pp 377–92

Marshall, P (1962) 'A British Sensation', in Bowman, S E (ed.), *Edward Bellamy Abroad* (New York: Twayne)

Mulvey, P Radicalism's Last Gasp? The British Liberal Party and the Taxation of Land Values. Accessed 28th March 2016 www.schalkenbach.org/scholars-forum/Radicalisms-Last-Gasp.html

Mulvey, P (2010) *The Political Life of Josiah C Wedgewood: Land, Liberty and Empire* (Woodbridge: Boydell and Brewer)

Murray, B (1980) *The People's Budget 1909/10* (Oxford: Clarendon Press)

Offer, A (1981) *Property and Politics 1870–1914. Landownership, Law. Ideology and Urban Development in England* (Cambridge: Cambridge University Press)

Packer, I (2001) *Lloyd George, Liberalism and the Land* (Woodbridge, UK: Boydell Press)

Peacock, A J (1961) Land Reform 1880–1919 (University of Southampton, UK, unpublished MA dissertation)

Skilletter, K (1993) 'The role of public utility societies in early British town planning and housing reform 1901–36', *Planning Perspectives*, Vol 8, No 2, pp. 125–65

Sutcliffe, A (ed.) (1981) *British Town Planning: The Formative Years* (Leicester, UK: Leicester University Press)

Sutcliffe, A (1981) *Towards the Planned City* (New York: St Martin's Press)

Sutcliffe, A (1900) 'From town-country to town planning: changing priorities in the British garden city movement 1899–1914', *Planning Perspectives*, No 5, pp 257–69

Swenarton, M (1981) *Homes fit for Heroes* (London: Heinemann)

Thane, P (1991) 'Labour and Local Politics: Radicalism, Democracy and Social Reform 1880–1914' in Biagini, E and Reid, A (eds), *Currents of Radicalism* (Cambridge: Cambridge University Press)

Tichelar, M (1997) 'Socialists, Labour and the Land: The Response of the Labour Party to the Land Campaign of Lloyd George before the First World War', *Twentieth Century British History*, Vol 8, No 2, pp. 127–44

Ward, S (2010) 'What did the Germans ever do for us? A century of British learning about and imagining modern town planning', *Planning Perspectives*, Vol 25, No 2, pp. 117–40

Whiting, R (2001) *The Labour Party and Taxation* (Cambridge: Cambridge University Press)

12 Radical and socialist influences on land, planning and housing reform

The introductory chapter set out a number of key themes:

1   The contrast between middle class philanthropic reformers and 'grassroots' campaigns originating within working class based radical and socialist organisations; the extent to which these represent distinct ideological positions and whether there is a clear separation of ideological traditions across the historical timescale;
2   Comparing utopian and pragmatic approaches to constructing a 'New Jerusalem';
3   The role of the State in initiating new settlements
4   The role of local initiatives relative to centralist reform;
5   The inter-relationship between policy on land and taxation, policy on housing and policy on planning and the inter-dependency of these three reform movements.

This concluding chapter will seek to relate the historical narrative presented to these key themes

The contrast between philanthropic reformers and working class radicals and socialists

One of the central themes of this study has been the contrast between on the one hand the working class radicals and socialists and on the other, the philanthropic reformers who have been the focus of attention in the standard histories of planning and housing reform. Studies of the histories of housing reform tend to start with Octavia Hill, while histories of planning often move from Christopher Wren through to the 'Great Estates' of Georgian London and John Nash, and the factory settlements of Owen, Salt, Cadbury, Rowntree and Lever before considering Ebenezer Howard, who is still seen by many as the founder of English planning, at least in relation to the planning of new settlements. Henry George is seen as the great land reformer, with his theories still the subject of vigorous debate and with his purist single tax vision still promoted by a group of cult like followers, while little attention is paid to the land nationalisation campaign promoted by Alfred Russell Wallace and to earlier working class led land reform initiatives.

This study has sought to demonstrate that there was also a tradition of independent radical and working class led written advocacy and campaigning on the issues of land, housing and planning reform, which should also be recognised as an important component of the history of British planning thought and action.

The early Puritan pioneers of the 17th century were a mix of artisans and members of the rural squirearchy, their main unifying feature being religious dissent rather than class. It could be argued that in the late 18th and early 19th centuries, arguments for social reform, including early interventions in what would now be termed town planning, were led by the group of radical intellectuals who were followers of Jeremy Bentham. This study has focused on the work of early utilitarians such as, J A Roebuck, J S Buckingham and the South Australian colonialists such as Rowland Hill, Robert Gouger and Edward Gibbon Wakefield. It should however be recognised that the Benthamite radical circles also included artisans such as Francis Place. While Robert Owen himself was a philanthropic industrialist, many of the Owenites were artisans, although communitarian leaders such as James Pierrepoint Greaves had middle class backgrounds and relied on aristocratic support. The Owenites rarely adopted a class based position, though many were uncomfortable with Owen's authoritarian leadership and his aristocratic connections. The Chartist leadership was also a mix of middle class leaders and artisans. Feargus O'Connor had an aristocratic background and was a lawyer. Ernest Jones was a barrister. Bronterre O'Brien had a more working class background and trained to be a lawyer before becoming a radical journalist. The clash between O'Connor and O'Brien reflected a difference of approaches to community settlement rather than being necessarily driven by different degrees of class consciousness.

It is however with the founding of the Land and Labour League in 1868 by O'Brien's followers, led by Martin James Boon, that an explicit class based argument in relation to land ownership first appears, an argument which directly challenged the utilitarian propositions promoted by John Stuart Mill and his Land Tenure Reform Association. The London Trades Council was a body which explicitly represented the working class, though in its early years, like the national Trades Union Council, it was dominated by craft unions. In contrast, Christian Socialists and positivists were both primarily middle class intellectual groups. While the Democratic Federation and the Socialist League were led by members of the middle class such as Hyndman, Belfort Bax and Morris, the first of this group in fact having an aristocratic demeanour, both organisations contained working class members, such as Jack Williams and John Lincoln Mahon, who were prominent in their leadership. The Independent Labour Party was a more explicitly working class based organisation and this determined its suspicion of middle class Liberals and radicals and influenced its support for collectivism against individualism. At its founding conference the ILP even discussed excluding persons who were not manual workers from its membership, a view also taken by some of the leaders of the TUC.

The circle around Ebenezer Howard was both middle class and Liberal. Similarly, the Georgites of the English Land Restoration League and the reform advocates of the National Housing Reform Council were middle class lobby groups who focused on influencing the Liberal Party. The Land Nationalisation Society, while led by the intellectual polymath Alfred Russell Wallace, nevertheless attracted more working class support. It was however, Fred Knee's Workman's National Housing Council that was explicitly based on the organised labour movement and which adopted an explicit collectivist approach to both land and housing ownership. It can be argued that there was an independent working class tradition, which can be traced from late Chartism through the Land and Labour League and the London Trades Council to the Democratic Federation, the ILP and the Workman's Housing Council.

This tradition had a distinct ideological commitment to collectivism and state ownership of land and housing. While the early Labour Party, including its parliamentary representatives, tried to incorporate both Georgite and collectivist policy positions within its platform, there nevertheless remained a distinctive collectivist position within the pre-war Labour Party, though it was not necessarily the dominant one.

Utopianism and pragmatism

The categorisation of any project or movement is contentious, especially in the light of the negative connotations given to 'utopianism' by Marx and others. To categorise a project as 'pragmatic' can also be a conscious critique of a lack of principle. Yet a plan which cannot be implemented is no more than a vision. It is important to recognise that a plan has to be capable of implementation if it is to be more than just a piece of paper and that the challenge for planners is to get the best balance between often competing objectives. The plans of the New England Puritan settlers were not short of vision. Basing their plans and governance on biblical texts, the settlers aimed for a perfect Christian society, whether it be the plan for New Haven based on the description of the Temple in Jerusalem in Ezekiel, or Winthrop's vision of Boston as the 'city on a hill'. The implementation of such visions proved problematic as the settlers faced real physical challenges and as different leaders disputed the appropriate biblical response. The narratives of the early settlements show the extent of disputation, with some arguing for theocratic autocracy, some for a recreation of early Christian communism, while others advocated autonomism.

The Benthamite planners were more pragmatic in their approach to governance and planning. The settlers in Freetown and South Australia had the advantage of applying utilitarian principles to a 'tabula rasa', having to a large extent dispersed any indigenous population. We therefore see the application of grid square plans, often devised in Whitehall before the departure of the colonists to the 'promised land', often ignoring the natural topography of the site, with the application of planning principles where the establishment of public buildings was prominent – the governor's house, the barracks, the town hall, the school and the prison. As Robert Home has demonstrated, planning of the colonial settlement was generally on the basis of explicit physical separation from the indigenous population, with the protection of the health of the colonisers the determining factor, and separation distances based on the maximum distance of flight of the mosquito. These plans were based on very practical objectives. Utilitarianism was a very practical philosophy.

Robert Owen is often categorised as a utopian socialist. While Owen was a supporter of the co-operative movement and promoted a form of socialism, in his early career he was very much a pragmatist, though in his later life he moved to a form of secular millenarianism, a tendency which is often confused with utopianism. While his working class followers in their promotion of co-operative settlements were very practical men, other communitarians such as Goodwyn Barmby and James Pierrepoint Greaves (influenced by Fourier and Cabet), and later settlement founders such as J C Kenworthy and Bruce Wallace (influenced by Tolstoy) tended to rely on a more religious basis for their communitarianism, and in so doing pursued a form of exclusivity. This limited their appeal and generated both friction within the communities and a failure to engage with the wider labour movement.

The Chartists, in contrast, grew out of the labour movement. O'Connor and O'Brien were both idealists, though it could be argued that O'Connor was stronger on polemic than on principle. His short work on the establishment of small farms, however, had a very practical focus. O'Brien was also a polemicist and in early years had a tendency to Jacobinical extremism. Later known as the 'schoolmaster of Chartism', O'Brien was to develop a far more sophisticated analysis than his rival, and was to leave a much more influential political legacy. While the early Chartist movement can be seen as mainly oppositional to the State and in effect anti-parliamentary, with no clear perspective on how a working class government would actually operate if it held power, the later Chartists with their advocacy of the 'charter and something more' seeking social and political reform, transform the earlier natural rights argument for a fairer distribution of land, to a class based argument that saw the collective ownership of land as the basis of political power and the role of state intervention in assisting the working classes in achieving their rights, achieved through the capture of power through democratic processes. This led some former Chartists into the Liberal party, and to some successes in engaging with local government institutions. It should not be forgotten that it was the Chartists who first organised working class candidates to stand for parliament and for municipal corporations and that Chartist–radical alliances had considerable success in winning local political power, for example in the city of Sheffield.

Both Christian socialists and positivists were idealists. While coming from very different ideological positions, they were often collaborators. Members of both movements, however, were not exclusive sectionalists and actively engaged in the practical politics of sanitary reform, co-operation, working class education and in the trade union movement. Some engaged directly with the governance structures of the central state, such as Ludlow's role as registrar of friendly societies; others such as Frederic Harrison, participated in local government structures – Harrison became an alderman on the London County Council. The Christian Socialist, Thomas Hughes, demonstrated a more utopian tendency with his attempt to recreate the English 'public school' on the American frontier with his Rugby settlement at Plateau City in Tennessee.

Martin James Boon can be seen as the most developed of the O'Brienites in having a set of clear political principles and objectives. He was a member of a cohort of working class socialist intellectuals, who had drawn on Owen and O'Brien as well as from active engagement with Marx and the international republicans and London trade union leaders within the First International. Boon, Alfred Walton, John Weston, William Maccall, and their trade union colleagues, Thomas Mottershead, Ben Lucraft, Henry Broadhurst, George Howell, John Hales and William Randal Cremer, were all very practical men and active participants in a wide range of political organisations; some worked within the Liberal Party; others such as Boon, Walton and Weston argued for a more independent politics. For many working class leaders it was Marx who was the utopian revolutionary, with his insistence that a proletarian revolution was a precondition of social and political reform.

The utilitarian philosopher, John Stuart Mill was also a pragmatist – engaging in politics through becoming an MP, though arguably less successful in this than his predecessors, Roebuck and Buckingham. Mill recognised that a laissez faire approach to government had its limitations and increasingly recognised the role of the state.

In establishing the Land Tenure Reform Association, he recognised the need for political alliances, and in the last years of his life moved towards a position which was socialistic if not socialist.

Many of the early campaigns for housing and social reform, and the development of both new settlements and improvement of existing settlements to include leisure amenities, were led by the practical men of Birmingham, Manchester and Leeds. These men were inspired by visions of a better life for all, but visions which could be practically implemented. The London County Council progressives, such as John Williams Benn, Charles Harrison and Sidney Webb, were also practical men and pragmatists.

Ebenezer Howard is often categorised as a utopian. His classic work, *Tomorrow – A Peaceful Path to Real Reform*, is based on a vision of a perfect society, but Howard was a practical man and a pragmatist rather than a philosopher. His work owes much to that of Buckingham and to the practical socialists such as John Richardson, engineer and author of *How It Can Be Done*. The famous diagrams in Howard's book perhaps imply a degree of eccentricity, yet Howard's book focuses on the detailed implementation of his vision and includes detailed costings which are not found in the works of earlier utopians such as Cabet and Fourier.

With the passage of the 1909 legislation, the visionaries were to be replaced by the practical men – the new bureaucrats of the civil service, the engineers and surveyors. As has been demonstrated above, the establishment of a new planning profession was to be based on collaboration of existing professions, and a struggle for dominance between architects, surveyors and engineers, who saw the implementation of the planning legislation as a matter for the technicians – Howard and his fellow planning pioneers being seen as amateurs who had little understanding of the practicalities of governance. The pragmatists had their victory. Planning was not only professionalised but the vision of a better quality of life was to a certain extent marginalised, as the planning pioneers were excluded from the professional institute as well as from the actual processes of plan making and plan implementation.

The role of the state

The Puritan settlements in New England considered at the start of the narrative were independent of state action, in fact consisting of an escape from the oppression of the powers, political and religious, of the English state. The Benthamite initiatives of the late-18th and early-19th century, with the settlements of Freetown, South Australia and New Zealand, were state sponsored, with the support of Government Ministers and the establishment of Colonisation Societies and Chartered Companies through parliamentary legislation. Owen and his fellow industrial philanthropists operated independently of the State, depending on both the profits of their enterprises and on the altruism of benefactors. The Owenite settlements, such as Ralahine in Ireland, operating independently of Owen's philanthropy and without State support, struggled to be self-sufficient and were all short-lived.

The Chartist land movement led by Feargus O'Connor was based on the principle of peasant proprietorship and operated independently of the state. It was the lack of viability due to this attempt to be self-sufficient that led to the demise of the Chartist settlements, to which a parliamentary enquiry contributed. In contrast, O'Brien and his followers argued for the collective ownership of land. Both O'Brien and his successors such as Martin James Boon recognised that the role of the state in raising taxation to fund new development and infrastructure was critical, a point which had been recognised as early as 1848 by J S Buckingham, who had rejected the utilitarian notion of a minimum role for the State. As has been pointed out above, Boon and his fellow Land and Labour Leaguers were more emphatic than Marx on the central role of collective land ownership, and in fact persuaded J S Mill to accept the need for State regulation of the land market and inheritance of land.

Ebenezer Howard shared many of the attitudes of the Benthamites and early-19th century philanthropists towards the State. He did not seek state sponsorship for his garden city vision and in fact depended on individual investors. As his Garden City concept depended on the trustification of land value, he was an opponent of state ownership of land as this would have destroyed the viability of his garden city. It was not that Howard's attitude to the state was anarchist in terms of being opposed to all forms of government authority. He was, after, all employed as a parliamentary clerk. Howard was also not a collectivist, in the sense that the anarchist communist Kropotkin was a collectivist – the garden city was to be owned by the shareholders in the company, rather than by the residents. The National Housing Reform Council shared many of Howard's views – it was also opposed to land nationalisation, supporting the co-partnership (collective home ownership or co-ownership projects) schemes developed at Letchworth, Hampstead Garden Suburb, Brentham in Ealing and other locations. It was the Workman's National Housing Council, with the ILP, that argued for a central role for the state and that housing for working people needed to be developed by local councils, and required positive state intervention through subsidised loans. The role of the progressives on the London County Council in both directly undertaking the development of council housing and promoting the case for the taxation of the value of private property showed the way forward, as well as pointing to the limited reach of philanthropic initiatives and housing projects where a requirement for a 4 per cent return to investors pushed rents beyond the reach of those on the lowest incomes.

Many of the housing reforms of the late-19th century, whether promoted by Conservative or Liberal administrations, recognised a role for the State – that in the interests of public health it was necessary to regulate housing conditions and to demolish slums. It was however the leading local authorities that forced central government to recognise that State intervention was necessary both to provide new homes and to plan for new settlements. The 1909 Housing and Town Planning Act represented a rejection of the voluntarist approach and explicitly put the State at both national and local level at the centre of both housing and planning policy.

Local initiatives and centrally driven reforms

The mid-19th century witnessed a growth of government intervention, which was generally driven by the central state. The utilitarian reformers of the period preceded the Fabians in seeing public health and housing reforms being legislated for in parliament and being implemented through a centralised civil service. This was largely a response to the perceived failure of local government structures to respond to cholera epidemics and slum housing. These reforms, symbolised by the role of Edwin

Chadwick, were resisted as contrary to British traditions of local governance and reflecting approaches to government seen in more autocratic countries such as Prussia. The rhetoric of the anti-centralising polemicist, Joshua Toulmin Smith, sought to promote a return to a mythical Anglo-Saxon age of local autonomy, somewhat spurious given that the Anglo-Saxon *witenagemot* was a council of nobles rather than an elected council or an assembly of all citizens.

Within the Chartist movement, there was an anti-parliamentary tendency, though the Chartist resistance was to the organs of the state – the magistracy and the yeomanry – rather than to parliament itself. The Charter was aimed at reforming parliament, rather than overcoming it, and the Chartists did themselves promote their own parliamentary candidates. Feargus O'Connor was himself an MP, originally elected in 1832 for an Irish seat but returned as a Chartist for Northampton in 1848.

Many of the radicals and socialists in the late Chartist and post-Chartist periods were London based, though some had started their careers in the provinces or in Ireland. The utilitarians were based in London, while the more working class organisations such as the First International, the Land and Labour League, the Democratic Federation and the Socialist League were all London based. The London Trades Council, the Metropolitan Radical Federation and the London progressives were all London-specific organisations. The Independent Labour Party, while having a northern origin, also soon moved its operational base to the capital. Of the influential socialist journals, it was only the *Clarion* which remained based in the north in Manchester. The study of the land reform campaigns within this book tends to focus on the London based organisations – the Land and Labour League, the Land Nationalisation Society and the English Land Restoration League. This is partly because this study has concentrated on urban politics and partly because the campaigns for rural land reform, especially in Ireland and Scotland, but to lesser extent Wales, have been the subject of other studies. While impacting on debates in the UK parliament and influencing the policies of UK-wide political parties, especially the Liberal party, those campaigns need to be related to the specific national politics of those three nations, which cannot be covered adequately in this work.

The campaigns for legislative reform however did originate, to a large extent, in cities other than London. It was Birmingham, Manchester and Leeds which first undertook planning initiatives and promoted housing reform and who in fact took the leadership of organisations such as the National Liberal Federation, the National Housing Reform Council, the Garden Cities Association, as well as promoting legislation through the Association of Municipal Corporations. However, it is important not to underplay the role of the progressives within the LCC, who had links to the Liberal party at national level as well as sharing key members, such as Saunders and Webb, with the Fabian Society. As has been shown, the role of London based Lib–Labs such as Henry Broadhurst, John Burns and W C Steadman was very significant. It is nevertheless notable that there was relatively little collaboration between the London radicals and the provincial radicals, with the former not being prominent in organisations such as the National Housing Reform Council and the Garden Cities Association, even though these organisations were London based. The working class based organisations did not participate actively in any of the middle class led reform bodies and, as has been demonstrated, were actively hostile to the NHRC and the Garden Cities Association.

The interdependence of land, housing and planning reform movements

The three reform movements are generally treated separately in historical studies. The history of housing reform in England in the modern era tends to start with Octavia Hill; the history of land reform with Henry George and the history of planning with Ebenezer Howard. Few historical narratives have examined the relationship between the three reform movements. The main objective of this study is to demonstrate that not only was there a prehistory to these late-19th century reform initiatives which can be traced back to the mid-and early-19th century and in fact to even earlier periods, but that in this prehistory there was a recognition of the inter-relationship, with campaigns on land reform and land ownership at the centre. For early and mid-19th century social reformers, some form of collective ownership of land was the essential precondition to the planning of a new settlement and the provision of good quality homes which were affordable by working class households.

The most forward thinking advocates, such as J S Buckingham, Bronterre O'Brien and Martin James Boon, recognised that state financing of new settlements was critical and that a system of progressive income tax, land tax and property tax was also necessary. Advocacy of a better built environment for all could not be pursued independently of advocacy of economic as well as of political equality. This was understood by the late Chartists, by the working class Owenites, by J S Mill as he moved from laissez faire to a form of socialism, and most clearly by the working class trade unionists in the First International, the Land and Labour League and their successor bodies. It is not a coincidence that the 1909 Housing and Town Planning Act was accompanied by income and land tax measures in the 1909/10 budget. The role of the pioneers studied in this narrative should be recognised and this history should no longer be hidden.

The lessons of history

History, if properly recorded, can speak for itself. Most current politicians appear to know little of history, and those who have studied history, tend to be selective about how they use historical knowledge. Contemporary policy discourse its notable for its ahistoricism. Most academic planning theory tends to use concepts derived from continental sociological and philosophical discourse. Debate as to the role of history in policy is often now disguised in the discourse of *path dependency*.

To this author, the importance of the past is self-evident. Knowing what happened in the past can only be a useful background for planning the future. The notion of planned settlements is hardly new, just as the need for good quality affordable homes is not a new discovery of the early 21st century. The role of land in urban growth is an issue of considerable historical significance, though it is only now, with the failures of governance of housing and planning policy difficult to deny, that we are again recognising that without control over land, planning will struggle to progress from plan-making, however visionary, to plan implementation. The narrative also shows that the role of the state at different scales is important and that autonomous activity in the form of self-contained communitarian settlement has its limitations and does not in itself deliver the fundamental changes in the economic and political framework necessary to achieve progressive objectives. The narrative should also demonstrate that the social justice agenda is not just central to radical and socialist ideology but should be central to the planning discipline. Planners need to reassert the core Benthamite principle of planning for the public good against the practice of planning to enable private gain. Planning has to be fundamentally a collectivist project and not an individualistic one.

The historical narrative is primarily a narrative of polemic and campaigns, although in the final decades of the long 19th century, radical and socialist ideas began to influence legislation and had an impact on what actually happened on the ground. To this extent, the lesson of history is that arguments for change can sometimes actually lead to the change taking place. Such positive outcomes are not achieved without passion, belief and hard work. Change does not come quickly – nor is it inevitable. This would be a lesson well learnt.

Index